Canoeing

Outdoor Adventures

Library of Congress Cataloging-in-Publication Data

Dillon, Pamela S.
    Canoeing : outdoor adventures / Pamela S. Dillon, Jeremy Oyen.
        p. cm.
    ISBN-13: 978-0-7360-6715-7 (soft cover)
    ISBN-10: 0-7360-6715-9 (soft cover)
    1. Canoes and canoeing. I. Oyen, Jeremy, 1970- II. Title.

GV783.D55 2008
797.122--dc22

                                    2008004392

ISBN-10: 0-7360-6715-9
ISBN-13: 978-0-7360-6715-7

This publication and DVD is written, published, and produced to provide accurate and authoritative information relevant to the subject matter presented. It is published and sold with the understanding that the author and publisher are not engaged in rendering legal, medical, or other professional services by reason of their authorship or publication of this work. If medical or other expert assistance is required, the services of a competent professional person should be sought.

Permission notices for photos reprinted in this book from other sources can be found on pages 249-250.

The Web addresses cited in this text were current as of February 11, 2008, unless otherwise noted.

Acquisitions Editor: Gayle Kassing, PhD; **Developmental Editors:** Melissa Feld and Ray Vallese; **Assistant Editor:** Martha Gullo; **Copyeditor:** Bob Replinger; **Proofreader:** Coree Clark; **Permission Manager:** Carly Breeding; **Graphic Designer:** Nancy Rasmus; **Graphic Artist:** Yvonne Griffith; **Cover Designer:** Keith Blomberg; **Photographer (cover):** U.S. Coast Guard; **Photographer (interior):** Mark Anderman/The Wild Studio unless otherwise noted. See pages 249-250 for a complete listing. **Photo Asset Manager:** Laura Fitch; **Photo Office Assistant:** Jason Allen; **Art Manager:** Kelly Hendren; **Associate Art Manager:** Alan L. Wilborn; **Illustrators:** Argosy and Alan L. Wilborn; **Printer:** United Graphics

Printed in the United States of America   10 9 8 7 6 5 4 3 2 1

Human Kinetics
Web site: www.HumanKinetics.com

United States: Human Kinetics
P.O. Box 5076
Champaign, IL 61825-5076
800-747-4457
e-mail: humank@hkusa.com

Canada: Human Kinetics
475 Devonshire Road Unit 100
Windsor, ON N8Y 2L5
800-465-7301 (in Canada only)
e-mail: info@hkcanada.com

Europe: Human Kinetics
107 Bradford Road, Stanningley
Leeds LS28 6AT, United Kingdom
+44 (0) 113 255 5665
e-mail: hk@hkeurope.com

Australia: Human Kinetics
57A Price Avenue
Lower Mitcham, South Australia 5062
08 8372 0999
e-mail: info@hkaustralia.com

New Zealand: Human Kinetics
Division of Sports Distributors NZ Ltd.
P.O. Box 300 226 Albany
North Shore City
Auckland
0064 9 448 1207
e-mail: info@humankinetics.co.nz

Canoeing

Outdoor Adventures

American Canoe Association

Editors

Pamela S. Dillon

Jeremy Oyen

HUMAN KINETICS

Contents

Preface

Welcome to *Canoeing*. In an effort to provide a resource to all outdoor enthusiasts, this introduction to canoeing has been developed for all current and future paddlers, including recreational paddlers who want to be safe on local ponds or streams and adventure seekers looking to move on to whitewater. The book also serves as a text for introductory canoeing courses taught at the university level.

This book was written in cooperation with the American Canoe Association (ACA). Founded in 1880 by a group of avid canoeists, the ACA has grown into the nation's largest and most active nonprofit paddlesport organization. Today the ACA is dedicated to promoting canoeing, kayaking, and rafting as wholesome lifetime recreational activities, accomplishing this mission by providing a variety of worthwhile programs and public services in such areas as event sponsorship, safety education, instructor certification, waterway stewardship, development of water trails, paddlers' rights and protection, and public information campaigns.

Canoeing contains nine chapters covering the principles and techniques needed for safe and efficient canoeing. Chapter 1 presents the history of canoeing as well as information on types of canoeing, outdoor ethics, and resources. Chapter 2 includes fitness requirements for canoeists, including stretching, nutrition, and components of a training program. Chapter 3 covers the equipment you will use while enjoying your canoeing adventure. Chapter 4 gets you ready for your trip by detailing all aspects of trip planning, including pretrip planning, on-water management, and canoe ethics and etiquette. Chapter 5 details safety aspects of paddle sports, whether you plan on being on a lake, pond, lazy river, or challenging whitewater. Chapter 6 introduces the fundamental canoeing techniques, strokes, and maneuvers, including concepts of paddling and boat dynamics in the water. Chapter 7 takes you to the river in order to illustrate the dynamics of moving water as they relate to a river trip. Chapter 8 provides information on properly planning a safe overnight experience, including choosing a campsite, setting up camp, and camping with children and dogs. Chapter 9 provides excellent resources on sharing paddle sports with others through use and stewardship of resources, paddlers' environmental ethics, and further paddling opportunities.

In each of the chapters you will find safety tips, paddling tips, and consumer tips highlighting interesting and important facts to remember about canoeing. Diagrams and photographs illustrate the techniques and concepts explained in the text. In addition, there are checklists to help you get organized as you plan for an outing. The book concludes with lists of Web resources for additional information on each of the topics covered in the book and success checks to test your retention of the information provided in the chapters.

Canoeing also includes the *Quick Start Your Canoe* DVD, which guides you through an introduction to paddle sports and basic safety and paddling techniques so you can enjoy a safe boating experience.

We hope that you find *Canoeing* a valuable resource as you start your own on-water adventure or continue the one already started. Be safe, happy, and smart on the water.

Note: This text includes a wealth of information about the sport of canoeing, including techniques, on-water information, and trip planning. However, it is not designed as a replacement for effective on-water instruction. As you enjoy the sport of canoeing, it is important to search out and participate in on-water instruction by qualified instructors.

Acknowledgments

Thanks to the many individuals and members of the American Canoe Association Safety Education and Instruction Council who helped put *Canoeing* together. With your expertise and input, we have created a valuable resource for outdoor enthusiasts interested in paddle sports.

Additional thanks to Northwest River Supplies (NRS) for supporting this project.

PART I

Preparing for a Canoeing Adventure

CHAPTER 1

Going Canoeing

There is nothing—absolutely nothing—half so much worth doing as simply messing about in boats.

Kenneth Grahame,
The Wind in the Willows

magine floating peacefully along the shoreline of a quiet lake. The sun warms your back and casts rays of light beneath the surface of the water. You are able to see through the water to view aquatic plants, large rocks, decaying logs, and schools of fish. As you reach out to place your paddle in the water, a large turtle pops up his head, momentarily startling you. He quickly pivots and swims away through the water like a hawk gliding through the sky. Paddling across the quiet water, you set your sights on the opening of the inlet ahead. The waterway narrows. Tall trees line the banks of the river as it twists and turns ahead of you. A beaver dam creates an obstruction, which you carefully scramble over, portaging your canoe. If you listen carefully, you can hear the rapids ahead. The river opens into a large pool, lined and speckled with smooth rocks. You pull the canoe onto shore, grab your lunch, and hop across the river from rock to rock until you find the perfect place for a picnic—a large, flat rock in the midst of the small rapids.

This is just one scene painted from hundreds of personal experiences that are readily available to you, the novice paddler. As you explore the pages in this book, take time to study, learn, and reflect on the information presented. The book will help you make the many decisions that you will face as you venture into the lifelong outdoor activity of canoeing. *Outdoor Adventures: Canoeing* begins with an overview of canoeing history and shows how canoeing has evolved from a means of transportation to a sporting activity. The book describes the different types of canoeing today and helps you determine the type of paddling that best suits your needs. Terminology, questions, and gear lists help you prepare to purchase your own canoeing equipment. To help you prepare for a trip, the text offers tips on fitness, safety and survival, trip planning, and paddling techniques.

Let's begin by answering the question, What is canoeing?

Canoeing, Kayaking, and Paddle Sports

Canoeing is the sport of kneeling or sitting on a raised seat in an open-decked boat and propelling oneself with a single-bladed paddle, using only human muscle power. In kayaking, a similar sport, the paddler propels either an open- or a closed-deck boat using a double-bladed paddle. The kayaker sits on the bottom of the boat and extends the legs in front of the body. Canoes can also be paddled with a double blade, like a kayak. *Paddle sports* is a general term used to include both canoeing and kayaking.

The canoe is a narrow boat with pointed ends. The canoe can be paddled solo (one person) or tandem (two people), or several people can paddle a large canoe called a dragon boat or war canoe. The average solo canoeist can paddle at a rate of 4 miles (6.5 kilometers) per hour.

Special fittings can be adapted to the canoe for sailing, rowing, or trolling.

- Sailing uses wind power. Sails vary in size and position in the canoe. The bigger the sail and the stronger the wind, the faster the canoe can travel.

- Rowing, like paddling, requires human power. The rower sits facing the back of the canoe, away from the direction of travel, and uses two oars to propel the boat.
- Trolling uses a battery-powered motor. Fishermen may add a trolling motor to the rear of the canoe to allow them to fish and also move the boat. Fishing and paddling at the same time is nearly impossible!

So, a canoe can be adapted to be similar to a kayak, rowboat, sailboat, or motorboat, but other watercraft have a hard time becoming a canoe. How does someone choose canoeing over other watercraft sports? Usually, it has to do with the purpose or the person's need to access water. Let's begin to look at this need as it relates to the history of canoeing.

History of Canoeing

Originally, canoeing met the simple need of moving across water. It was a means of transportation and survival—getting from one place to another, hunting for food and pelts, or harvesting wild rice crops. Dugouts, made by shaping and hollowing out a large tree trunk, are thought to be the earliest canoes (figure 1.1). They were built to fit local needs. Some were crude and some were quite

Figure 1.1   Dugout canoe.

sophisticated, both in construction and design. Dugouts were heavy and difficult to carry on land, so users often deserted them at the destination point and made new ones at the next location where the need arose. Archeologists have been able to trace dugout canoes back to the Stone Age.

Birch bark canoes originated in northern Canada in the 1800s. They arose in response to the need for a canoe that was strong enough to carry large loads yet light enough to be carried over land. Builders used strips of wood to create a skeleton and birch bark as a "fabric" to cover the ribs. Birch bark is lightweight and waterproof, and it was an abundant resource. The birch bark canoe was durable enough to run rapids, and a damaged canoe could be easily repaired because the material was readily available. The fur trade drove the need for larger, stronger birch bark canoes.

Canoe makers were able to make variations to canoes, in both shape and materials, to adapt boats for different purposes and make them better suited for a variety of waters. Today, canoes are made for open lake water, slow-moving rivers and streams, rapids, and deep, rough, open water. In chapter 3, you will learn more about how canoe shapes are altered to adapt to different water and the variety of materials used to build canoes today.

Canoeing Today

With the advent of roads and railroads, canoeing as a means of transportation became less efficient, and often impractical. Recreational paddling thus became the main kind of canoeing.

John MacGregor is credited with popularizing canoeing as a recreational sport for the middle class in Europe and North America in the mid-1800s. MacGregor used his boat, the *Rob Roy*, which was fitted with a sail, to travel around Europe. He promoted canoeing in books and lectures. Various canoe clubs cropped up across Europe, Canada, and America.

- In 1865 MacGregor founded the Canoe Club, a group of prestigious British sportsmen and travelers.

- The American Canoe Association (ACA) was founded in 1880 and is the oldest paddlesport organization in the United States, following three strategic tenets: education, stewardship, and recreation.

- The Canadian Canoe Association was founded in 1900.

- The Internationale Repräsentanschaft für Kanusport (IRK) was founded in 1924, and canoeing was a demonstration sport at the Paris Olympics. Through the effort of the IRK, canoeing became a full-fledged sport in 1936. After World War II, the IRK was reconstituted as the International Canoe Federation, in 1946.

- In 1936 the British Canoe Union (BCU) became the governing body of the many British canoe organizations.

Canoeists today are recreational paddlers. We can divide recreational canoeing into three major subcategories: general recreation, canoe camping, and competition.

Types of Canoeing

The type of canoeing that you choose to do will depend on your access to water, your personal interests, and your level of confidence or competence on the water. Whether you are using the canoe as a means for something else, such as fishing, or are competitive and looking for a new sport, canoeing offers a range of options that will fit almost anyone.

General recreation is a broad category of canoeing. It includes flatwater and river touring, whitewater paddling, and hobbies such as fishing, birding, and photography (see figure 1.2). Ponds, quiet lakes, and gentle streams or rivers are ideal environments for the recreational paddler. Recreational canoeists paddle to improve fitness, to experience nature, to participate in a group activity, or to pursue a hobby. A skilled recreational paddler may choose a larger lake, adding the challenge of wind and waves, or a swift-moving, frothy (whitewater) river filled with rocks and rapids that create a challenging obstacle course. A whitewater paddler may run a river from point to point or continually work a small section by running it, climbing out on shore, walking back to the put-in spot, and repeating the run. This whitewater activity is called park and play.

Canoe camping, or tripping, combines the activities of canoeing and camping. It is like backpacking, but the traveler loads gear into the canoe instead of carrying it on his or her back. A canoe camping trip can be a short paddle

Figure 1.2 Paddlers can enjoy a broad range of recreational activities, including hobbies such as fishing.

across a lake to a campsite destination or a multiday paddle that could include short carries over land, between waterways, and around rapids or waterfalls. Canoe camping gives the paddler access to places unreachable by other forms of transportation, such as hiking or motorized craft. Designated campsites and lean-tos are usually indicated on recreational or paddling-specific maps.

Competition includes a variety of skill levels, speed, and individual and paired performance. Racing and freestyle are the major categories in canoe competition.

Racing includes marathon, sprint, slalom, and canoe sailing.

- Marathon: Like marathon running, marathon canoeing means racing over a long distance at a consistent speed, but on lakes or slow-moving rivers. The length of the race can vary from 5 to over 100 miles (8 to 160 kilometers). Racers are divided into categories according to age, ability, gender, type of boat, and number of paddlers.
- Sprint: Flatwater racing from 200 meters to 5 kilometers; individual and paired events.
- Slalom: A competitive sport in which the competitor guides a whitewater canoe through a series of course gates on river rapids in the fastest possible time.
- Canoe sailing: Racing a canoe under sail power.

Freestyle involves precision paddling. It is like obedience training for you and your canoe. The competitor links together strokes and maneuvers, choreographed to music and performed in a .25-acre (.1-hectare) area of calm, flat water. Freestyle is the flatwater version of a whitewater park and play.

Benefits of Canoeing

Canoeing, a low-impact activity that strengthens the upper body, offers physiological, sociological, and psychological benefits. Paddling at a rate of 4 to 5 miles (6.5 to 8 kilometers) per hour can expend up to 400 calories per hour. Besides allowing the participant to be outdoors and enjoy nature, canoeing helps the mind and body relax and unwind. Canoeing provides a healthy alternative to the standard fitness routine.

For those seeking social situations, canoeing provides an opportunity to paddle with friends and family. Many local outdoor clubs have a paddling group, and outfitters schedule paddle demo days, day and overnight trips, and paddling instruction. As you become more involved in canoeing, you may find yourself wanting to protect, preserve, and maintain your favorite lake or river. Perhaps you will become involved in water trail maintenance or water rights legislation. A river cleanup event, for example, allows participants to clean up their favorite river, develop their outdoor ethic, and give back to the community.

As leisure time becomes more of a luxury, we need to find activities that meet our needs for psychological wellness. Canoeing provides an opportunity for personal growth in skill development and the achievement of new experiences. Personal values and identities develop from these experiences as others recognize unique skills and abilities. Fitness, stress reduction, and social support are aspects available day to day or during a life crisis. Lastly, canoeing is pleasurable and contributes to overall well-being, both mentally and physically—just ask any seasoned canoeist.

Outdoor Ethics

Outdoor ethics is a subject that is important to all outdoor enthusiasts and is vital for the paddler to understand and follow. Outdoor ethics deals with aspects of respect for self and others along with proper stewardship and protection of the resources that we as a society need for continued recreation and quality of life.

As you continue your journey as a canoeist, hiker, photographer, or general outdoor enthusiast, it is essential that you understand the impact you can have on the environment and conditions around you, whether you are in a remote wilderness area in the Boundary Waters, on your local pond or stream, or even in your own backyard.

The best known outdoor ethics program is called Leave No Trace (www.LNT.org). Leave No Trace is based on seven principles, which form the framework of the program's outdoor ethics message:

1. Plan ahead and prepare.
2. Travel and camp on durable surfaces.
3. Dispose of waste properly.
4. Leave what you find.
5. Minimize campfire impacts.
6. Respect wildlife.
7. Be considerate of other visitors.

Courtesy of the Leave No Trace Center for Outdoor Ethics www.LNT.org

For a detailed overview of the Leave No Trace principles specifically adapted for canoeing, please refer to chapter 9 of this text.

Where to Canoe

Water, water, everywhere, yet you don't know where to paddle? Finding safe, accessible, usable waterways is a challenge for the novice canoeist. Estimating the appropriateness of a sea, lake, reservoir, pond, river, or canal for your paddling excursion is difficult. Find a local expert or guide to assist with your search for paddling venues. Web addresses for several water trails are provided in the "Web Resources" section that follows chapter 9, and you will find more information about choosing the right boat, selecting gear, and planning your trip later in this book. As you try new aspects of canoeing, from camping to whitewater, continue to seek the advice of experts. As a beginner, you should choose a quiet, protected lake or a slow-moving canal, creek, or river, with minimal motorboat traffic. As your skill level and experience develop beyond the novice level, you may add advanced water venues.

Quiet Water (Novice)

A quiet-water lake, pond, or reservoir has relatively calm water with an almost glasslike surface (see figure 1.3). A small body of water that is sheltered from the wind and has restrictions or limits on motorboat traffic is ideal for the novice paddler. A protected shoreline and minimal boat traffic will minimize the waves created by wind or boat wake. Your safest route on a lake is along

Figure 1.3 Canoeing along the shoreline of a quiet lake is a safe route for the novice paddler.

the shoreline, within safe swimming distance from shore. In the event of a capsize, you will be able to swim to shore with your canoe in tow and then reenter the canoe.

A small, 1- to 5-acre (.4- to 2-hectare) pond is large enough to practice paddle strokes, to fish, and to offer ample images to the photographer. The shoreline of a 650-acre, 3-mile-long (250-hectare, 5-kilometer-long) lake could be explored in an afternoon or paddled extensively for exercise, or it could be a great place for a family picnic—paddling, swimming, and a meal. A 10,000-acre, 15-mile-long (4,000-hectare, 24-kilometer-long) lake attracts the traffic of larger boats, is more exposed to wind, and is less suitable for quiet-water canoeing, unless you are paddling short distances, along the shoreline, from a camp or cottage.

Gently Moving Water (Novice)

Rivers, canals, and large streams or creeks are often canoeable. What is the definition of gently moving water? A slow-moving river is one that you can paddle upstream, against the current, without much effort. It has little or no current, and no riffles or rapids. It is not classified as moving water or whitewater (see chapter 7 for more information on river classifications). A river classified as class I, the lowest classification of whitewater, has fast-moving water with riffles and small waves and few obstructions, all easily missed with little training; the risk to swimmers is slight and self-rescue is easy.

Many people paddle a river using a there-and-back method; they paddle upstream for about an hour, turn around, and paddle back. Starting the paddle by heading upstream allows a less-strenuous return with the current. The water needs to be deep enough to float the canoe and to submerge the blade of the paddle completely, while clearing the bottom of the waterway. At 3 to 6 inches (7.5 to 15 centimeters), canoeing is only fair, and you will find yourself getting out of the canoe to drag it through the shallows. A depth of 6 to 12 inches (15 to 30 centimeters) is good, and water 1 to 3 feet (30 to 90 centimeters) deep is excellent for canoeing a river.

Lake Inlets and Outlets (Novice to Advanced)

The marshy areas of lake inlets and outlets are often exceptional canoeing venues. An explorer can zigzag among reeds and lagoons, getting close to birds, fish, and other aquatic wildlife (see figure 1.4). The relatively shallow water and narrowness of such waterways make access ideal for the canoeist. A word of caution: The boggy bottom of a marsh can sink a paddler thigh deep into muck, making a reentry into a capsized canoe messy. Review the safety and survival skills outlined in chapter 5 and remember that safe practices suggest never paddling alone.

Figure 1.4   Canoeing in a marshy area can offer paddlers a good vantage point for observing birds and other wildlife.

Open Lakes and Seas (Advanced)

Open lakes and seas are larger bodies of water. A canoe camping or tripping adventure often includes a passage through a large, open stretch of water. Open bodies of water are often gateways to quiet inlets or mouths of pristine rivers. Many beautiful island camping destinations are in the middle of larger waterways. Lakes, exposed to wind, are subject to waves, which will vary in height and frequency with wind speed. Paddling in wind and waves requires endurance and efficient paddling technique. A well-trained tandem team can make paddling in wind and waves look almost effortless.

Whitewater (Advanced)

Rivers, creeks, and canals are subject to change as water levels rise and fall with change of season and precipitation. A gently flowing river can become a dangerous flooded waterway after a rainstorm. A lazy river that passes over a drop in elevation can become a raging field of rapids. For experienced moving-water canoeists, the challenge of a swiftly moving river provides the adrenaline rush that makes them feel alive (see figure 1.5) (see chapters 6 and 7 for more information about paddling rivers).

American Whitewater posts a national database of rivers and their classifications on its Web site (www.americanwhitewater.org). Some rivers are monitored by a regional stream keeper, who updates water flow and offers paddling

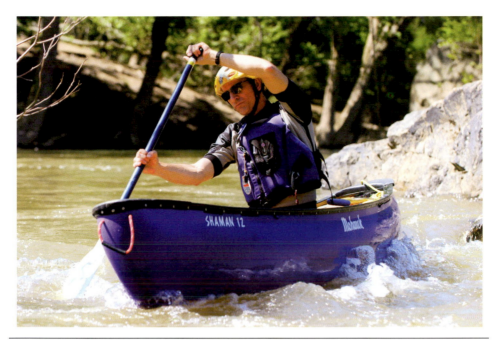

Figure 1.5 Experienced moving-water canoeists enjoy the challenge of a swiftly moving river.

recommendations for the river. Many rivers and reservoirs are dammed, and dams may be subject to timed water releases. Paddling on a river below a dam can be life threatening because the flow and swiftness of the water can change rapidly after water is released.

SAFETY TIP
Motorboats: A Water Hazard

Motorboats create a water traffic hazard for the canoeist and therefore the frequency of boat traffic can be frustrating. Motorboats often use canals and rivers to gain access to larger waterways. Dodging boat traffic and dealing with wakes (the water turbulence that follows the boat as the boat moves through the water) can be a challenge for the beginning canoeist. In large lakes, multiple boat wakes create a wavy cross-chop that is difficult to navigate. On canals and rivers, the wake of a single boat can range in height from 6 to 12 inches (15 to 30 centimeters). Wakes can be paddled through safely at an angle, but the unsuspecting canoeist whose canoe remains parallel to the wake may find the wake rolling over the side of the canoe and swamping the boat. Respectful boaters will slow their speed to reduce the wake. When choosing your waterway, be aware of boater traffic patterns and understand the rules of the road as they pertain to navigating local waterways. See chapter 4 for information about sharing waterways with other boats.

Paddling Venue Resources

Do you have a water venue in mind, such as a protected lake or gently moving stream? If not, you may need to seek information from local guides and experts, guidebooks, and Internet resources.

Local Guides and Experts

So how do you find safe, accessible, usable waterways for paddling? Your best resources are local guides and experts. These experts can be found through retailers, outdoor clubs, or other paddlers. Many retailers offer training classes, day trips, and product demo opportunities (see figure 1.6). Local outdoor clubs may have a paddling committee or links to a paddling club. Join the local paddling club and participate in paddling outings.

Experienced paddlers are your best source for up-to-date information about put-in locations (where you park and launch) and take-out locations (the end of a river trip), a place to rest or picnic, or a hazardous section of a river that can be avoided by carrying the canoe over land. Knowledgeable paddlers can also provide water or trip difficulty ratings, whitewater river classifications, and hazard references.

Figure 1.6 Novice paddlers should rely on experts for instruction and advice.

Guidebooks

When searching for a new place to paddle, it is recommended that you seek out local published canoeing guides as a resource for paddling trips in your area. Many outdoor groups and paddling experts have written descriptions and classifications of their favorite paddles within a specific geographic area. Guidebooks are a reliable source for developing a list of potential outings. Most outdoor retailers stock local guidebooks. Community paddling clubs are also a great resource, as they often have a list of recommended guidebooks and have insight about areas that have been paddled. Canoeing guidebooks may include driving directions, descriptions of waterways, a difficulty rating or scale, and maps of parking areas and launch sites (put-in and take-out).

Internet Resources

You may want to research waterways available in your area and then find a guide to lead you on a trip. Check out the following Internet resources.

The American Canoe Association has created a directory of water trails in the United States and Canada and a listing of Paddle America clubs. Check out www.americancanoe.org for information on water trails and clubs in your area. You can search by state or province, click on a water trail, and in most cases find a link to detailed information. Some trails are designated as ACA recommended, which means that the waterway meets certain criteria that make it a good destination for paddlers.

The British Canoe Union (BCU) Web site at www.bcu.org.uk is an excellent resource for finding paddling clubs in England, Northern Ireland, Scotland, and Wales. Many waterways in the United Kingdom are privately owned, and the landowner must grant permission to use specific routes. The BCU offers members a reduced rate on a British waterways license and access to a full list of the British waterways available to canoeists. The list includes canals, broad rivers, and quiet stretches of water, to meet the varied needs and skill levels of canoeists.

Paddle Canada is the national organization responsible for the management, coordination, development, and promotion of paddle sports in Canada. The Paddle Canada Web site, www.paddlingcanada.com, offers information on paddling education programs and paddling in Canada.

Internet search engines such as Google provide an opportunity to explore paddling resources within your community or around the world. Most Web sites include links to clubs, education, waterways, retailers, and other informative links in the area. Additional Web sites worth exploring include the following:

- Australian Canoeing at www.canoe.org.au
- European Canoe Association at www.canoe-europe.org
- New Zealand Recreational Canoeing Association at http://rivers.org.nz
- Confédération Africaine de Canoë at www.kayakafrica.org
- Asian Canoe Confederation at www.canoeacc.com

SAFETY TIP

Nature is subject to change. Be smart and check with local experts to verify information listed in a guide or on the Web before you venture out on your own.

Summary

What is it that draws you to canoeing? A childhood memory? The lure of the natural world? The potential health benefits of a new recreational activity? Understanding the history of canoeing and relating the use of the canoe to the activities and water available to earlier people can help you define how and where you will be using your canoe. Are you a recreational paddler, a canoe camper, or a potential competitor?

As with any new adventure, we usually find that the more we learn about canoeing, the more aware we become of how much we don't know. Let the experts who are willing to share their knowledge and experience in this book, in your local community, and on the Internet guide you in making decisions about your adventure in canoeing.

CHAPTER 2

Getting Fit for Canoeing

If you don't do what's best for your body, you're the one who comes up on the short end.

Julius Erving

Physical fitness is a crucial component of canoeing. Being physically fit goes beyond having enough energy to make it from the put-in to the take-out. Physical fitness means a safer activity for you and those around you. It can help prevent injury, and most of all it allows you to spend more time having fun.

If a situation arises that requires a rescue, whether a capsize in open water or an unexpected swim through a deceiving rapid, self-rescue is the best method of recovery. Being physically fit enables you to take care of yourself on the water and not have to rely on the skill and ability of others. Being fit enough to rescue yourself also means that you are less of a risk and worry to the group you are with. Those who are physically fit can more easily lend a hand to other paddlers in trouble.

As with any physical activity, injury may occur when canoeing. Although unavoidable and unforeseeable situations may occasionally lead to injury, most injuries can be prevented with proper paddling technique and physical fitness. Many accidents and injuries are a direct result of paddler fatigue. Being mentally exhausted can lead to poor decision making when reading the river, and physical exhaustion could cause the current to take you places you had no intention of going.

Physical fitness is an integral component of a safe, injury-free, and enjoyable canoeing experience.

Four Components of Physical Fitness

Before beginning a fitness program, you need to evaluate your current level of physical fitness. Consult with a doctor to make sure that your body is in appropriate shape to begin whatever program you choose. Deciding what program works best for you requires a basic understanding of the components of physical fitness. Fitness comes in four varieties: strength, flexibility, endurance, and cardiorespiratory fitness. These four ingredients, when combined, are a recipe for success on the water.

Strength

Although strength is a requirement for canoeing success, body builders will not necessarily be better paddlers than marathon runners. Strength can mean different things to different paddlers, depending on what they want to get from their experience. Whitewater slalom racers and sprint canoeists will need more sheer strength than will recreational paddlers or even marathon racers.

Flexibility

A paddler who is flexible is less likely to be injured than a paddler who is stiff and cannot easily adapt to a variety of circumstances. A flexible paddler is also likely to last longer on the water and perform more efficient strokes. Torso rotation is a critical component of an efficient paddle stroke. The more you are able to rotate your torso, the more efficient the power phase of your stroke will be and the fewer strokes you will need to cover a given distance.

Endurance

Most people can repeat a simple motion a few times without sacrificing technique or power, but the lasting repetition of those motions determines a person's endurance. The better a paddler's endurance, the longer that paddler can stay on the water without putting him- or herself, or the group, at risk. The amount of endurance required depends on how much time you plan to spend on the water and how strenuous the exertion during that time is going to be. Paddling downstream will be much less difficult than paddling upstream, which requires a higher level of endurance.

Cardiorespiratory Fitness

Simply stated, cardiorespiratory fitness refers to how well the circulatory and respiratory systems are able to supply oxygen to skeletal muscles during sustained physical activity. If you have good cardiovascular health, your heart pumps with little effort, providing the parts of your body the oxygen that they require to burn energy used to perform whatever task you are doing. If you have poor cardiovascular health, your heart must work harder, tiring more quickly and shortening the active portion of the task. Attaining cardiovascular health is not only a critical step toward becoming a physically fit canoeist; it is also a great way to reduce the risk of heart attack, heart disease, obesity, and a myriad of other health concerns.

A paddler's strength, flexibility, and endurance depend on how efficient the body's circulatory system can distribute blood and oxygen to the parts of the body that need it most. This distribution of oxygen and energy is determined by a person's level of cardiorespiratory fitness. Without a steady flow of oxygen to the muscles and tissues, a paddler's strength, flexibility, and endurance will be compromised.

Flexibility In and Out of the Canoe

A lot of discussion has occurred in the fitness community about whether people should warm up before beginning any sort of strenuous physical activity. This is the time to pay attention to your own body—how it behaves and when it performs best. Jumping jacks or a slow jog gets the blood pumping through the muscles, but if your body tells you no, begin with a less strenuous warm-up to increase your heart rate.

A good rule of thumb when stretching for paddling is to work your way from head to toe. That way you can be sure that you won't miss any key muscle groups. While you stretch, breathe deeply and consistently, holding your stretches for 10 to 15 seconds. Bouncing may allow you to touch your

TECHNIQUE TIP

Use what is at hand to make stretching easier. Use a paddle for balance or as a lever against a stationary object to release tension.

toes, but doing so may pull a muscle. Rather than touching your toes for a split second, gradually release tension in your muscles. Slowly relax your gluteal muscles, your hamstrings, and your calves until your toes are within reach. Consistent, proper stretching leads to increased flexibility—one of the four major components of good physical fitness.

Specific Stretches

Many stretches can be used for the various muscle groups. Although some may work well for you, they may not be effective for others. Listen to your body and experiment. If a stretch hurts, don't do it. Try another stretch that engages the same muscle group. Practice the routine before and after you paddle.

Head and Neck

Paddling demands familiarity with your surroundings, and you must be able to monitor the rapid changes that can occur in those surroundings. Keep your head on a swivel, but only after stretching. Press your ear toward your shoulder and feel the stretch on the opposite side of the neck. Use your hand to press on your head to increase the tension. Switch sides and repeat.

Chest

Power strokes engage the pectoral muscles while paddling. Place your hands behind your back, grab your wrist, and slowly lift upward. Alternatively, find a tree or buddy, hold your arm out to your side, press your palm against the friend or tree, and slowly turn your body outward, facing away from the tree or your buddy. Switch sides.

Back

Hold your arm out in front of you and cross it over your chest. Using your other hand, squeeze your arm into your chest just above the elbow. Feel the stretch between your spine and shoulder blade.

Grab a partner and stand facing each other. Reach out and hold each other's wrists and then lean away from each other. Feel the stretch in your lower and upper back.

Shoulders

Shoulder injuries typically result from extending your arms where your body is not accustomed to going. Keep your shoulders loose by doing arm circles. With your arms out to your sides, parallel to the ground, draw circles in the air. Start out small and gradually increase the diameter. Reverse directions.

Biceps

Hold one arm out in front of you, palm facing up. With your other hand grab your outstretched fingers from below and pull them down toward your body. Switch sides. This stretch is also a good way to loosen your forearms if they tighten up after paddling long distances.

Triceps

Raise one arm above your head. Then, bending at the elbow, lower your forearm behind your head. With the other hand, grab your elbow and slowly pull so that your fingers extend down your spine. Switch sides.

Groin

Stand with your feet far apart, slightly wider than your shoulders. Keeping your spine perpendicular to the ground, lunge to one side, keeping the opposite leg fairly straight. Feel the stretch on the inside of your straight leg. Switch sides.

The Core

If you are new to canoeing and learn to paddle correctly, you will be amazed at how much your abdominal muscles, obliques, and ribs are engaged in the activity.

With your feet shoulder-width apart, place your hands on top of your head and slowly bend to one side, feeling the stretch along the other side of your body. Switch sides.

Place your hands on your hips and slowly bend backward at the waist so that your chest faces the sky. Remember to breathe!

Gluteal Muscles

Lie down on your back. Bend one leg at the knee and bring your knee to your chest, feeling the stretch just above your hamstring.

Quadriceps

While standing upright, bring your heel to your buttocks and hold at the ankle. Be sure to point your knee straight down at the ground while holding this stretch. Focus on a blade of grass to keep your balance or use a paddle to support yourself.

Hamstrings

Stand with your feet a little farther than shoulder-width apart. Being careful not to lock your knees, bend forward at the waist. Grab both ankles and pull your torso toward your legs. Pull your torso into your legs again to increase the intensity. Stand up, breathe, and then bend forward at the waist. Grab one ankle with both hands and press your chest to your knee. Stand up and switch sides.

Calves

Begin on the ground on your hands and knees. Plant the balls of your feet in the ground and slowly straighten your legs until your body forms an inverted V.

Ankles

You never know when you will find yourself out of the canoe, scrambling over rocks and rough terrain. Paddlers are not immune to ankle sprains. Draw slow, wide circles in the air with your toes, rotating at the ankle. Change directions and then switch feet.

Stretching in the Boat

We would all like to be flexible all the time, but our muscles will inevitably contract, especially after extended use. This muscle contraction can happen while you are paddling as well, but you may not have the luxury of pulling on shore to run through your routine. Discover ways to stretch while still in the boat; just be sure to do so safely, in a controlled environment.

Stretching after you get in the boat not only increases your flexibility and reduces the possibility of injury; it is also an excellent way to test your range of motion while in the boat. Knowing your limits can make the difference between catching an eddy and pulling a muscle. While in the boat, simple techniques such as extending your legs in front of you will increase blood flow.

Try rotating your torso so that your shoulders are parallel to the keel line and grab the gunwales (the upper edges of the canoe sides), stretching your sides, abdominal muscles, and back. Bend at the waist and reach for the bow or thwart (cross brace attached to the gunwales) in front of you and stretch out your back. Instead of holding on to a tree or buddy, reach one arm behind you and press your palm against the inwale (inside upper edge of the canoe), rotate your torso toward the opposite side of the boat and feel the stretch in your chest. You can do many of the upper-body exercises that you performed on land while in the boat. Be creative, stay limber, and stay hydrated.

Stretching After You Paddle

After a long day on the water, often all we want to think about is loading the boats and getting home. Although it may feel better at the time to sit and catch your breath, spend 15 minutes stretching and cooling down your muscles. While on the water you spent a lot of energy making the boat do what you wanted it to do, and lactic acid has built up in your muscles. A postworkout stretch will make you feel better and perform better the next time you ask your body for extra output. Simply repeat your prepaddle flexibility routine, but spend a bit more time on the muscles and joints that feel most sore.

Key Components of an Effective Training Program

Being physically fit undeniably leads to a more successful paddling experience. The process of becoming physically fit and maintaining fitness can be fun and exciting. Lifting weights to exhaustion will not necessarily make you a better baseball hitter. You might become stronger, but to become a better hitter, you will also need to evaluate swing mechanics and spend time in the batting cage. Paddling is no different. Spending time in the gym will make you stronger and less susceptible to injury, but that is no substitute for spending time on the water. Wherever and however you decide to spend your training time, an effective training program includes four components: action, quality, variety, and fun.

Action

No training program, no matter how intricate or intense, will be effective unless you actually do it. You could have a complete weight set, several pieces of training equipment, and a caloric monitor, but unless you engage regularly in a fitness program, your success will be limited. A systematic approach works well for some, but a more laid-back approach may work better for others. The key is discovering a method that works for you.

Quality

Training hard every day does not guarantee success. The quality of your workouts can affect the outcome much more than the number of workouts you perform. At the same time, training without allowing your muscles adequate rest between workouts can do more damage than good. Find a balance that's right for you and give targeted muscles at least 48 hours of rest between workouts.

People who live busy, hectic lives often have difficulty finding time for a fitness program. Targeted training, in this case training that focuses on specific muscle groups used when paddling, will produce the best results. Get the most from the time you spend getting in shape by making sure that your workouts are quality workouts. Perform exercises precisely and pay attention to how your body responds to the various motions. This mantra holds true both in the weight room and on the water.

Variety

Boredom can be a killer when it comes to fitness routines. If your workouts start to become stale, the likelihood that you will continue the activity declines. Switch it up. Pick new locations and activities to put some variety in your sessions. Instead of running on a treadmill, try going for a jog along the river. Play basketball instead of doing squats. Paddle backward rather than forward. Engage similar muscle groups by choosing different activities. By keeping your muscles guessing, they will grow stronger, with greater flexibility, and at the same time you will stay sane.

Fun

Make sure that you enjoy your workouts. Find a buddy and exercise together. Bring along a music player to add some life to your on-water workouts. The workouts will be more exciting, and you will be more likely to work out again on your next scheduled day. After all, paddling is supposed to be a fun activity; there is no reason you cannot have fun getting in shape, too.

TECHNIQUE TIP

Know yourself. Understand your own tendencies so that you gain the most from your workout. Are you a morning person or evening person? Do you enjoy a regimented schedule, or do you prefer impromptu activity? Understanding who you are can help you find your own path toward physical fitness.

Cross-Training and Off-Season Training

Outdoor sports can be invigorating, but the fun will last only as long as your body can endure the activity. In addition, participating in outdoor activities has a number of limiting factors, including weather, dependence on others, and the always-nagging time factor. However, being in good physical condition helps guarantee that when the clouds part to offer you a chance to have some fun on the water, your body is just as willing as your mind.

Canoeing can sometimes be problematic to do alone, so you cannot always train in the boat. Cross-training is a way to stay in shape while at the same time participating in some sports that you have not yet enjoyed. Most cross-training activities include both cardiorespiratory and strength training, but a few sports emphasize one or the other.

Cardiorespiratory Fitness

Cardiorespiratory fitness is crucial to any athlete. When training to enhance cardiorespiratory fitness and increase the flow of oxygen throughout your body, start slowly. Build up some endurance first and establish a baseline. After you are comfortable with your current level of cardiovascular health, advance toward sprints and more difficult workouts.

Swimming is an excellent alternative sport for paddlers. Getting involved in canoeing is easy and requires few prerequisite skills, but the ability to swim is essential. Knowing how to swim, and how to swim while wearing your gear, is the best way to be safe. Swimming not only boosts your on-water safety; it also does wonders for your fitness level. Swimming is a low-impact (meaning few jarring motions on your joints) aerobic activity that builds strength, endurance, flexibility, and cardiovascular health (see figure 2.1). Whether you train

Figure 2.1 Besides improving your fitness level for canoeing, swimming for exercise also improves your ability to be safe on the water.

PADDLER TIP

Swimming is a great way to train for paddling. To tailor your workout to canoeing, try the backstroke or butterfly to focus on the powerful back muscles.

in-season or off-season, swimming keeps you in shape and prepares you for the unexpected capsize. If you happen to find yourself out of the boat, you will be more comfortable in the water and self-rescue will be easier.

Muscular Fitness

Cardiorespiratory fitness is an important contributor to paddling effectiveness, but so is muscular strength. Having strong muscles is important not only for enhanced performance, such as paddling up rapids, or attaining, but also for reducing the likelihood of injury.

In-season, sprints while in the boat are an effective way to build muscular strength. Try sprinting for 1 minute, take a 2- or 3-minute rest, and then sprint again. Continue this routine for approximately 30 minutes.

Off-season muscular training can do wonders for your paddling stroke and your general health. You will find that once-tiresome turning strokes are a snap, that you travel farther under the power of a single forward stroke, and that minor course and turning adjustments seem effortless.

The more muscle mass you have, the higher your metabolism will be and the easier it will be for you to burn calories and lose weight. Increasing your muscle mass and strength does not have to mean pumping iron at the gym. You just need to add some resistance to whatever activity you choose and exercise with enough intensity to reach momentary muscle failure.

If you live near a sandy beach, run sprints on the beach rather than the pavement. Winter blues got you down? Go for a hike in the snow or put on a pair of snowshoes. Whatever activity you choose, make sure that you are challenging your body. Think about the message that you are sending your body while you work out. Try to convince your body that it needs to be stronger and ready to repeat that performance when you call on it again.

Take your workout a step further by tailoring it to canoeing. Focus on twisting rotations of the torso and pay a little more attention to the upper body. Go to the gym and try to mimic movements that you would make on the water, only do so with weights. Be sure to balance your workout to achieve symmetry in the way that your body works and to reduce the likelihood of injury (for example, chest and upper back, biceps and triceps, quadriceps and hamstrings, abdominal muscles and lower back).

Cable machines and elastic tubing are great ways to simulate the paddling movement with added resistance. Pull-ups and chin-ups are good exercises for paddlers because they focus on the biceps, triceps, and back, muscles that

The river delights to lift us free, if only we dare to let go. Our true work is this voyage, this adventure.

Richard Bach

are regularly engaged during the paddling stroke. Push-ups work the triceps, shoulders, and chest, which are also engaged during many paddling strokes. Set up two chairs facing each other, about shoulder-width apart, put your hands on the seats, and slowly lower your body between the two, working your triceps and lower chest. There are many creative ways to build strength, both in the gym and at home.

An often ignored but critical muscle group is the abdominal region. There are few movements you make, in either canoeing or everyday life, that do not engage your abdominal muscles. Washboard abdominal muscles are not a prerequisite for good paddling, but a strong core reduces the stress on other muscle groups, increases endurance, and reduces the risk of injury.

For a more challenging workout, train with a partner or consider hiring a trainer or coach. Working out with another person can motivate you to work hard and maximize the time that you spend conditioning.

As you work in the off-season, keep your workouts simple but effective—4 to 5 days a week, 1 hour per session. This routine, done properly and effectively, will put your body in a great position to grab the paddle and go as soon as the river is running.

Be careful not to overexert certain areas of your body. As you train, try to alternate muscle groups. An overworked muscle or tendon can lead to injury.

PADDLER TIP

Enter a triathlon. The variety of sports will keep you interested in your workouts and help improve total body fitness. Then, during the paddling season, look for a paddling triathlon (bike, paddle, run) and let your hard work in the off-season help you take home the trophy.

Rather than training your entire body in one session, switch it up. Even better, change exercises and movements to keep your body guessing. Introducing new movements trains your body to respond favorably in difficult situations on the water.

Many free resources are available to help you get started. Do a search online (see "Web Resources" on pages 229-234), check a book out of the library, ask a friend, or ask your doctor. Many people are enthusiastic about physical fitness and are typically happy to offer advice.

Most important, decide what you want from canoeing and determine what level of training you need to achieve those goals. Be selfish. Find a routine that fits your schedule, your goals, and your body. The result will be longer and more enjoyable injury-free time on the water.

Nutrition

Canoeing requires effort, and effort requires energy. To maximize your time on the water, you need to understand the basics of nutrition. Understand, too, that different foods work better for different people. Think about the myriad of automobiles on the market. Some require diesel fuel, some premium gasoline, some regular. The point is that different engines need different fuel to run most efficiently. The human body is no different. Experiment to find the fuel, or food, that makes you feel and perform best.

Six major nutrients are essential to canoeing and, indeed, to healthy living: water, vitamins, minerals, protein, carbohydrate, and fat. The ideal balance of these six nutrients depends on what activity you will be asking your body to perform and how strenuous that activity will be. Nutrition is a complex science because proper nutrition is different for everyone. In addition, experts are constantly updating recommended daily allotments for what and how much you should eat.

Generally, try to match the number of calories (energy) going into your body with the number of calories that you are burning. If you plan on working or paddling hard, for example, by attaining, or paddling up a set of rapids, you will need significant energy to complete the task. If you plan to lounge in the bow on a lazy river, your body will require fewer calories. Unfortunately,

CONSUMER TIP

Having a few sweets while on the water is OK, but beware of the sun. Chocolate lovers should substitute hard-shelled candy, such as M&Ms, for chocolate chips in their GORP (good old raisins and peanuts) to avoid a midafternoon meltdown.

proper nutrition is not as simple as balancing calories in to calories out. The quality of the calories is just as important. Minimize your intake of processed foods and maximize your indulgence in fruits, vegetables, and whole grains. Treat your body like a finely tuned machine; give it the best fuel possible and drink plenty of water.

Staying energized and hydrated means that you will not only have more energy on the water; you will also be more alert. Canoeing sometimes requires quick judgment. Make proper nutrition a priority.

Nutrition for the Recreational Canoeist

To stay properly energized and hydrated, you should eat before you are hungry and drink before you are thirsty. Tarot card reading and seeing the future in a crystal ball may work for a few of us, but the truth is that we just need to develop a talent for guessing. If you wait to eat and drink until you feel the urge, it is a little too late because your body is indicating that it is already in deficit. Eat and drink often! Pack high-energy snacks such as peanuts, granola, raisins, sunflower seeds, and dried fruits. Many kinds of energy bars are available. Some taste great, whereas others taste like sandy chalk. Find the ones that you like and take them along. These foods are not likely to spoil on the river, they taste good, and they keep your spirits high.

Proper hydration is essential to your awareness on the water and your safety on the trip. You lose water by sweating, urinating, defecating, and breathing. Take whatever water you think you'll need and then take a little more. Although it is possible to overhydrate, doing so is difficult. Drink just enough water so that your urine runs clear. Secure water bottles to the thwarts of the canoe with rope or straps to prevent their loss should you capsize (figure 2.2). Hydration packs that offer a water bladder and "straw" for drinking are a great way to have water easily accessible and keep fluids in the body. Strap one below the seat or to your back for easy access.

Food and water won't do you much good unless you actually eat and drink, so keep them accessible. Rather than stowing food in the bottom of a big dry bag, bring along a smaller bag and lash it to the thwart in front of you. That way, every time you look down you will be reminded to keep snacking.

Figure 2.2 Staying hydrated is easier if you keep a water bottle accessible and attached to the thwarts or seat of the canoe. And you won't lose the bottle in the event of a capsize.

Nutrition for the Competition Canoeist

Some paddlers decide to take their on-water experience to the next level and participate in local, regional, or even national competitions. Whomever you face and wherever that may be, proper nutrition is critical to a successful outcome.

Competitive paddlers take training and nutrition seriously. They read articles and books on techniques and strategies. Some hire trainers or consult with physicians to determine exactly how many calories they need and how often they need them. If competitive canoeing intrigues you, consult with a physician or personal trainer to develop a diet that will meet your needs. Online resources can help you calculate calories burned and even plan your diet for you; see "Web Resources" on pages 229-234. Invest in a heart rate monitor to be sure that you are training at optimal levels and plan your diet accordingly. Remember, no one diet works well for everyone, so experiment and discover what works best for you and your body.

Relearn the Fundamentals

Remember back in grade school when your teacher dressed in a giant grape costume and made you memorize the food pyramid? It wasn't all fun and games. Your teacher knew something about healthy eating. Nutritionists today know even more than they did 20 or 30 years ago. The size of the portions and the levels of the pyramid may have changed a little, but the principles are the same: Eat natural foods, eat a variety of foods, and minimize fat intake. Every sport has some fundamentals that the best athletes and coaches focus on. Learn the fundamentals of nutrition and apply them to how you will be spending your time on the water. Go to www.MyPyramid.gov for assistance in creating an eating plan customized to your level of activity.

Summary

As your canoeing skills improve and your taste for adventure increases, remember that your journey can go only as far as your body will take you. Pay attention to the four components of physical fitness (strength, flexibility, endurance, and cardiorespiratory fitness) to maximize your potential as a canoeist. Train appropriately, eat properly, and treat your body with respect. If you follow the basic fundamentals of fitness and nutrition as detailed in this chapter, you will have energy and desire helping you on your paddling adventure. With poor nutrition or poor fitness, you may have a difficult time on a longer trip.

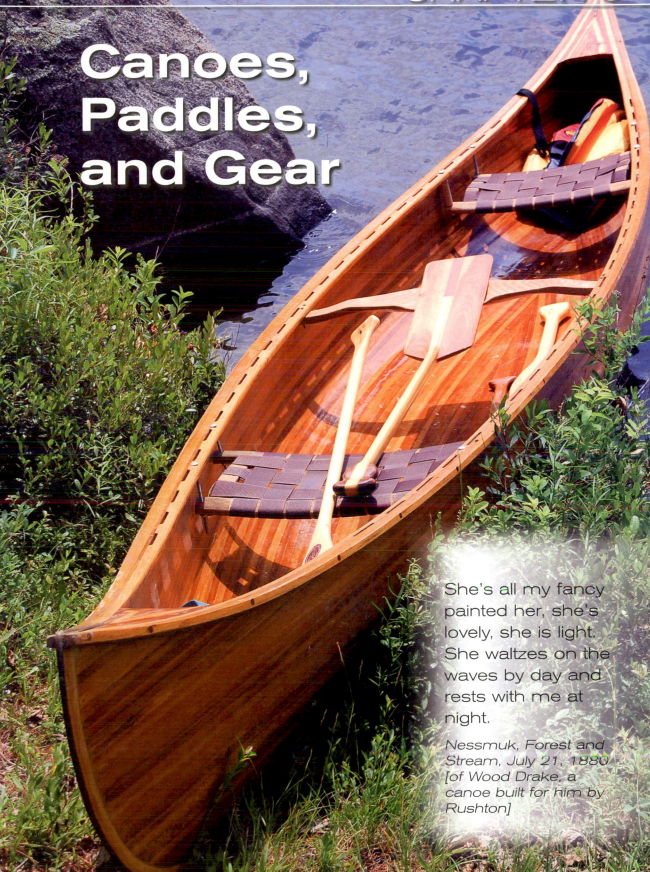

CHAPTER 3

Canoes, Paddles, and Gear

She's all my fancy painted her, she's lovely, she is light. She waltzes on the waves by day and rests with me at night.

Nessmuk, Forest and Stream, July 21, 1880 [of Wood Drake, a canoe built for him by Rushton]

Thunder rumbled overhead. A canoe adventure was taking a turn for the worse. The sky opened, and buckets of water filled the canoe. We quickly paddled to shore. Squatting on the balls of our feet, we took cover under our overturned canoe and waited out the storm. Our cotton clothing was soaked through to our underwear. We were both wet and cold. Luckily, we were not far from camp, the storm was brief, and sunny skies soon returned.

Experience is a great teacher. Being unprepared can be scary and dangerous! Understanding what gear is available, determining what is necessary, and defining your individual gear needs will prepare you to make your purchases. This chapter includes information about the canoe—the names of its parts, materials used to make canoes, and variations on canoe design as they relate to performance on different water venues (from chapter 1). The chapter also covers paddles and PFDs (personal flotation devices, otherwise known as life jackets). You will have to choose from among different classes of PFDs and consider a variety of features.

Beyond the fundamental purchases of canoe, paddle, and PFD, you will need a car-top rack system or trailer to transport the boat, appropriate clothing for paddling, and storage or packing gear for day trips or overnight camping. Again, do your research and seek the advice of experts. A well-educated consumer will save time and money.

This chapter will also help you learn the jargon and terminology used by seasoned paddlers, retailers, and outfitters. Use the information to develop your personal criteria and create your own gear list to take with you as you shop.

Canoes

Hundreds of variations of the canoe are available today. How do you decide what type of canoe is right for you? It is best to start with the fundamentals. First we will define the parts of the canoe. Then we will examine the hull design, or the shape of the canoe. Canoes vary in shape to adapt their performance to

CONSUMER TIP

Your personal criteria are the attributes that you value as they relate to canoeing. Answer the question, What is important to me about _____ as it relates to canoeing? For example, What is important to me about how much gear I can load into my canoe? A racer who carries only a spare paddle would not care much about gear, but a canoe camper who brings everything but the kitchen sink on his or her excursions would consider the answer extremely important.

different types of water (i.e., flatwater versus river), so choosing a canoe that suits the type of water to be paddled is an important step toward ensuring a pleasant time on the water. Another option to consider is the materials used to build the canoe. Like automobiles, most canoes are available in an entry-level model, but as features and materials improve, the cost of the canoe increases—as does the performance.

Canoe Parts and Nomenclature

Having an understanding of the parts of the canoe (see figure 3.1) is extremely useful when learning strokes and maneuvers or when communicating with a partner in a tandem canoe. Proper terminology can also be helpful as you determine what type of boat to use in specific paddling conditions.

- **Amidships**—Midway between the bow and stern.
- **Beam**—The width of the canoe at its widest point. A wider-beamed boat is more stable but slower to paddle.

Figure 3.1 Parts of the canoe.

- **Bow**—The front end of the canoe. The bow can be determined by examining the seating arrangement. In a tandem canoe (two seats) the bow seat is placed farther from the end of the canoe to provide legroom for the bow paddler. In a solo boat, the seat is often pitched toward the front of the boat. The bow paddler's primary responsibilities are providing power and scouting for obstacles.

- **Chine**—The area of the hull where the bottom of the canoe turns up and becomes the sides.

- **Deck**—A triangular shaped piece of wood, vinyl, or aluminum at the bow and stern of the boat. Decks can be used as handholds for carrying the canoe or may have a place to tie a rope (painter or end line) to the canoe.

- **Draft**—The depth of water required for the canoe to float. Draft is measured as the distance from the waterline to the bottom of the keel.

- **Entry lines**—The front part of the canoe that slices through the water. The sharper the entry line, the cleaner the boat will slice through the water.

- **Flare**—The outward curving of the sides of the canoe near the gunwale. Flare helps keep water from splashing in over the sides of the canoe.

- **Freeboard**—The distance from the gunwales to the waterline.

- **Gunwales**—The upper edges of the canoe sides. Materials may be wood, aluminum, or vinyl. Gunwales can be divided into inwales (the inner half) and outwales (the outer half), depending on construction and design.

- **Hull**—The main body of the canoe that displaces water and provides buoyancy.

- **Keel**—A structural or imaginary line that runs through the center of the boat from bow to stern. Keels are visible from the underside of the hull. Builders originally added keels to canoes to provide support and protection for the canvas bottom.

- **Kneeling thwart**—A tilted piece of wood used in place of the seats and normal thwarts to enable kneeling paddlers to take weight and stress off their knees and ankles. Replacing seats with kneeling thwarts will reduce the weight of the canoe.

- **Length**—The greatest distance from the bow stem to the stern stem.

- **Port**—The nautical term for the left side of the canoe.

- **Portage yoke**—A yoke-shaped thwart designed to fit the contours of the neck and shoulders, to assist in a solo portage (carry) of the canoe. The portage yoke replaces the center thwart.

- **Ribs**—U-shaped pieces of wood or aluminum that push outward from the inside of the hull to add strength and rigidity. Kevlar or fiberglass canoes may have diamonds of additional fabric or foam to provide core support.

- **Rocker**—The upward sweep of the keel line toward the bow and stern. The more pronounced the rocker is, the easier the canoe is to turn. More rocker means faster turning and maneuverability. The trade-off is poorer tracking and more vulnerability to wind.

- **Seats**—Molded, caned, or webbed. In tandem canoes, bow seats are placed closer to the center and are usually wider than the stern seat. The stern seat is placed close to the rear of the boat and is usually narrower than the bow seat. Solo canoes have one seat placed amidships. Some tandem canoes are fitted with a third center seat to provide solo or tandem paddling options.

- **Solo**—Paddling a solo canoe, paddling a tandem canoe from the center thwart, or paddling a canoe stern first while sitting in the bow seat are paddling options for the solo canoeist.

- **Starboard**—The nautical term for the right side of the canoe.

- **Stem**—The curved end of the bow and stern of the boat. Canoes may be fitted with brass, aluminum strips, or stem bands to help prevent wear and relieve the stress of impact. Another term for stem bands is skid plates. They are made of composite materials and often used in whitewater canoes.

- **Stern**—The back end of the canoe. Most of the steering is done from the stern.

- **Tandem**—Like a bicycle, a tandem canoe is built for two.

- **Thwarts**—A cross brace attached to the gunwales to provide structure and support to the gunwales and the shape of the hull. Thwarts are useful for tying down gear.

- **Tumblehome**—The inward curving of the sides of the canoe near the gunwale. Tumblehome makes it easier for the canoeist to get his or her hands over the water when paddling.

Canoe Design

Canoes are designed for optimal performance in one of four areas: speed, carrying capacity, maneuverability, and stability. Understanding these features will help you purchase the best canoe for your needs.

Speed

How fast do you want to travel? Will you be racing or paddling across large lakes toward a camping spot? A canoe designed for speed has a long, narrow hull with little rocker and sharp entry lines. Look at the canoes used in marathons—long and pointy—and compare the length and width of a racing canoe to those of a rowboat, which is short and stout.

Carrying Capacity

A boat designed to haul gear and heavy loads will be long and wide with a flat or shallow-arch bottom for greatest stability. As you add weight, the performance of the canoe changes. The boat sits lower in the water. If gear is loaded above the gunwale line the canoe can become less stable and catch more wind. How much will you carry in your canoe? Think people, kids, pets, and gear.

Maneuverability

A shorter canoe with rocker (picture a banana) will be responsive (in turns) in winding creeks, in fast-moving water, or for freestyle paddling. A longer boat

TECHNIQUE TIP

Sit in the canoe on flat water, then gently rock the canoe back and forth and side to side to test both initial and secondary stability.

with less rocker will track better and is more suitable for traveling long distances on open bodies of water. A whitewater canoe can literally spin in place, whereas a touring canoe will create a large arced circle when made to turn.

Stability

Initial and secondary stability are features of hull design. Initial stability is the amount of stability that a person feels when first stepping into a canoe. Many first-time canoeists grab the side of the canoe and hold on with white knuckles as the canoe rocks back and forth in the water. (Compare this sensation to that felt when stepping into a rowboat, which is relatively stable in comparison.)

Secondary, or final, stability is the way that the canoe feels and performs when the boat is loaded or heeled over on its side. A boat with good secondary stability stands a better chance of being righted after being tipped on its side.

Tippiness can be good or bad, depending on how the canoe is used. An angler will want a boat with strong initial stability, sacrificing secondary stability. Secondary stability is an important feature for canoes used in rivers and wavy conditions.

Hull Shape

A canoe that is cut in half from port to starboard will reveal a cross-section of the hull. Hull shapes have four major variations: flat bottom, round bottom, shallow arch, and shallow vee (see figure 3.2). These four hull shapes influence the performance of a boat and its initial and secondary stability. The designs also relate to the various categories of canoeing.

- **Flat bottom.** A flat-bottom boat is stable. It also has a great deal of initial stability. Flat-bottom boats are typically designed for general recreation—fishing, photography, or paddling short distances with pets or kids.

- **Round bottom.** Most round-bottom boats are whitewater designs. Because they are designed for the dynamic aspects of rivers and currents, these crafts have less initial stability but strong secondary stability. The round hull feature makes them adaptable in the rough water conditions that a canoeist encounters when running rapids on a river.

- **Shallow arch.** This popular hull design offers continuous initial and secondary stability. The length and rocker of the canoe will determine its ability to track in open water or meander through a winding stream. The shallow-arch hull is one of the most versatile canoes.

- **Shallow vee.** Wooden, sailing, racing, and some touring canoes are apt to have a shallow-vee hull. This design allows the boat to float lower in the water and helps it track on a straight line. Canoes with shallow-vee hulls have moderate initial stability and greater secondary stability and are stable under a variety of conditions.

Hull Design: Categories of Canoeing

How does hull design relate to the various categories of canoeing? By using what you have learned about hull design and performance, you can determine the type of canoe and the attributes best suited for certain types of canoeing.

General Recreation

Flat-bottom canoes are steady, maneuverable, and easy to control. They tend to be shorter in length, 16 feet (4.9 meters) or less, and at least 36 inches (90 centimeters) wide. General recreation canoes are designed for stability, slower speeds, and all-around fun. Ideal for short day trips and perfect for carrying smaller amounts of gear, pets, or children, this style of canoeing is an ideal choice for anglers, photographers, and families.

Flat bottom

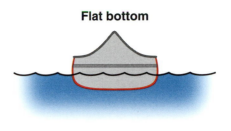

Round bottom

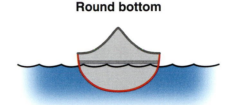

Shallow arch

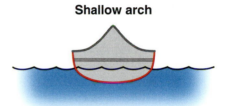

Shallow vee

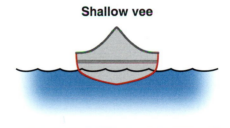

Figure 3.2 Various hull shapes: *(a)* flat bottom, *(b)* round bottom, *(c)* shallow arch, and *(d)* shallow vee.

Flatwater and River Touring and Canoe Camping

Whether used for a day trip or an extended camping trip, a touring boat is designed to carry people and gear over time and distance. The weight, number, and age of people on board and the amount of gear carried dictate the size, length, and width of the boat. Flatwater and river touring and canoe camping are activities that can easily be enjoyed with just a few folks or with a larger group tripping together. As on-water groups increase in size, outdoor ethics and local regulations must be followed closely to properly maintain the resources all paddlers enjoy when on the water.

Shallow-arch or flat-bottom hulls may be suitable for day touring or extended trips. The type of water influences the design features of the shallow-arch or

> At times on quiet waters one does not speak aloud but only in whispers, for then all noise is sacrilege.
>
> *Sigurd F. Olson*

flat-bottom hull. A dropped or skegged stern influences the ability of the canoe to track a straight line on open water. A boat with more rocker will perform better on a river. A flared hull keeps water from sloshing in over the sides on the river, and on flatwater in wind and waves. Tumblehome creates greater volume and carrying capacity and allows the paddler to get the paddle over the sides of the canoe more easily.

Whitewater Paddling

Whitewater paddlers choose round-bottom canoes with lots of rocker. These canoes offer high maneuverability for negotiating rocks and rapids. Whitewater canoeists may run a long stretch of river with varying classes of rapids, or they may choose a short stretch of rapids with deep pools and eddies that they run repeatedly. Running the rapids and then carrying the canoe back upstream along the shoreline is a type of whitewater activity called park and play.

CONSUMER TIP

Rocker, flare, and tumblehome are all design features of a canoe hull. Rocker influences turning ability—more rocker aids spinning; less rocker allows straighter tracking. Flare keeps water out, but high sides catch wind (sail). Tumblehome brings wide sidewalls into the gunwales, making it easier for the paddler to reach the water.

Freestyle Canoeing

Freestyle canoeing is technical, quiet-water paddling. It emphasizes smooth, efficient paddling and precise boat control on flat water. Freestyle technique achieves precise results by integrating body, boat, and paddle to execute maneuvers in harmony. It blends basic paddle strokes with weight shifts and static paddle placements to create its own vocabulary of maneuvers, with specialized names like Axle and Christie. Freestyle includes maneuvers in all four quadrants of the canoe. So anything you can do on one side, you can do on the other side. Anything you can do forward, you can do backward.

Freestyle paddling requires no special equipment other than a boat, a paddle, a PFD (life jacket), and usually a kneepad. Freestyle techniques can be applied in many different types of canoeing situations. In fact, freestyle can add efficiency, grace, and fun—especially fun—to almost any paddling experience. Many freestylers even paddle to music, making freestyle canoeing an expressive, interpretive art form. Freestyle canoes have a shallow-arch hull, symmetrical stems, and a fair amount of rocker.

Race

Sprint and marathon canoeists use long, narrow, lightweight boats with a shallow-arch or shallow-vee hull.

Solo Versus Tandem

A solo canoe has one seat, and a tandem canoe has two. Some tandem canoes can be paddled solo by adding a center seat or kneeling thwart, or by simply sitting in the bow seat and paddling the boat while facing the stern. Fishing, photography, bird watching, and exercising are all activities that the solo canoeist can enjoy. Hauling gear, paddling with children, or covering long distances are activities more suited to the tandem option. A solo canoe is generally shorter and has less beam (width) than a tandem canoe.

Table 3.1 lists the canoeing classifications as they relate to the performance factors of speed, capacity, and maneuverability. The hull design features (length, width, rocker, and hull shape) can serve as a general reference guide when

Table 3.1 Canoe Classification Chart

Canoe classification	Performance factors			Hull design features			
	Speed	Capacity	Maneuverability	Length	Width	Rocker	Hull shape
Recreation							Flat bottom
Flatwater touring							Shallow arch
River touring							Shallow arch
Camping or tripping							Flat bottom, shallow arch
Whitewater							Round bottom
Race							Shallow arch, shallow vee
Freestyle							Shallow arch
Sail							Shallow vee

low, moderately low, moderate, moderately high, high

choosing a canoe. Canoe manufacturers offer extensive material both in print and on the Web to help you evaluate the alternatives.

Canoe Materials

Like the shape of the canoe, the materials used in the construction of canoes have changed over time. Manufactured materials now dominate production. The five types of construction materials available in today's market are wood, wood and canvas, aluminum, plastic, and composite material (fiberglass, Kevlar, or carbon fiber). After describing the materials, we will examine five criteria that you can use to choose the optimal material for your canoe.

Wood and Wood and Canvas

Wooden canoes are steeped in history. Most wooden boats are handmade by artisans who produce a limited number of them. Stunningly beautiful, wooden canoes perform exceptionally well. A wooden strip canoe is made from strips of wood nailed around a skeleton and sealed with polyurethane. A wood and canvas canoe has a wooden interior. A canvas skin is stretched and nailed to the outside of the hull, sealed, and painted. Early settlers used sail canvas to replace the birch bark formerly used to cover the skeletal structure of the canoe.

Most wooden canoes require periodic maintenance. Because of their historic value or individual artisanship, wooden boats are probably the most expensive boats on the market.

Aluminum

Aluminum canoes evolved from the aircraft industry after World War II. They require almost no maintenance, last forever, and can be found en masse at camps and many liveries. But hull shapes are limited, and the number of models being produced has declined over the years.

Plastic (Polyethylene, Rotomold, Royalex)

Plastic boats are made from large sheets of plastic that are heated and fitted into molds. The result is a durable craft that is low maintenance and virtually indestructible. Blunt entry lines make them less precise than canoes made of fiberglass, carbon, or Kevlar.

Composite Material

Composite boats are made from layers of woven fabric bonded with resin. Most composite boats have an outer gel coating to protect the hull from abrasion. They are efficient in the water because of their sharp entry lines and stiff hulls. They are easy to repair (though the repairs may not be cosmetically attractive) and require little maintenance.

The composite materials used include fiberglass, Kevlar, and carbon fiber. Fiberglass is the least costly of the composite materials and is the heaviest of the three. Kevlar and carbon fiber hulls are lighter in weight and resist damage

CONSUMER TIP

The weight of the canoe does not affect its strength and ability to carry a heavy load or larger person. Lightweight canoes are tough and are able to carry large loads, but they are not designed for river running—they do not have the durability for it.

better (based on similar lay-up, or layers of fabric), but are more expensive. To increase structural support of composite materials, multiple layers of cloth or a foam core are added in the hull construction process.

Regardless of what material is used for canoe construction, general care and maintenance tips include:

- Store your canoe out of the sun.
- Clean the hull as needed with a biofriendly cleaner (check with your outfitter or manufacturer to see what is best for your canoe).
- Properly maintain all components of your canoe (seats, thwarts, gunwales, etc.).

Major manufacturers usually offer canoe designs in at least two different materials. Small boat shops specialize by limiting hull design and manufacturing canoes in a specific material (wood, fiberglass, carbon, or Kevlar). So how do you choose the best material? For most people, the choice comes down to cost, but you should consider all five criteria in making your decision.

Criteria for Choosing Materials

The five major criteria for choosing canoe materials are durability, weight, performance, maintenance, and cost (see table 3.2). Answer the following questions to start narrowing the field.

1. **Durability.** While paddling, what sort of impacts and abrasions will occur? Will you use the canoe in rocky rivers or quiet lakes? Will you store it outdoors or keep it sheltered? Will you drag it to the beach? Will you transport it on top of a vehicle? Will several paddlers use the boat?

2. **Weight.** How strong are you? Will you have to carry the boat from the canoe shed or car to water, or will you be portaging from one body of water to the next? Will the boat be stored at a camp and simply dragged out to use?

3. **Performance.** Are you seeking to take a leisurely paddle along the lakeshore? Do you need a boat that will travel quickly over long distances? Do you live in an area with winding creeks and rivers? Will you be taking children or pets out and thus need greater stability? Will you be using your canoe for training and exercise?

4. **Maintenance.** How much maintenance are you willing to do? Are you handy? Can you fix the canoe if it is damaged by wind, rocks, or abuse? Do you have the time to maintain your canoe, or can you pay to have it done? Where will you store your canoe?

5. **Cost.** What are you willing to spend in money and time? Consider the whole package—canoe, paddles, PFDs, clothing, and racking for transportation.

The answers to the preceding questions will start to define your personal criteria for a canoe.

Table 3.2   Canoe Materials Comparison Chart

Material	Durability	Weight	Performance	Maintenance	Cost
Aluminum	High	Heavy	Limited	Low	Low
Rotomold	High	Heavy	Limited	Low	Low
Royalex	High	Moderate	Good	Low	Moderate
Fiberglass	Moderate, repairable	Moderate to light	Excellent	Moderate to low	Moderate to high
Carbon or Kevlar	Moderate, repairable	Light to ultralight	Excellent	Moderate	High
Wood	Moderate to low, restorable	Moderate to light	Excellent	High	High

Caring for Your Canoe

A little TLC will go a long way when caring for your canoe. Proper storage, preventive maintenance, and adequate care are the basics.

A good practice is to wash or wipe down your canoe after use. Simply hosing it down will take off any grit or grime picked up in the water or on the road. If you need to scour the boat clean, avoid abrasives and check with your local marine supplier to find an environmentally friendly product. This time is also a good time to inspect your hull for cracks, dents, or deep gouges. If your canoe needs repair, take it to a dealer or, if you are handy, make the repair yourself.

Another important point to consider is UV protection. The sun's rays cause fading and brittleness, and can weaken the hull. Apply a UV inhibitor (e.g., 303 Protectant) to the hull to absorb the UV rays. Simply spray it on and wipe to apply an even layer to the hull. Let it dry and wipe with a soft cloth. UV protectant wears off with use or abrasion, so apply it according to how much you use your canoe. Apply it monthly if you use your boat regularly. At the very least, apply protectant at the start of the season and before you put the boat away in storage.

Wood seats and gunwales need special care. Wood will fade to gray when exposed to the environment; if left alone, it will rot over time. Maintain your wood by lightly sanding and oiling it annually, or as needed. When sanding or oiling, tape the hull along the gunwales to protect it from accidental sanding and oil drips. Use a fine-grit sandpaper and sand with the grain. To control drips, use a foam brush and soft rag when applying the oil. Watko is a popular brand of oil.

> The canoeist always maintains that the canoe of which, for the time being, he is the owner is as nearly perfect as any canoe can be.
>
> *William L. Alden,*
> *The Perfect Canoe*

Proper maintenance also means finding the right way to store your boat. Ideally, your canoe should be stored inside. Although a canoe was designed to perform in the elements, it should be stored in a protected environment, away from the sun, rain and snow, wind, and extreme temperature. Store your canoe upside down (with the gunwales down). Place the canoe on a rack, sawhorses, two slings suspended from the ceiling, or on two supports placed on the floor. A misshapen hull will result if you store the canoe right side up or tipped on its side.

If you can't store your canoe indoors, protect it with a waterproof tarp, carefully placed and tied to avoid trapping moisture. If you can't cover your boat, store it at a slight incline so that water runs off the hull and gunwales. Be sure to tie down the boat; a strong wind can take it for a ride and cause costly damage. Royalex, wood, and fiberglass materials expand and contract at different rates when exposed to freezing and thawing temperatures. Wood gunwales on a Royalex canoe will pop their screws and possibly crack the gunwales. Loosen the gunwale screws if you are storing your canoe in a cold environment, whether it is indoor or out. Always make sure that your boat is clean, dry, and in good repair before putting it away in storage.

Buying a Canoe

By now, you may have a clearer understanding of the paddling category you fit into, an idea of where you might paddle, a broad idea of canoe shape and hull design, and perhaps a preference for canoe materials. By being armed with this information when you begin your shopping trip, you will help the retailer or outfitter identify the right canoe for your needs.

Always test-paddle a canoe before you buy. Take time to compare hulls, materials, boat designers, and manufacturers. Local retailers often offer demo days to provide canoeists an opportunity to test-paddle and compare a variety of boats. Some dealers have rentals available, so that you can test a boat during a daylong paddle. Used canoes are available in the secondary market. Many dealers and outfitters sell used and demo boats at the end of each season. Individuals list boats for sale on the Web. The Web site www.paddling.net posts canoes for sale and consumer reviews of many boats.

Have you determined your preferred canoe classification? Answer the following questions to determine the what, where, how, and who of using the canoe:

- What will you be doing with your canoe? Taking day trips, fishing, camping and hauling gear, running rivers, doing fitness routines, training for canoe marathons?

- What type of water will you paddle on? A lake or a river? In calm, windy, or wavy conditions? On a river with gently moving water or rapids?

- Do you want a boat that tracks well in flat water, maneuvers easily on a winding river, or remains stable when hauling gear and children?

- Who will be paddling the canoe? Will you bring children or have them paddle with you? Will you paddle tandem, solo, or with the family? Is stability an issue?

Transporting Your Canoe

After you buy a canoe, you will need some form of racking and tie-down system to transport the canoe on the top of your vehicle. Transporting a canoe in this way is called cartopping. Two options are custom-fitted car racks or rope and foam blocks.

Car Racks

The most secure option for transporting a canoe on top of your vehicle is to install a custom-fitted rack with gunwale blocks and tie-down straps. Place the boat upside down (gunwales to the roof of the car), running parallel to the vehicle. Loop two straps around the canoe—midbow and midstern—using the crossbars as anchors. In addition, you should attach lines from both the bow and stern of the canoe to the frame of the vehicle under the bumpers. Otherwise, strong winds may move and lift the canoe right off your vehicle. Always have four separate tie-down points.

Foam Blocks and Ropes or Straps

A less expensive, temporary system uses foam blocks and ropes or straps. The foam blocks are attached either to the gunwales of the boat or to an existing luggage rack. (Most luggage racks are not made for cartopping a canoe.) The foam blocks protect the car and canoe from rubbing and scraping. Straps or ropes are tied over and around the canoe, anchoring to the rack or to the frame of the vehicle (but only in vehicles with frameless windows). Tying the doors shut is not recommended.

Ropes are an affordable way to secure the boat to the vehicle. Be sure to hone your knot-tying skills. Use knots that won't slip and loosen up but that are easy to untie, especially if they tighten up or are exposed to weather. Canoe straps are a better option because the fabric is less apt to fray, snap, knot, or slip. The cam buckles make cinching the boat a cinch!

Carrying Your Canoe

Learning to carry the canoe is an essential paddler's skill, whether you carry it from your garage to your car, from your car to the water, or over a longer distance, usually between two waterways, a carry known as a portage. Factors that influence the type of carry that you use are your personal fitness level and upper-body strength, the weight of the canoe, the amount of gear that you have to haul (day trip versus an extended camping trip), and the distance that you have to carry the load. For descriptions and illustrations of ways to carry your canoe, refer to chapter 6.

Paddles

Paddles, like canoes, come in a variety of sizes, shapes, and materials. Unlike the canoe, a paddle can make or break a trip, because it is the paddler's connection between the body, the water, and the boat. You will be carrying your paddle for the entire trip, so comfort and performance are critical. Criteria for choosing a paddle include the type of paddling that you will be doing, the weight and durability of the construction materials, the performance of the blade design and shape, and most important, the comfort and fit of the grip and shaft.

PADDLER TIP

Carrying a spare paddle will keep you from being "up a creek without a paddle" in the event that a paddle cracks or is accidentally dropped overboard. Having an inexpensive wooden or plastic paddle available for rocky areas or near the shore will reduce wear and tear on a more expensive paddle. Being able to switch paddles to adjust to changing wind or wave conditions or to reduce hand fatigue on extended trips is another good reason to carry a spare.

Paddle Parts and Nomenclature

As with the canoe, it is important to know and understand the terminology associated with your equipment. Figure 3.3 shows two paddle designs side by side, with the various parts labeled. Descriptions of the parts of this vital piece of equipment follow.

- **Back face**—Opposite the power face.
- **Blade**—The wide, flat end of the paddle.
- **Grip**—The top of the paddle. The most popular grips are the pear-shaped, or squashed-ball, grip and the T-grip. Whitewater paddlers prefer T-grips for a strong handhold. The pear-shaped grip allows flexibility in the handhold, including palming and palm rolls.
- **Power face**—The side of the blade that catches the force of the water during the forward stroke. The power face is said to be loaded with the force of the water. Some canoe paddles are designed with a scooped blade, indicating a specific power face, but the majority do not have a specific power face.
- **Shaft**—The long, tubelike part of the paddle between the grip and the blade. Shaft length varies according to the paddler's torso height and arm length, sitting or kneeling style, position in the canoe (bow, stern, solo), and the beam (width) of the craft.
- **Throat**—The point where the blade meets the shaft. The shaft hand rests slightly above the throat of the paddle. An efficient paddle stroke will bury the blade in the water up to the throat. The throat is tapered to minimize resistance in the water.
- **Tip**—The end of the blade, opposite the grip.

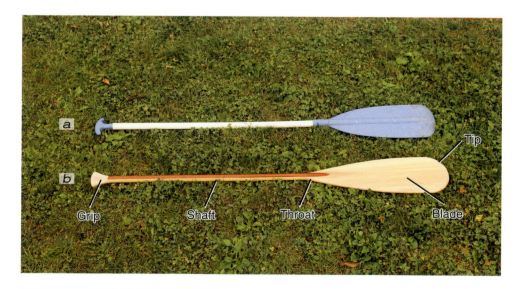

Figure 3.3 Two paddle designs: (a) T-grip plastic paddle and (b) pear-grip wooden beaver tail paddle.

Paddle Design

The two most popular grip shapes are the T-shaped grip and the pear- or palm-shaped grip (see figure 3.4). A T-grip provides a strong handhold to control the paddle angle. This grip shape is preferred by whitewater paddlers, who use short, quick strokes repeatedly to work with the current in strong steering maneuvers. A pear-shaped, or squashed-ball, grip is ergonomic and more comfortable for longer periods on the water.

Shaft

Shafts come in a variety of sizes in both length and diameter. Round shafts are more popular in production, and oval shafts are more comfortable in the hand. An oval shaft fits comfortably in the crotch of the hand (the curve between the thumb and index finger) and allows the paddler to align the knuckles to the blade, providing a reference point regarding the angle of the blade in the water.

Bent-shaft paddles are designed to enhance the efficiency of a seated paddler's forward stroke. The angled blade in a bent-shaft paddle compensates for the limited torso rotation available to the seated paddler. Bent-shaft paddles have a dedicated power face, which makes draws, sculls, cross strokes, and underwater recoveries a challenge. The paddle is used in a manner similar to moving the backside of a spatula or snow shovel through water, not like moving a spoon through ice cream.

Length

Paddle length is measured from grip to tip. Therefore, when comparing two brands of 54-inch (137-centimeter) paddles, you may find that although the paddles are comparable in overall length, the shaft and blade length vary greatly between the two.

Blade Shape and Size

The ideal blade width and length vary with the type of paddling.

- A whitewater paddler typically uses a paddle with a wide, short blade.
- A recreational tripper may choose an elongated, narrow beaver-tail blade, which offers less resistance and therefore alleviates neck and shoulder pain.
- A freestyle paddler opts for a wide, long, thin blade, which allows precise placement for maneuvering and slicing back through the water in an underwater recovery.

The length and width of the blade, along with the stiffness of the paddle shaft, affect the power of the stroke, resistance in the water, and the amount of muscle the paddler needs to use when paddling. A short, wide blade is more desirable for the moving-water paddle and a long, thin blade creates a more traditional touring paddle. See figure 3.4 for various types of paddles.

Figure 3.4 Various types of paddles.

Paddle Materials

Paddles, like canoes, are made from a variety of materials. The construction materials affect weight, durability, strength, flexibility, and cost.

Aluminum and Plastic

Aluminum and plastic paddles are economical and durable. They tend to be heavier, and the aluminum shaft is cold in cooler weather.

Wood

Wooden paddles are a very popular choice. They are buoyant, flexible, and durable. Wood retains warmth when cold, so it is comfortable to hold. The type of wood used affects weight, strength, and durability. Some paddles are made with a tip guard to protect against abrasion. Others have a coating of fiberglass over the blade for added strength. Grip, shaft, and blade shape vary, as does pricing. A wooden paddle may require sanding and varnishing on occasion.

Fiberglass

Fiberglass materials allow flexibility and precision in the design of paddles. Fiberglass is lightweight, strong, and relatively maintenance free. Blades can be shaped or scooped for competition. Whitewater paddles are usually made from fiberglass. Fiberglass is more expensive than wood or aluminum.

Carbon

Carbon paddles are the lightest, least fatiguing, and most expensive type of canoe paddle. Like their fiberglass counterpart, carbon paddles can be shaped

CONSUMER TIP

You can paddle a canoe with a shovel, but a paddle is more efficient. If you are torn between spending more money on a canoe or a paddle, your best bet is to invest in a better paddle.

and designed for precision and performance. Carbon paddles are virtually maintenance free; nicks can be wet-sanded, and epoxy can be used to fill deep scrapes.

Paddle Design: Categories of Canoeing

How do paddle designs relate to the various categories of canoeing?

Recreational

Recreational paddles are general-purpose, low-cost, all-around canoeing tools. They are made from less expensive wood, aluminum, or plastic. The durable but heavier materials limit performance.

Flatwater Touring or Tripping

Flatwater paddles are designed for thousands of repetitive strokes on open water. They are generally made of wood and tend to have long, narrow blades, shaped like a beaver tail, or voyager style. Grip and shaft style will vary along with craftsmanship and lightness of the wood used.

Whitewater

Whitewater paddles are built to handle the abuse of river rocks. Materials vary, but the design is usually a short, square blade with a T-grip. The blades are shorter than those on flatwater paddles, but the shafts are usually longer. Whitewater paddles tend to be made from composite materials, but are occasionally made from wood.

Performance

Performance paddles are built for speed or efficiency. A racing canoeist will look for a lightweight paddle, possibly a bent shaft, and a freestylist will want a high-volume blade with fine edges for precise entry. Performance paddles are made from wood, fiberglass, or carbon using a variety of grip, shaft, and blade designs.

Fitting Your Paddle

For a paddling experience that is as good as it gets, a proper fit of your paddle is essential. If you use a paddle that is too long or too short you will not be paddling with efficiency, and you will be using more energy than necessary. A properly fitted paddle provides the comfort and ease necessary to maintain your strokes throughout the trip.

Shaft Length

Shaft length is an important component of a good paddle fit. Factors that determine proper shaft length include the height of the paddler's torso and the length of his or her arms, the paddling position used (sitting or kneeling; bow, stern, or solo seating position), and the beam (width) of the boat.

One method to fit a paddle is to sit in a chair and hold the paddle vertically with the grip end down, placed between your legs, and resting on the chair seat. The shaft at the throat of the paddle should measure somewhere between your eyebrows and hairline.

A second method starts with the placement of one hand on the grip. If you prefer to paddle on the right side of the canoe, your left hand is the grip hand. Place your other hand on the shaft near the throat. To determine the distance between your hands, hold the paddle horizontally over your head and create 90-degree angles with your elbows (see figure 3.5).

Figure 3.5 One method of fitting a paddle.

Shaft Diameter

As in fitting a tennis racket, you want to find a paddle shaft with a diameter that fits comfortably in your hand. To determine the size paddle shaft that is best for you, make a circle by resting your pointer finger on the side of the knuckle of your thumb. You can also measure from the tip of your longest finger to the heel of your hand. A small-diameter shaft fits a glove size of extra-small to medium. A standard-diameter shaft fits large to extra-large. Some paddle manufacturers have hand measurement charts. Your shaft hand will slide up and down when you perform maneuvers, as it does when choking up on a baseball bat, so along with fitting the size of the diameter, check for a comfortable feel to the sliding movement up and down the shaft of the paddle.

Hand Placement

The recommended hand placement for recreational canoeing is to hold the paddle with one hand on the grip and the other on the shaft with your hands slightly more than shoulder-width apart. Depending on personal preference, paddling style, and venue, this position may change.

Grip

The grip hand is your control hand in paddling. A 45-degree or 90-degree cock of the grip-hand wrist changes the angle of the blade in the water for steering or movement abeam (sideways). You hold the grip with your palm braced against the shape of the grip and your fingers wrapped around the top end, as you would to palm a tennis ball or grab the rung of a ladder. Grips will vary in fatness or thickness. Find one that fits your palm and grip-hand size.

Some grips have nondedicated palms that can be palm rolled, from one side to the other, so that the back becomes the front. Actually, there is no front or back! A dedicated grip is more comfortable to hold one way and may be designed with a dedicated power face. A bent-shaft paddle is an example of a paddle with a dedicated power face and grip.

Personal Flotation Devices

Federal law requires that one personal flotation device, or PFD, per person be on board your canoe. The U.S. Coast Guard (USCG) and the ACA recommend that the PFD be not only on board but also on your body! In the event of a capsize, the PFD could make the difference between life and death. Laws differ by state, but most states require children 12 years old and younger to wear a PFD at all times while on the water.

Fit and Selection

Each of the various types of PFDs has an intended use. Fit is critical; PFD size is based on chest measurement. Make sure that your PFD is the proper size and wear it zipped, buckled, and cinched.

Figure 3.6 *(a)* A properly fitted PFD; *(b)* an improperly fitted PFD.

When fitting a PFD, loosen all the straps, slip on the vest, and zip or buckle it up. Tighten the straps, beginning at the waist belt, working up the sides, and saving the shoulder adjustments, if it has any, for last. A partner can help with the fitting process, cinching straps and tugging upward on the shoulders, checking to see whether the jacket rises above your head (see figure 3.6). A well-fitted jacket is snug and does not rise above your head, but it is not so tight that it restricts your breathing. Be sure to cinch the jacket while standing and then check for comfort in a seated position.

When shopping for a PFD, fit it as described and then use mock paddle strokes to check for range of motion and freedom of movement. Take time to note the presence of (or, you hope, the lack of) chafing or rough spots along the armholes and sides. Also look to see how far up the jacket rides when you sit down. Some vests have deep V-necks to keep the chin from rubbing against zippers or buckles.

Although color is a personal choice, brightly colored PFDs (orange, yellow, red) are more visible on the water.

Types of PFDs

Manufacturers are required to meet certain regulations to obtain USCG approval within the categories listed here. A comfortable choice for paddling is a type III PFD.

- **Type I: offshore life jacket.** This type of PFD is usually found aboard ships at sea. A type I PFD is intended for extended use in rough, open water. Due to the design of the PFD, an unconscious person will usually be turned face up. This type of PFD is extremely bulky and uncomfortable for paddling.

- **Type II: nearshore buoyant vest.** Designed for use in calm inland water near the shore where quick rescue is imminent, this is the classic PFD. The orange horse collar fits this category, as do other standard PFDs. They come in several sizes for children and adults. Some styles will turn an unconscious person face up. Type II PFDs are less expensive than type I PFDs, but they too are bulky and cumbersome for paddling.

- **Type III: flotation aid.** Type III PFDs are the most comfortable type for paddling. The streamlined fit, large armholes, and variety of styles—from vests to pullovers—offer options for personal comfort and fit. An increased range of motion gives paddlers a sense of freedom. These vests are designed for quick rescue in inland water, where the wearer must be able to assume a face-up position in the water. Jackets are available in a variety of sizes for children, women, and men.

- **Type IV: throwable.** These buoyant cushions and ring buoys are not USCG approved for use in canoes. They are intended to be tossed to a swimmer who is already wearing a PFD.

- **Type V: special-use device.** This category includes rescue vests, wind-surfing vests, waterskiing vests, work vests, deck suits, and hybrid vests that may contain an inflatable bladder for added internal buoyancy. Some are designed to protect against hypothermia; other vests may offer freedom of movement or are specially designed for a particular sport.

- **Types III and V: inflatable devices.** Inflatable jackets are comfortable to wear, highly visible when inflated, and turn most people face up faster than do traditional PFDs. The user wears the jacket deflated but can rapidly inflate it by pulling a tab on a cartridge of CO_2. Some inflatables have a backup oral inflation valve. Inflatable vests are only approved for flatwater settings and are not to be used for moving or whitewater paddling.

Other Features

PFDs are not a one-size-fits-all product. The more comfortable the fit is, the greater the likelihood that the person will wear the PFD. Look into specialty and optional features.

- **Flotation.** The average adult requires 7 to 12 extra pounds (3.2 to 5.4 kilograms) of flotation to keep the head out of water. Small child and infant vests provide 7 pounds (3.2 kilograms) of flotation. Children's vests must provide 11 pounds (5 kilograms) of flotation. Check the tag inside the PFD to see whether it meets USCG standards.

- **Women.** Manufacturers have designed specialty jackets with princess seams, shorter waists, and fitted foam that conforms to a woman's shape.

- **Children.** Children should always wear their PFDs on and around the water. Check the laws of your state for local requirements. Infant and toddler jackets often have a crotch strap, a flotation collar to keep the child's head out of water, and a grab loop to haul the wearer back into the boat.

- **Dogs.** If you take your dog with you in a canoe, consider getting a canine PFD. They fit around your dog's torso like a harness, and the most useful feature is the grab loop that helps you get the dog near or back into the canoe. Avoid tying your pet into your boat, a true hazard for you and your pet.

Optional Features

Consider the style of the PFD. Modern vests offer many options, such as zippers, buckles, pullover or front-opening styles, ribs of foam panels, and mesh backs. The shape can be short and bulky, or long and smooth.

Consider PFDs that have pockets and space for attachments. If you want a place to stash small items like lip balm, a whistle, a knife, and bug repellent, look for a vest with zippered pockets and loops or rings. Mesh pockets drain better than nylon pockets. Some PFDs are specifically designed for fishing, with extra pockets, loops, and attachment points.

Maintaining Your PFD

A well-maintained PDF can last for years. Wear your vest instead of using it as a cushion, because sitting on it can compress the foam and decrease buoyancy. Rinse and then let your PFD dry before you put it away, especially if you use it in saltwater. Store your vest away from UV rays, which can damage the nylon. If your PFD becomes sun-faded, ripped, or torn, it is no longer USCG approved and you should dispose of it properly.

Personal and Safety Accessories

Adding safety and personal gear to your boat makes it comfortable, fun, and safe to paddle (see figure 3.7).

Figure 3.7 Properly outfitted canoe.

Seats, Kneeling Thwarts, Pedestals

A number of options are available for sitting or kneeling in your canoe. Most novice paddlers begin in a seated position, choosing molded plastic, webbed, cane, or lightweight carbon or Kevlar molded seats. Comfort, durability, weight, and aesthetics are the criteria to use for choosing your seat.

Kneeling offers more stability by lowering your center of balance. It also enhances paddling efficiency because you can transfer energy from your leg muscles to the canoe. You kneel by tucking your feet under the seat and resting your buttocks on the edge of a webbed or cane seat, or by resting your buttocks against a kneeling thwart. Some boats can be fitted with a kneeling thwart in place of the center thwart or yoke, which transforms a tandem canoe into a solo craft.

Whitewater paddlers use pedestals made from stiff foam, which is custom fitted to the paddler and glued into the bottom of the canoe. Thigh straps help to hold the whitewater canoeist in place.

Kneepads

Kneepads are designed to protect the kneeling paddler from abrasion and to insulate the knees and feet from cold water. Removable kneepads come in strips, T-shapes, and large rectangles. The most comfortable pads have a soft polyester top, foam cells, and a nonslip bottom. Minicell foam squares or strips can also be glued directly to the bottom of the canoe.

Foot Pegs

Foot pegs make paddling more efficient and comfortable. The seated paddler is able to increase paddling efficiency by transferring energy from the leg muscles to the canoe. The pegs or braces can be glued or drilled into the hull. Trippers, marathon racers, and whitewater paddlers often opt for this accessory.

SAFETY TIP

Always have a repair kit along with you on any paddling trip. When assembling a repair kit, think about patching holes; repairing cracked wood gunwales, thwarts, and seats; refastening seats or gear; and strengthening a cracked paddle. Assemble your repair kit based on how far you will be from civilization and according to the materials that you might need to repair.

Yokes

Portage yokes are shaped to fit the contours of the neck and shoulders. Some yokes come with shoulder pads to increase comfort. A portage yoke replaces the center thwart in a tandem canoe. A solo canoe can be carried overhead by resting the seat on the shoulders. A more comfortable option for solor canoeists is to use a removable portage yoke that can be attached as needed. If you will be carrying your boat solo over long distances, the investment is worthwhile.

Lines

Lines are tied to the bow and sometimes to the stern of the boat. The lines, called painters or end lines, are half the boat length. Lines used for other purposes, such as lining canoes up or down rapids, are 20 to 25 feet (6 to 7.5 meters) in length. The rope should be buoyant, strong, and water-resistant. Painters are used to secure a boat to a dock or shore, to tie more than one canoe together while rafting up for a picnic or break, or to tow other boats or equipment, especially during a river rescue. The line can also be used to tie down the canoe during car-top transportation.

Gear lines, made up of a series of D-rings and lashing rope, will help secure gear in the canoe for rough water or an unintended capsize. Loop and toggle bungees and Velcro straps securely attach loose gear such as extra paddles, fishing gear, and water bottles to thwarts or seats.

Flotation Bags

Flotation bags are used by whitewater canoeists to minimize the amount of water that collects inside a canoe in rough conditions. A swamped boat is difficult to paddle or to rescue if capsized. The bags are filled with air and attached at the bow and stern, or at the center of the canoe. Most canoes have built-in flotation chambers in the bow and stern, an arrangement that is adequate for the average paddler in a nonwhitewater venue.

Gear Checklist

The list of personal and safety gear available for outdoor recreation is extensive. Use the gear checklist at the end of the chapter to determine what gear you need to buy and later to keep your gear accessible and organized. Having a bag dedicated to paddling and preloaded with necessary gear saves time and reduces the "Oops, I forgot it" factor.

Gear needs will change depending on the extent of your trip. First, evaluate the conditions of the trip. Determine what you need to bring based on the weather, length of the trip, and access to civilization. With these major factors as planning criteria, use the checklist to make sure that you have everything you need.

PADDLER TIP

Sharing equipment lightens everyone's load. Typical shared items are cooking equipment, water purification systems, stoves, lanterns, and a first aid kit. With proper planning, meals can be coordinated and simplified by cooking for the group rather than the individual or family. If you are river canoeing, each canoe should carry a rescue kit, including a throw rope.

Clothing

Plan on getting wet when paddling. Because of the nature of the sport, getting wet is always a risk. With this in mind, factors to consider when dressing for paddling are the weather, the length of the trip, the distance from shore or the starting or take-out point, and whether a portage is involved. Be sure to check the weather forecast for air temperature, wind velocity, chance of precipitation, and water temperature. Think about dressing from head to toe in preparation for a potential, unexpected capsize. Extra clothing secured in a dry bag is recommended.

Layering: The Three Ws

How do you stay comfortable in the unpredictable outdoors? The best way is to dress in layers. The key to layering your clothes is the order and function of the layers—wicking, warmth, and weather (see figure 3.8). The advantage of layering is that the layers can go on or come off as the weather or your body temperature changes.

Wicking

The wicking layer is the layer next to the skin, often referred to as the base layer. This layer is needed for moisture management and UV protection. Highly breathable wicking fabrics work to remove moisture from the skin, through the fabric, and into the air. Choose a wicking short-sleeve T-shirt for warm weather and a long-sleeve shirt for colder days. You may also want wicking underwear, and women may consider a wicking bra. Some products have UV protection or bug protection woven into the fabric. On a hot day, a long-sleeve, button-down synthetic shirt can be dipped in the water and placed over your PFD for cooling and UV protection.

Warmth

The second layer is your insulation layer. Wool, fleece, or pile works best. Most insulating fabrics are breathable and allow moisture to move through the fabric. If the weather is too warm to wear your warmth layer, pack it in an accessible

Figure 3.8 Layering: *(a)* and *(b)* base layers (wicking), *(c)* insulation (warmth); and *(d)* outer protection (weather).

SAFETY TIP

Precipitation or an unplanned capsize can present the risks of cold-water shock and hypothermia. Hypothermia is a condition brought on by an abrupt drop in body temperature due to exposure to the elements. If the combined air and water temperature is below 120 degrees Fahrenheit (50 degrees Celsius), hypothermia is a distant possibility. If the water temperature is below 65 degrees Fahrenheit (18 degrees Celsius), the possibility of cold-water shock (gulp reflex, hyperventilation, and increased heart rate and blood pressure) is high. Evaluate the risk, plan to swim, and dress accordingly.

place so that you can retrieve it in the event of a change in temperature or an unanticipated swim! In cold weather, consider packing an extra or thicker warmth layer. Think about protecting yourself from head to toe by including a hat, shirt or pullover, gloves, pants, and socks.

Weather

The third layer, or outer layer, protects you from the elements, keeping wind, rain, and splash water away from your body. Clothing in this category comes with varying degrees of comfort, protection, and, of course, cost. Key words here are water resistant, waterproof, wind resistant, windproof, and breathable. Water-resistant breathable layers are worn to protect from the wind and will repel mild precipitation. A heavy rain will eventually soak through a water-resistant layer. The fabric is usually a tightly woven nylon, treated with a water resistant coating on the outside. DWR (durable water resistant) is a product used to treat and retreat these products. As water resistance declines over time (that is, you start getting wet), you can re-treat the product with DWR, which you can spray on or apply during the wash cycle.

Waterproof breathable layers are designed to keep rain and splash water out yet allow the body's moisture and heat to pass through. Some rain jackets are lined with a netting material that allows the moisture to move away from the body, but the moisture may remain trapped inside the garment. Gore-Tex is a popular waterproof breathable fabric that allows water vapor to travel through the membrane, but does not allow water droplets to do the same. This "breathability" helps disperse the water vapor trapped beneath the garment but prevents the precipitation from penetrating it.

Waterproof nonbreathable layers are relatively inexpensive coated nylon or PVC. Although such fabrics are extremely durable and will keep you dry from the elements, they do not let moisture out. Your sweat and body heat will be trapped underneath the garment. Some jackets have armpit zippers or back flaps to allow heat and moisture to escape. Rain pants may have a side zipper that can be used for ventilation.

Dress From Head to Toe

When dressing for paddling, think about dressing from head to toe. If it rains, all your garments will be exposed to the elements—rain hat, jacket, pants, and booties. Layers are a paddler's best friend. A heavy jacket on a cold morning may seem like a wonderful idea until the sun warms you up and your body starts sweating because of the exercise. Layering provides a wide variety of options. If the breeze picks up you may opt for wind protection without the warmth layer. As the temperature drops, the fleece goes on. Rain pants with waterproof side zippers allow for venting and easy-on, easy-off adjustments. You can paddle with the side vents fully open in the sun and zipped up as the wind picks up and the temperature drops.

CONSUMER TIP

As you shop for accessories, be sure to read the labels and hangtags. Outdoor clothing manufacturers usually provide technical information beyond the typical fabric content, cleaning, and care instructions. Hangtag information may include technical fabric design and benefits, recommended product usage, and suggested temperature ranges.

A lake carries you into recesses of feeling otherwise impenetrable.

William Wordsworth

Choosing Fabrics

Manufacturers offer an array of clothing and a variety of fabrics designed for the outdoors. Read fabric labels and hangtags to determine the functions and performance of the garment. Knowing the basics will help you select the right garment for your activity.

Cotton

Cotton (i.e., T-shirts and jeans) is not recommended for paddling in cool or cold temperatures because it absorbs and retains moisture, takes too long to dry, and works to cool the body. Wet, cold, or damp cotton underwear is uncomfortable too. However, during a hot, steamy summer day, wearing cotton can help your body stay cool while paddling.

Wool

Wool has long been popular as a fabric for outdoor use because of its insulating properties. Traditional wool products trap some of your body heat when they are wet, but the downside is that their big woolen yarns absorb water and become extremely heavy, making swimming or rescue difficult. Manufacturers, however, have reworked wool so that it can compete with fleece or synthetic fibers in the outdoor market. They have created a superfine merino wool thread and woven it into lightweight, soft, washable fabrics that can serve as either a next-to-skin layer or an insulating layer. Manufacturers state that the superfine merino wool fibers are better at temperature regulation, moisture management, odor resistance, and strength than the synthetic fibers. Moreover, they claim that the garments are itch-free. Smartwool and Ibex products are examples.

Spandex (Lycra)

Spandex, often known by its most famous brand name, Lycra, is a synthetic fabric made from rubber. Its major property is its ability to expand. Lycra is found in most active wear, especially women's bathing suits and workout clothing. If Lycra gets wet, it will dry out when exposed to the sun. Lycra bathing suits make a good base, or next-to-skin, layer in warm weather. Workout clothing fits well under fleece and rain gear.

Polyester

Polyester refers to cloth woven from polyester fiber. Polyester clothing was all the rage in the 1970s because of its no-wrinkle properties. Polyester fibers are often combined with cotton fibers to produce a cloth with some of the better properties of each. Such fabric is a better choice than 100 percent cotton. Lightweight, synthetic polyester fibers are a good choice for base layers. Polyester is used for next-to-skin garments such as T-shirts and long underwear tops and bottoms.

Fleece or Synthetic Pile

Fleece was invented in the 1980s. Lighter than wool and more compressible, it maintains its insulating properties when wet and dries much faster than wool

CONSUMER TIP

Synthetic fabrics are known by many different names: Duofold, Under Armour, Capilene, Coolmax, Supplex, Dryline, Polypro, Polar Tec, Synchilla, Polar fleece, Gore-Tex, and others. Many of the fabrics have similar technical characteristics, tweaked by the various manufacturers.

because it does not absorb any moisture. Woven from 100 percent polyester, using as much recycled plastic material as possible, basic fleece is a fabric that offers durability, warmth, breathability, wind resistance, odor resistance, and protection from the elements.

Fleece is woven in a variety of thicknesses. Microfleece, the lightest, is often found in linings of gloves or jackets. Fabrics in the 100-weight series are about the weight of sweatshirt fabric. Medium-weight fleece, the 200-weight series, is probably the most common and versatile fleece on the market. The 300-weight series is designed for cold-weather wear. There are even fleece garments that offer wind protection, blocking up to 95 percent of the wind.

The insulating properties of fleece are tremendous. When wet, fleece is warm, remains lightweight, and dries out relatively quickly. To speed the drying process, fleece can be wrung out and swung around. Fleece is usually worn as an insulating layer. Although fleece may protect the wearer from the wind and resist water, it will not keep a person completely dry. For maximum protection from the elements, fleece is best worn over a wicking layer and under a wind- or waterproof layer.

Nylon

Nylon fabrics are wind and water resistant. Some nylon fabrics are brushed to be as soft as cotton. Nylon is a good choice for shorts, pants, and wind jackets.

Extreme Protection

If you choose more extreme types of paddling such as whitewater rivers or open lakes with wind and waves, or if you will encounter very chilly temperatures, you should invest in outerwear protection made specifically for paddling in extreme conditions. When the risk of immersion is high, or when hypothermia and cold-water shock are risks because the combined air and water temperature is below 120 degrees Fahrenheit (50 degrees Celsius) or the water temperature alone is below 65 degrees Fahrenheit (18 degrees Celsius), the need for high-performance insulation and water protection increases. Spray wear, neoprene wet suits, and dry suits are three types of extreme wear designed specifically for paddling.

PADDLER TIP

Give yourself a treat by leaving a clean set of fleece pants and a pullover in your car to change into after paddling in cooler weather.

PADDLER TIP

A paddler wearing just a rain jacket will experience a cool flow of rainwater every time he or she raises an arm to paddle. Water will trickle down the inside of the arm to the armpit and slowly soak the paddler's undergarments. The benefit of a paddling jacket or paddling shirt is that the cinched cuffs keep rainwater out.

Spray Wear

Whitewater and open-sea paddlers may need more protection from the splash of waves and surf. Specially designed spray jackets, shirts, and pants with neoprene cinch cuffs at the wrist, ankles, and neck collar seal out water. Although spray wear protects the paddler, it will not keep the wearer dry in the event of a capsize.

Neoprene Wet Suits

Neoprene is a synthetic rubber compound with insulating properties used for making wet suits. A nonbreathable fabric worn next to the skin, neoprene keeps the wearer warm by trapping a thin layer of moisture between the fabric and the body. Thicker neoprene will be warmer than a thinner fabric but has less stretch, and therefore limits mobility. Neoprene products are available in traditional tops and bottoms, jumpsuits called Farmer Johns or Janes, and full bodysuits. In warm weather and cold water, insulating the core with a neoprene vest and neoprene shorts is an option. Neoprene can be worn alone or under an insulating layer like fleece or under rain gear or a spray jacket, depending on the weather and the temperature of the water.

Dry Suits

Dry suits are made of both breathable and nonbreathable, waterproof fabrics and feature waterproof zippers and latex gaskets at the neck, wrists, and ankles. They are the best choice for protection during immersion. A dry-top and dry-pant option may leak a little at the waist, but will keep you relatively dry in the event of a quick swim. Dry wear gives paddlers year-round paddling options. A dry suit is often the choice of whitewater paddlers, arctic paddlers, and year-round paddling enthusiasts who paddle on open water in colder spring, fall, and winter weather. Staying dry when you capsize in cold conditions is a real benefit! When paddling in cold water or cold weather conditions, paddlers must still layer appropriately under the dry suit.

What to Wear Versus What to Pack

Packing and carrying a dry bag with extra layers and spare clothes to change into is a recommended practice. The farther you are from shore, your car, or shelter where a warm, dry change of clothes is available, the more critical this practice becomes.

If the weather is too warm to wear all your layers or if there is a threat of precipitation but it is not raining, stow your extra layers in a watertight dry bag. Be sure to have the bag accessible for a quick change while paddling. If your insulating layer and wind or rain gear is roomy enough, you can wear it over your PFD, allowing easy adjustment to conditions.

Pack and carry an emergency dry bag with you in the canoe. The emergency dry bag should include an extra set of cool-weather clothing to change into in the event of a capsize (imagine all your layers being wet)—a fleece or wool shirt, fleece pants, wool socks, a fleece or wool cap, and gloves. If it is warm and the sun is out, you won't mind air drying. Remember, prepare for the risk of getting wet, not just the air temperature!

Packing a change of clothes for après canoe activities—traveling home, hiking, or camping—is a recommended practice. Leave a bag in your car or have one ready for your next activity at the take-out.

Accessories

Don't forget to dress the other parts of your body—head, hands, eyes, and feet.

- **Head.** Wear a waterproof, wide-brimmed hat to protect you from the sun and rain. Carry an insulating wool or fleece hat in your warm-gear bag. You can lose up to 75 percent of your body heat through your head.

- **Hands.** Hands are exposed to wind, rain, and sun. Gloves can relieve fatigue, provide a layer of insulation, and protect your hands from UV rays. Fingerless paddling gloves are an option for anglers, photographers, and bird-watchers. Find a fabric that is water resistant, quick drying, or comfortable when wet.

- **Eyes.** The glare of the sun off the water can be blinding. Get a good pair of polarized sunglasses and an eyeglass strap to hold them on your head if you take an accidental swim.

- **Feet.** You should protect your feet from rocks, glass, fishing lures, and other sharp objects that you may step on while launching or in the event of a capsize. Wet, soggy shoes or socks are tolerable in warm weather but become a hazard on cooler days. Although water sandals are appropriate for most paddling activities, consider portage shoes with sturdy soles, ankle support, and drainage features if you will be carrying your canoe over land. One cool-weather option is to wear wool or fleece socks inside your shoes or sandals. Another option is to wear neoprene booties, which retain heat when wet.

Storing Your Gear

Choosing the right storage options for all your gear is important. The basic rule of thumb, again, is to plan on getting wet. Somehow, water usually manages to find its way into your gear. Dripping paddles, sloshing water, or an unexpected rainstorm can put a damper on a picnic or camping outing. Worse yet, a dry bag packed but left open will dump all its contents as the boat capsizes.

Storage Options

Basic storage options range from daypacks to plastic bags. Waterproof storage is more specialized and is specifically designed to keep water out. Your waterproof options range from dry bags to pouches.

Daypacks and Duffle Bags

Traditional daypacks and duffle bags can be lined with garbage bags, or the gear can be packed in the garbage bag and stored inside the pack or duffle. The handles and straps make carrying, portaging, and lashing manageable. Packs designed for snow sports offer a water resistant or waterproof fabric, but the zippers aren't waterproof, so gear will get wet if the bag is immersed.

Nylon Stuff Sacks

Nylon stuff sacks will keep your gear protected from light rain or splashes. Stuff sacks are good for compressing gear, like sleeping bags and clothes, or organizing small items within a larger, waterproof bag. It is good practice to line the stuff sack with a small garbage bag to help keep the items dry.

Mesh Bags

Using mesh bags is a great way to organize within a larger bag because the mesh allows you to see what is inside—cookware, clothing, toiletries, camp stakes, dirty laundry. Mesh bags can be hung up when you set up camp and are ideal for organizing and drying wet gear when off the water.

PADDLER TIP

When packing for an extended trip, you may want to pack gear in a number of smaller bags and then combine them into larger transportation bags. Weight is also a factor, for carrying the load and distributing it in your canoe. Remember to keep essential and emergency gear—throw ropes, first aid kits, and logistics (map and compass)—readily accessible.

SAFETY TIP

Wilderness first aid kits come preassembled and packaged in portable packs. If you want to make your own, Nalgene bottles make an excellent waterproof container. Remember to replenish your kit after each use and to update it annually.

Plastic Bags

Zippered plastic bags come in a variety of sizes, are basically water tight, and can be used to store clothes, food, papers, and so on. Resealable and lightweight, they are easy to pack and useful for organizing. Plastic garbage bags are often used to line larger packs. Heavy-duty trash bags are your best choice. Pack extra bags so that you will have a replacement in the event of a tear or puncture.

Dry Bags

Dry bags are made from a tough plastic and have a collar that you roll and buckle to make a watertight seal. They are tube shaped and come in a variety of sizes and colors, including clear, which allows you to view the contents.

Pelican Boxes and Cases

These hard-cased boxes are designed to protect equipment from impact. Some have foam inserts that can be customized to provide close-fitting padding for cameras, cell phones, binoculars, and other fragile items. O-rings create a watertight seal.

Pouches

A variety of custom-sized pouches and cases are available for maps, GPS units, wallets, cell phones, and car keys. Some are designed to float. They provide watertight seals for gear items that may be left out or stowed in larger bags.

Canoe Bags and Packs

When packing for your trip, there are numerous types of packs and bags to choose from. What you should use depends on the length of your trip and what you need to take with you. Using the right type of bag can make things much easier.

Portage Packs and Duluth Bags

These heavy duty PVC plastic or treated canvas bags are made specifically to stow in a canoe. The large bags are top loading and fitted with shoulder straps for portaging. Some might even have tump lines.

Thwart and Seat Bags

Specially designed bags can be fitted in the bow, under the center thwart, or under or behind the seat. These bags serve as a glove compartment for your canoe, providing a good place to stow small items—gloves, lip balm, snacks, GPS unit—that you may want to access while paddling.

Securing Gear in Your Canoe

Most gear will not float. If you don't want your food, tent, or cooking equipment to end up at the bottom of the lake, you must lash it into the canoe. Some bags have clips that easily attach to thwart bars. Lightweight gear can be attached with Velcro straps or bungee cords.

For longer trips or whitewater paddling, tie gear securely in the boat to prevent it from hanging out and becoming caught on rocks or strainers in the event of a capsize. There are two ways to tie down your gear.

1. **Basic Tie-Down.** Wedge the gear into the canoe. Secure a tie-down line to the thwart and work the line over, under, and around the gear until it is tied securely into place.

2. **Custom Tie-Down.** Drill a series of small holes just below or through each gunwale and fit them with loops or D-rings. With this system, you can easily and efficiently string tie-down line from point to point to keep gear snug and well fitted in the canoe.

Food and Water

"Be prepared" is an apt slogan for all outdoor activities. With this in mind, bring food and water as needed for the trip you plan as well as an emergency stash. What you bring and how much space the food and water take is related to the length of your trip. A bottle of water, an energy bar, and a piece of fruit may be all you take for an hour-long paddle on a local canal. A picnic lunch and snack work well for a day trip. An overnight trip requires more planning (see chapter 8, "Overnight Camping Skills").

Food

Food items can be heavy, take up valuable space, and are perishable and crushable. Energy bars, nuts, cheeses, apples, and peanut butter all pack well and provide much-needed nutrition. Buying or creating your own one-bag meals is a good alternative. Repackage items into resealable zippered plastic bags, premeasure ingredients, and bundle by meal. Search for items that can be prepared by just adding water, such as juices, oatmeal, and rice dishes. For overnight trips, be sure to have some meals that do not require cooking and pack at least one extra meal, just in case.

Water

Staying hydrated is a basic principle of survival in the outdoors. We all know that the body can survive longer without food than it can without water. Dehydration can cause the body to become fatigued. In extreme conditions, a well-hydrated person is less apt to become chilled or to develop heat stroke. For day trips you can carry all you need. For extended trips, you will want to consider water treatment options to ensure that you have access to enough water and to lighten your load.

Taking Water

For day trips you should drink water before you launch, during your outing, and at the end of the trip. Pack extra water in your vehicle. Stow water bottles in the canoe and make sure that the sipping surface is not exposed to dripping lake water. Plastic Lexan water bottles withstand a great deal of outdoor abuse. Wearable hydration packs are a convenient, hands-free option. Some PFDs are fitted with a pocket for a water hydration bladder; other hydration systems are made to attach to the straps of your PFD, or even under the canoe seat. A sipping tube that runs from the bladder can be clipped to the front of your PFD for easy access.

Water Treatment

Fresh lake or river water contains bacteria, protozoa, and viruses. Although drinking from the river may not kill you, the water can make you sick enough to feel as if you are dying. To prevent waterborne illness, you must treat water before drinking, cooking, cleaning your dishes, or even brushing your teeth.

To treat water, you can boil it, filter it, or chlorinate it. Boiling will eliminate most germs but won't get rid of dirt and minerals. Boiled water is generally safe for cooking, washing dishes, and brushing teeth. Drinking water is best when filtered and chlorinated. Consider investing in a good water filter. To use a filter, you drop a line into the lake and pump the water through the filter to eliminate sediment and most bacteria. After you add a few drops of chlorine-based water treatment solution, the water is ready to drink. An herbal tea bag or unsweetened drink mix will mask the chlorine taste.

Summary

This chapter covers the technical nature of much of the equipment that one can (or should) use when paddling a canoe. As the individual paddler's experience, skill level, and paddling venue changes, more equipment may be necessary to maintain a safe and enjoyable trip. Simply grabbing a canoe, a couple paddles, and a couple life jackets is not sufficient. Be sure to take into account the many factors that will make the trip the best it can be, and remember the 6 Ps: Proper, prior preparation prevents poor performance.

Gear Checklist

Basic Canoe Gear

- ☐ Boat
- ☐ Paddle or paddles (spare paddle)
- ☐ PFD
- ☐ Signaling device (whistle, mirror, flares)
- ☐ Knife
- ☐ Throw rope
- ☐ Light
- ☐ Maps and guidebook
- ☐ Compass
- ☐ Weather radio
- ☐ Two-way radio or cell phone

Personal Essentials

- ☐ Water
- ☐ Food or snack
- ☐ Sunscreen
- ☐ Hat
- ☐ Sunglasses and eyeglass straps
- ☐ Cold- and wet-weather gear
- ☐ Change of clothing
- ☐ Water shoes or portage boots
- ☐ Paddling gloves
- ☐ Dry bags
- ☐ Bug spray
- ☐ Emergency blanket
- ☐ Matches or lighter
- ☐ Money for emergencies

Shared Gear

- ☐ Cooking equipment and kitchen items
- ☐ Water purification system
- ☐ Stove
- ☐ Flashlight or lantern
- ☐ Group first aid kit
- ☐ Rescue kit
- ☐ Food
- ☐ Shelter

Repair Kit

- ☐ Duct tape
- ☐ Extra bolts, nuts, and pins
- ☐ Screws and wood screws
- ☐ Multiuse tool
- ☐ Saw blade
- ☐ Plastic bags
- ☐ Epoxy adhesive
- ☐ Nylon cable ties
- ☐ Bailing wire
- ☐ Vinyl patch and cement
- ☐ Fiberglass repair kit
- ☐ Resin

First Aid Kit

- ☐ Emergency contact information

First Aid Tools

- ☐ First aid manual
- ☐ Safety gloves
- ☐ CPR face shield

- ☐ Emergency blanket
- ☐ Magnifying glass
- ☐ Matches or lighter
- ☐ Tweezers
- ☐ Safety pins
- ☐ Razor blade
- ☐ Knife
- ☐ Scissors
- ☐ Thermometer
- ☐ Duct tape

Bandages and Pads

- ☐ Band-aids of various sizes
- ☐ Butterfly bandage
- ☐ Triangle bandage
- ☐ Large compress
- ☐ Gauze pads
- ☐ Gauze wrap
- ☐ Adhesive tape
- ☐ Moleskin
- ☐ Sam splint

Medications

- ☐ Antibiotic ointment
- ☐ Hydrocortisone cream
- ☐ Antiseptic wipes
- ☐ Nonaspirin tablets
- ☐ Aspirin
- ☐ Ibuprofen

☐ Antihistamine tablets

☐ Bee sting swabs

☐ Burn gel

☐ Calamine lotion

☐ Antibacterial soap

☐ Lip balm

☐ Bug spray

☐ Sunscreen

CHAPTER 4

Getting Ready to Paddle

Everyone must believe in something. I believe I'll go canoeing.

Henry David Thoreau

Whether you're planning a trip for yourself and a friend or a larger group, the fundamentals of trip planning remain constant. Planning is critical to a safe and successful trip. You must keep several factors in mind as you plan your trip: the skills and experience of the group, water and weather factors, the safety of the route, and gear needs. Extended trips require a pre-event planning meeting to coordinate trip details, designate cooking and gear assignments, and assign individual roles and responsibilities among the group. Remember, prior, proper planning prevents poor performance.

Planning a Trip

The first step in trip planning is to assess the skills of the group. After you have determined each person's paddling ability, you can make the remainder of your plans accordingly. The route or the type of water that you paddle must fit the skill level of all individuals in the group. Taking a first-time paddler along on a winding river trip will be frustrating for experienced paddlers and slow the entire group. A wide, lazy river or a quiet, protected lake would be a better option.

Paddler Skills and Experience

The canoeing event should be geared to the skill level of the weakest paddler. Answer the following questions to assess the ability of your group.

- What paddling experiences have they honestly had?
- What formal instruction have they had, or what certification do they have?
- Are any similarities present among the group?
- What is the emotional commitment of the group (excited versus apprehensive)?
- Are they novices, beginners, or advanced paddlers?
- Can they swim?
- Has the group practiced assisted or self-rescue? Are they competent in performing rescue techniques?
- Is anyone afraid of weather, water, bugs, water snakes, or lightning?

Use the following skill level classifications to determine the level of each group member.

- **First-time or amateur.** The paddler is paddling for the first time or has recently been introduced to paddling sports. Experience and confidence are low.
- **Beginner.** The paddler can perform basic strokes to maneuver a boat in a straight line and avoid obstructions. He or she is comfortable on quiet water and negotiating twists and turns on a gently moving river. River paddlers should be able to negotiate class I rapids.

I will up and get me away where the hawk is wheeling lone and high, and the slow clouds go by. I will get me away to the waters that glass the clouds as they pass.

Richard Hovey

- **Intermediate.** The paddler is proficient in all basic and some advanced strokes. He or she is able to maneuver safely in moderate wind and waves, and can perform an assisted canoe-over-canoe T-rescue and deep-water reentry. Whitewater paddlers can negotiate class II rapids.
- **Advanced.** The paddler has solid paddling techniques and is able to perform self-rescue and assisted rescue. He or she is comfortable in large bodies of water, wind, and waves. Whitewater paddlers can paddle up to class III and IV rapids.

As the trip leader, your role is to ensure the safety and success of every paddler. Do not put yourself or others at risk by making exceptions for paddlers who are enthusiastic but unskilled. Instead, rethink the trip so that it meets the needs of the weakest paddler, or create a series of events to prepare participants by building their skills and competence.

Determining the Route

After you have assessed the skill, experience, and desires of the group, you will match these criteria with an appropriate waterway. Chapter 1 covered different water venues (quiet water, rivers and streams, whitewater, and open lakes and seas) and their appropriateness for the novice or advanced paddler.

As a trip leader, you have the responsibility to rate or know the difficulty of the route that you choose. Experience is your best resource, so the best approach is to be familiar with a route before you take others along with you. The trip difficulty is determined by the type of water that you paddle, the length of the paddle (distance and time), the location, the weather, and the number and length of carries (portages) included in the trip. Consult tables 4.1 and 4.2.

Note that precipitation, strong winds, and even heat can increase the difficulty of a well-planned trip. Alternative routes or time schedules should be part of your contingency plan to accommodate changes in weather. In the event of severe weather, you may need to cancel the event.

Paddling guidebooks often rate the level of difficulty of outings. Check publication dates to make sure that the information is current. Guidebooks may provide details for parking, lake or river access, and specifics about put-in and take-out sites. The narrative description may help you determine whether a destination is appropriate for your group.

Local guides or experts can provide up-to-date information on water levels, hazards, man-made obstacles, launching and landing sites, and portage routes. Local guides may also be able to provide information on campsites, local attractions, and side trips.

You can search the Internet for current paddling or canoe maps of your location. If paddling-specific maps are not available, a topographic map of the

Table 4.1 Water Classification

Water type	Description
Flat water	Protected from wind and waves. River, canal, or creek with negligible current, no rapids.
Open water	• Class 1—easy • Class 2—moderately challenging • Class 3—challenging • Class 4—difficult • Class 5—very difficult • Class 6—extreme
River classification	Rivers are given a difficulty rating under different conditions based on the force, flow, and difficulty of the moving water. • Class I—easy • Class II—novice • Class III—intermediate • Class IV—advanced • Class V—expert • Class VI—extreme Negotiating moving water requires experience with strokes, negotiating obstacles, and assisted and self-rescue. (See chapter 7 for more details on river paddling and classifications.)

Table 4.2 Trip Rating

Level	Length	Carries	Water classification
C	Less than 6 miles (10 kilometers)	No carries	Flatwater
B	6-12 miles (10-20 kilometers)	Short carries, less than .5 mile (.8 kilometer)	Class I water—moving; moderate wind and wave exposure
A	12 miles (20 kilometers) or more	Long carries, more than .5 mile (.8 kilometer)	Class II water and above; moderate to heavy wind and wave exposure

Additional trip rating qualifiers:

+ Trip will be more strenuous than a normal rating because of longer distances, open water, rapids, or carries.

− Trip will be less strenuous than a normal rating because of shorter distances, fewer classified rapids, or short carries.

SAFETY TIP

If you are traveling in a remote area, be sure to have contact information for rangers, emergency facilities, or civilized areas so that you will be prepared in the event of an emergency.

area would be an adequate resource because it shows features not seen on standard road maps. However, road atlases do offer a wealth of other pertinent information. Launch sites are usually noted by a boat icon, campsites by a tent or lean-to icon, and fishing access by a fish icon. Check the shoreline for public property that you can use for picnics or breaks (take-outs). Respect private property and access it only in an extreme emergency.

Paddling clubs often maintain a local database of paddling destinations. The American Canoe Association (ACA) offers an up-to-date national database and provides reputable information for the trip planner. The ACA Web site, www.americancanoe.org, publishes links to ACA-approved water trails that meet a set of basic criteria and stand out as good destinations for paddlers. To be eligible, a trail must meet the following requirements:

- The trail must be a contiguous or semi-contiguous waterway or series of waterways that is open to recreational use by paddlers;
- The trail must have public access points for paddlers;

- The trail must be covered by a map, guide, signage, or a Web site that is of reasonable quality and detail and available to the public;
- Published or printed materials for the trail (e.g., guidebook, map, signs, Web site) must communicate low-impact ethics to trail users; and
- The trail must be supported or managed by one or more organizations.

ACA-recommended water trails earn the right to use a special ACA logo in maps, signs, and other printed material related to the trail. They also receive special recognition in the ACA's water trails database. The ACA names a new group of recommended trails during the summer of each year.

Float Plan

After you have planned your trip, write down the details and file it with a friend, a ranger, or the Coast Guard. Include details about the route: starting, stopping, and camping points; final destination; estimated departure and arrival times; and a list of participants. Have an agreement in place with your designated contact about what action he or she will take if you fail to make contact before the designated time. Then be sure to contact the person when the trip ends.

Pre-Event Planning Meeting

Now that you have decided you are ready to go out on a canoe trip, it is essential that you plan accordingly, so that the elements of surprise and danger are minimized. Using the tips that follow, you will be able to plan a safe and fun trip for all those involved.

Emergency Plans

An emergency action plan (EAP) should always be discussed, especially if threatening weather (e.g., lightning) is possible or a potential medical emergency (i.e., bee allergy) exists among the group. When developing your EAP, be sure to take into consideration how you can seek shelter, contact the necessary medical or emergency agencies, or simply evacuate the area. This plan should include all the necessary contact information, not only for individuals on the trip, but also for those at home with whom you have left a copy of your trip plan.

Individual Paddling Roles

Beyond the roles of trip planner, first aid provider, handyman, meal planner, and camp equipment and gear inventory person, four safety roles should be assigned to the group for the on-water segments of the trip: leader, sweep, rescue, and group. The roles can be explained and assigned at the pre-event meeting and later restated and clarified prelaunch for a day trip. Like the person who occupies the exit seat on an airplane, a person who accepts a role

SAFETY TIP

Pack two stoves and two water purification systems. If something happens to one, you have a backup.

must understand the role, be willing to execute it for the entire trip without becoming distracted, and be trained and capable of fulfilling the responsibilities of the role.

Leader

The trip leader organizes the trip, assesses skill levels, enforces safety practices, and performs gear and equipment checks. The leader must carry the map, compass, safety and rescue gear, and extra paddle, as well as a repair kit. The leader sets the pace and determines the route throughout the paddle. The leader initiates communication and river signals for the group (see chapter 5). The trip leader is not necessarily the trip planner. The planner may be the right person to handle the particulars, but depending on the group's strengths, he or she may not be the ideal candidate to take responsibility for on-water leadership and safety.

If anyone in the group has medical, physical, or emotional limitations, the trip leader and one other responsible member of the group should be aware of them. The leader needs to designate a qualified assistant who would act on his or her behalf should the leader require emergency or rescue assistance.

Lead and Sweep

The lead boat sets the pace. Sometimes this boat has the trip leader aboard, but not always. One of the most important functions of a good lead boat is to keep the group together. The paddler in the lead boat looks back to make sure the group is moving as a unit and is not too spread out. A spread-out group can lead to unsafe rescue situations and it can be a major hazard when paddling in areas with other boat traffic.

The sweep boat brings up the rear, often encouraging and motivating weaker paddlers. The sweep's key function is to make sure that no one gets left behind. The sweep should be a strong paddler, trained and competent in rescue procedures.

Rescue

When the trip is under way, one or two canoes may be designated as the "rescue boats." Their paddlers should be individuals who have experience handling rescue situations. These boats are not typically assigned to the lead or sweep positions.

Alternatively, in some instances, all the members of the group can be considered the rescue team. In this scenario, the two boats closest to the troubled paddler should respond first. Priorities are in this order: people, boat, and gear. The remaining paddlers should gather nearby and assist as necessary without interfering. Rescue techniques are described in detail in chapter 5.

Group

All paddlers are assigned responsibility for the group. Participants need to understand that they are part of a group, are expected to adhere to the guidelines set forth by the leader, and are to remain part of the group throughout the paddle. Communicating, keeping eyes open for obstacles and hazards, and practicing safety and personal responsibility will affect the success of the trip.

Once all the roles and responsibilities of the group members have been defined, it is recommended that the group review the trip plan. This exercise allows all paddlers to know and understand the trip ahead, ask questions, and express concerns or excitement over the upcoming adventure. Reviewing the trip plan also gives the individuals in specific roles the opportunity to assess the group further, keeping in mind the special responsibilities that come with their roles.

Day of the Trip

Today is the day! All the planning is complete. Now it's time to pack the cars, load the boats, and head to the water. It can appear to be as simple as that, but there are other factors paddlers must consider even while the adrenaline and excitement of the moment is upon them. There are some things you can't plan for and you must evaluate them on the day of the trip.

Wind, Weather, Water

On the day of the trip, reassess the safety conditions and determine whether the trip should still take place. If so, determine how far you will travel. Wind, weather, and water are the major factors to consider. A well-thought-out plan to respond to potential adverse weather scenarios will help you react quickly and safely to changing circumstances. Consider these factors:

- **Wind.** What is the strength and direction of the wind? Will you be protected from the wind? Will you be paddling into or against the wind? How much will the wind slow you down? Can you make your destination by dark?
- **Weather.** Evaluate current and predicted weather. Are you prepared to ride out a storm? What are alternative take-out sites in the event of an emergency? Will shelter be available?
- **Water.** Assess water temperature, the size of the waves, and the strength of any current, rapids, or tides. Are water levels too high or too low? Have storms come through the area, felling trees and creating river hazards?

Figure 4.1 A prelaunch meeting gives the group an opportunity to review the route, the plans for the day, and any known risk factors.

Assess the paddlers' skills against the environmental conditions. If you have any doubt about safety, postpone the trip until conditions improve or until the paddlers involved gain the necessary skills and experience to participate successfully.

Prelaunch Meeting

Gather the group and share the itinerary for the day, including break and lunch times (see figure 4.1). Review the route, highlighting known hazards, emergency shelters or take-outs, and the end goal or take-out. Discuss skill levels of the group, including individual participants' swimming ability and medical conditions. Identify the trip leader(s) and the lead and sweep boats, and discuss emergency and first aid plans.

Gear Check

Before launching, conduct a gear check to make sure that everyone has the basics—PFDs, paddles, food and water, extra clothing, and inclement weather gear. Trip leaders are responsible for carrying maps and guides, compass, a first aid kit, and safety and rescue gear. Your personalized gear checklist from chapter 3 will come in handy here.

When paddling as a group you can lighten individual loads by divvying up the items on the gear list from chapter 3 and the camping equipment list from

TECHNIQUE TIP

Coordinating meal preparation among the whole group is easier than having every person pack individual meals. Meal responsibility can be divided among the group, but you must be sure that you (or whoever is responsible for cooking equipment) have all the cooking utensils and ingredients necessary for meal preparation. For day trips, pot-luck style makes for an interesting meal.

chapter 8. Each person is responsible for his or her basic canoe gear, personal essentials, and personal camping and sleeping gear. An additional first aid kit, a repair kit, kitchen items, and other items on the list of shared equipment can be split among the group. The person with the highest level of first aid certification should be assigned to this first aid kit.

Once all the gear has been loaded in the canoes, check the boats to be sure that gear is appropriately stowed and tied down. Is each boat trim, that is, floating level, in the water? If not, adjust gear or people so that the boat is loaded and weighted properly.

Sharing the Waterways

As with driving and navigating highways, rules and rights of passage govern the navigation of waterways. You are responsible for knowing the U.S. Coast Guard's navigational rules for the waterways that you paddle.

Be Aware

Always assume that other boaters do not see you. Canoes do not show up on radar, and they can get lost on the horizon. Large motor craft are not as maneuverable as canoes and have long stopping distances. Be aware and use your ability to stop or get out of the way.

Collision Course

To determine a collision course with another boat, take and hold a bearing off your bow. If the bearing changes as the range decreases, that is, if the other craft moves one way or another relative to your bow, you are not on a collision course. If the bearing stays constant as you draw closer to the other boat, you are on course for a collision. You should change course, stop, or do whatever

Figure 4.2 Buoys delineate channels for larger boats. By staying outside the buoys, closer to the shore, canoes can avoid traffic and wakes.

it takes to get out of the way and let the boat pass. Use a signal device (horn or whistle) if necessary.

Right of Passage

Channels are marked for larger boats with buoys and red or green lights (figure 4.2). If you stay between the shoreline and the buoys, you are less apt to encounter wake and traffic. If you need to cross a channel, do it as a group, crossing the channel at a right angle to the direction of the powerboat traffic, not as a long line of stragglers.

Since 9/11, many harbors, bridges, dams, and drinking water supplies have restricted access and may be patrolled. Respect the authorities and report suspicious activities.

Paddling at Night

If you are paddling between sunset and sunrise or under conditions of limited visibility (fog, rain, haze), you must have a light on your canoe. The law requires paddlers to have a visible white light. Some preferred lights include headlamps, handheld flashlights, or small lights you can fasten to the shoulder strap of your PFD and hold overhead if a motorized craft approaches (figure 4.3). Motorized crafts have a red light portside (bow left) and green light starboard (bow right). The position of the lights helps you determine which way the motorboat is traveling.

Figure 4.3 When canoeing at night, regulations require you to use a visible white light to alert others to your position. Headlamps or shoulder-mounted lights are recommended.

Canoe Etiquette and Ethics

You can maximize safety and minimize social and environmental impacts by adhering to the following guidelines.

Safety Guidelines

Adherence to these practices will minimize potential personal risk and risk to others.

- Wear your PFD—on, zipped or buckled, and cinched.
- Avoid drug and alcohol use while canoeing.
- Paddle with a friend—never alone. File a float plan.
- Avoid a capsize!
    - Don't overload the canoe with people or gear.
    - Remain seated. Do not stand in a canoe.

- Paddle in control. Be able to steer and control the speed and direction of the canoe.
- Leave space between yourself and other paddlers.
- Know your limits. Paddle in situations at or below your skill level.
- Be a competent swimmer or practice swimming in your PFD.
- Know how to perform self-rescues and rescues to assist others.
- Dress for changing weather conditions.
- Keep an eye out for water hazards and alert others to them.
- Know how to read the signs of changes in weather and water, and respond accordingly.
- Know and adhere to land and water regulations in your area.
- Be familiar with the rules for sharing waterways with other boat traffic.

Social Guidelines

Adherence to these practices will minimize the effect that our presence has on the privacy of others and their personal enjoyment of outdoor resources.

- Respect private property.
- Don't be noisy when encountering others on the water.
- Give anglers and swimmers a wide berth.
- Change clothes privately.

Environmental Guidelines

Adherence to these practices will preserve and protect our natural resources, ensuring that green and blue spaces will be available for future generations.

- Participate in local river cleanup days.
- Bring a garbage bag and collect litter along your route.
- Practice water conservation at home.
- Avoid introducing invasive species.
- Use environmentally friendly products on the hull of your boat.
- Properly dispose of waste.
- Protect shorelines by treading lightly and spreading foot and boat traffic on land to keep plants and wildlife intact. This practice reduces shoreline erosion.

Summary

Making the decision to get out and enjoy the sport of canoeing is an exciting and positive first step. Like many before you, canoeing may actually become something you will be passionate about. Knowing how to plan and prepare for an on-water excursion is an essential skill for all paddlers and it should be one you acquire at the very start of your paddling experience. Regardless of the length of the trip you are taking, planning is a basic requirement for a safe and successful trip. You must keep in mind the skills and experience of each individual in the group, environmental factors such as water and weather conditions, the safety of the route you will be taking, and what gear you will need. Work out all the details and include every participant in the process to ensure the safety of everyone in the group.

CHAPTER 5

Water Safety and Survival Skills

There is no such thing as bad weather, only bad clothes.

Old Norwegian adage

They planned to enjoy a short, relaxing trip. Seth and Alex were eager to try out their new canoe, so they packed only a few items, making sure that they had their new paddles and life jackets. They headed to Grand Lake, launching on the western shore. The late-day temperature was rising fast, and Seth and Alex did not notice the clouds building up behind them. Soon the west wind was pushing them farther into open water, much faster than their new paddling abilities could handle. When the thunderstorm erupted, they found themselves scared and cold, and they panicked in the lightning and hard rain. They laid low in the bottom of the canoe to keep from capsizing. Strong winds pushed them past the warning buoys and toward the overflow of the Grand Lake dam. Not knowing what else to do, they dove into the 60-degree Fahrenheit (15.5-degree Celsius) water and swam to the anchored warning buoy, away from the danger of the dam. From the water, they watched the wind blow their canoe over the rim of the overflow. They huddled together for warmth and awaited rescue.

Know Your Boating Abilities and the Waters

Paddling in moving water requires special skill and knowledge. Good boat control on a lake or river is mastered through knowledge of the various forces involved and the application of those forces in a given situation. Your movement with wind or river current could cause you to come upon obstacles too fast to react in time. By knowing the proper strokes and maneuvers, you can slow your speed and assess the situation so that you can stay out of harm's way.

Paddling in rapidly moving water or high wind is a complex skill that requires extensive knowledge of the boat and the power of the water. If you are not experienced in boat handling under these conditions, you should obtain training and travel with someone who is. Through that person's experience, your observation, and your study of the characteristics of wind, waves, and moving water, you will soon be able to paddle with confidence.

"Know before you go." This slogan means that you should read guidebooks, check with outfitters, or talk with paddlers who have experience on the river that you intend to paddle. You'll need to know about hazards, difficulty, water levels, the locations of put-ins and take-outs, and more. Make sure that everyone in your group has the skills appropriate for the river or lake that you intend to paddle. Formulate a float plan and leave a copy with a friend, family member, or other responsible party.

Learn to recognize potential hazards and use good judgment to avoid them. Inclement weather, flood waters, and natural or man-made obstructions are all danger signs.

Be conservative! Paddling can be safe, and it should be fun. Walk around or leave a wide margin around hazards. Reschedule the trip when conditions are simply too dangerous—for instance, during floods or extreme cold.

A lake is the landscape's most beautiful and expressive feature. It is earth's eye; looking into which the beholder measures the depth of his own nature.

Henry David Thoreau

Weather

Paddlers must have a basic understanding of weather and weather patterns. To the paddler, weather is a primary concern, and knowledge of some simple weather prediction tools can be invaluable. Weather forecasting, although based on scientific analysis, can be relatively easy to accomplish with some know-how. Several practical tricks can help you predict the weather with considerable reliability. And all you really have to do is look up to the sky.

For example, the formation of jet vapor trails is a key indicator. The high-altitude air is frequently crisscrossed with trails left by planes. On some days the trails are invisible. On other days they last for a few minutes before vanishing. But at times they seem to last for hours. Some spread slowly and seem to change into clouds. The lingering vapor trail is noteworthy because a trail that remains in the sky usually foretells a change in the weather.

Read the Clouds

An interesting method of weather forecasting is cloud reading. Each type of cloud carries a weather message. From cloud clues you can get a good idea of the type of weather to expect in the next few hours to the next few days.

The simplest message comes from the perfectly clear day. This sky condition means that the chance of rain or snow is absent. On a partly sunny, partly cloudy day when the sky is filled with loose, fuzzy cumulus clouds, you should watch for any firming up of the clouds. Loose and cottony clouds are harmless. When firm edges start appearing and the clouds take on a definite shape, showers may develop. The faster the clouds develop, the greater the chance that rain will fall. Generally, the weather will take a turn for the worse when small clouds gather and change into larger clouds. A shifting wind and clouds moving in different directions at different heights is also a good indication that rain will follow.

Watch for Signs

Some signs that fair weather will continue include summer fog clearing before noon, clouds decreasing in number, wind blowing gently from the west or northwest, the sky remaining clear, the sun appearing as a ball of fire, and the moon shining brightly.

Signs that the weather will change for the worse include clouds increasing and lowering, clouds moving in different directions, wind shifting from south to east, clouds darkening the western horizon, the barometer falling, and wind blowing strongly in the early morning.

The weather will clear when the cloud bases increase in height, a cloudy sky begins to clear, the barometer rises rapidly, and wind shifts to a westerly direction.

Obtain Weather Reports

Being able to forecast can be fun and possibly save the day. But you should obtain a reliable weather report before going paddling. Local newspapers often print one- to three-day forecasts. Radio and television broadcasts include weather reports with short- and long-range forecasts. The Internet provides a reliable source of weather information any time of the day.

And, of course, don't forget the special 24-hour weather broadcast by the National Weather Service, a branch of the National Oceanic and Atmospheric Administration (NOAA). Transmitters placed across the country provide the latest weather broadcast directly from the office of the National Weather Service. All you need is a radio with a weather band and you are able to receive regularly updated forecasts for your region. For links to international weather information, visit www.weather.com.

Be Weather Wise

Regardless of how you obtain weather information, heed the warnings. Being weather wise is a basic rule of safe paddling. If you are planning a day on the water, check the local forecast. Remember that you can get into bad weather even with a fair forecast. Squalls and thunderstorms are unpredictable and can cause an enjoyable outing to turn into a dangerous situation. Keep a weather watch and make the decision to go into shore if conditions become threatening.

River Reading

Moving water has power. A canoeist who understands the principles of moving water can harness this power to have fun on the river. On the other hand, a canoeist who doesn't understand and respect these forces can be harmed or even killed by the power of moving water. This section of the chapter covers river dynamics, which provides the foundation for river reading. The dynamics of moving water covered in this section include river currents, river obstacles, and river hazards.

Having an understanding of river dynamics is important for canoeists to ensure an experience that is both safe and enjoyable. Rivers are our drainage systems. Eventually, everything upstream is carried downstream, including natural and man-made debris. The difference between a river feature that can provide endless hours of fun and one that might be dangerous is sometimes subtle. The description of river features and hazards in this chapter can help the paddler have a safe and enjoyable experience.

River Currents

River flows can be quite complex since gravity, inertia, and obstructions change the way water flows within the banks of any given stream. This section covers many of the ways water reacts to the surrounding environment.

SAFETY TIP

A person standing thigh deep in a 5 mile-per-hour (8 kilometer-per-hour) current can easily have 100 pounds (45 kilograms) of pressure placed on his or her body. This amount of pressure is often enough to upend the person. The great pressure exerted by fast-flowing water also explains why the moderate drowning-trap flows are potentially dangerous.

SAFETY TIP

Drifting along in a 5 mile-per-hour (8-kilometer-per-hour) current may seem tame. But a swamped canoe filled with water can easily exert a force of 2,400 pounds (1,100 kilograms). For this reason you want to be upstream of a swamped canoe so that you do not become caught between a rock and the swamped canoe. Some rivers are measured in cubic feet per second (CFS), representing the volume of water passing a given point at a given time.

Primary Current

The primary current, the current found in the main channel, refers to the general direction in which the river is flowing. The primary flow is illustrated by a cross section of the river indicating the speed of the flow at various levels (laminar flow). The slowest-moving water is next to the bottom, and each successive layer of water toward the surface flows faster than the layer below it. The fastest-moving water is found just below the surface, because the air next to the surface creates friction that slows the surface water slightly.

A way to conceptualize this principle is to imagine sheets of plywood stacked on the floor with wooden dowels between the sheets (figure 5.1a). Push the stack of plywood. Each sheet of plywood on the stack will travel at the speed of the next lower sheet plus its own speed. Hence, the higher the stack of plywood, the greater the speed that the plywood will travel.

The primary flow can also be illustrated by a top view (figure 5.1b) showing the linear, or surface, flow of the river. As in the laminar flow, the water closest to the river bank is slowest, while the unobstructed center flow is moving fastest.

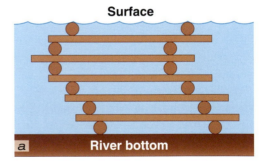

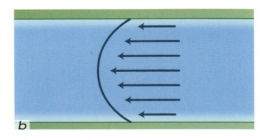

Figure 5.1 Primary current illustrated as *(a)* laminar flow and *(b)* surface flow.

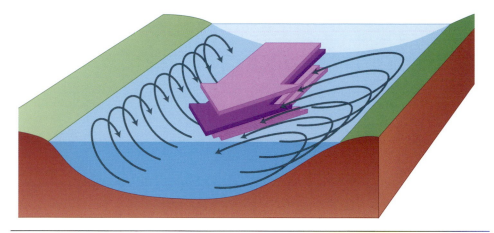

Figure 5.2 Shore-to-center (helical) flow.

Shore-to-Center Flows

Shore-to-center flow refers to the currents moving at the surface of the water from the riverbank to the center channel. Because the water at the surface is traveling slower than the water underneath it, a slight depression is created at the surface. To fill the void, water is drawn in from the sides of the river. These flows are sometimes referred to as helical flows (figure 5.2). Because these currents are going away from the shore, a victim who is self-rescuing in higher-volume flow situations may need to swim actively toward the shore to reduce the likelihood of being carried away from shore.

Bends

Rivers tend to meander. When the river bends, inertia forces the main current toward the outside of the bend (figure 5.3). As the deeper,

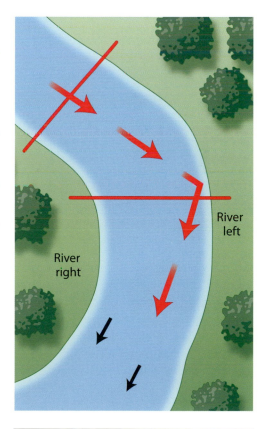

Figure 5.3 Current at a river bend.

faster, and more powerful current reaches the outside of the bend, it turns downward and creates a spiraling effect off the bottom of the river that leaves more room for surface water on the outside of the bend. The force of the water tends to erode the outside of the bend, causing trees and other debris to fall into the river where they can form strainers.

In contrast, the slower, shallower, and less powerful current is found on the inside of the bend. A cross section of the current speeds shows the difference between a straight section of river (figure 5.4*a*) and a bend in the river (figure 5.4*b*).

Canoeists need to approach bends cautiously. The current can force the canoe to the outside of the bend and into any strainers or obstructions that may be present. Also, if the current is powerful enough, it will tend to push the canoe toward the outside shore of the bend. In addition, the slower water on the inside of the bend can create an effect that can turn the canoe as if it were caught by an eddy. Because the current is going faster toward the outside of the bend, canoeists need to "set" the canoe around the bend to prevent the current from forcing the canoe to the outside of the bend. To set the canoe properly, position it so that the bow is facing the direction of the downstream current just past

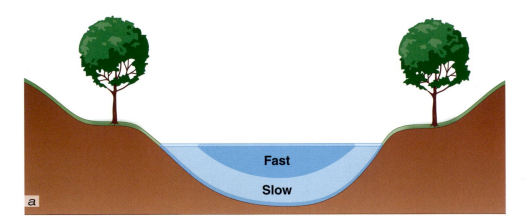

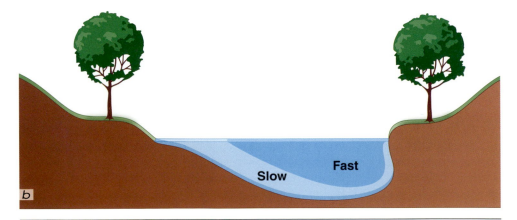

Figure 5.4   Current at a river bend (side view).

the inside of the bend (figure 5.5). Once the canoe clears the slower-moving current on the inside of the bend, paddlers can then accelerate forward, avoiding the obstructions and faster current on the outside of the bend.

Chutes and Waves

A constriction forces the water to increase its speed as it passes through it. This water usually forms a smooth tongue of water, or a chute (figure 5.6). After the water passes through the constriction, its deceleration into a deeper and slower state results in a series of uniformly spaced, scallop-shaped standing waves. The

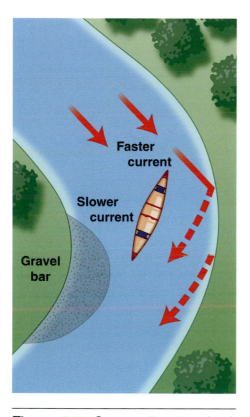

Figure 5.5 Canoe position at river bend.

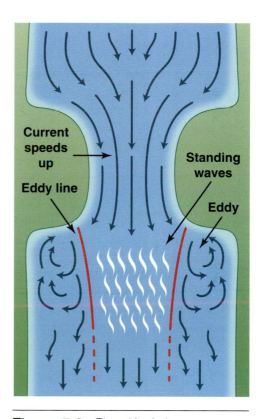

Figure 5.6 Riverwide chute.

SAFETY TIP

Approach a bend in the river on the inside of the bend where the current is slower and where you can avoid the fast current and any strainers on the outside of the bend.

constriction can vary in width from a boat length to the width of the river. The former can create a simple drop with small waves that the canoe simply drops through. A riverwide constriction can create large standing waves that can swamp a canoe going through them. On the other hand, these waves often provide ideal waves for surfing the canoe.

Downstream and Upstream Vs

Two rocks or other objects can create a constriction in the water where the water flows between the rocks to form a small chute. The chute of water funnels between the rocks and forms the shape of a V (figure 5.7). The rocks form the two upstream points of the V, and the chute between the rocks forms a downstream point of the V. Often there is a difference in vertical height. Because the water creates a cushion against the rocks, the upstream V will be slightly higher than the chute forming the downstream V where the water is dropping off. Steer clear of the upstream points and position the boat to travel down the V for the deepest water.

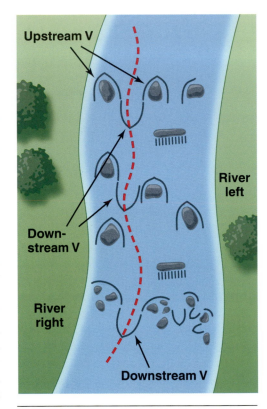

Figure 5.7   Downstream and upstream Vs.

River Obstacles

Rocks are the main obstacles found in rivers. The depth of the rock in the water and its size are key factors in determining its effect on river dynamics. Pillows, holes, and eddies are closely related. A totally submerged rock may have little or no effect on the surface current while a rock that is closer to the surface will force the water passing over it upward to the surface, creating a small wave, or pillow, downstream from the rock. If the rock is wide, water from the side cannot fill in behind it, creating a depression or void behind the rock. The water flowing over the rock attempts to fill the void, creating a hole, or hydraulic, behind the rock. If the rock is exposed, the water can no longer flow over it and can only fill the void behind the rock from the sides. Eddies are created by the water filling in the void from the sides behind an exposed rock.

Pillows

Water passing over a rock close to the surface is forced upward to the surface, which creates a pillow, a small rounded wave downstream of the rock. The deeper the rock, the farther downstream the pillow is located (figure 5.8*a*). The closer the rock is to the surface, the closer the pillow is to the rock, until the pillow is directly over the rock (figure 5.8*b*). With experience, the paddler will be able to recognize which rocks are close to the surface and need to be avoided and which ones are deep enough not to pose a problem.

A rock that is partway out of the water creates a pillow of water that flows up against it and forms a cushion (figure 5.8*c*). A paddler floating up on a well-developed cushion can use the cushion to avoid broaching on the rock. Regardless, the paddler should avoid the upstream sides of rocks and might have to think and react quickly to keep from being broached (pinned sideways against the underlying rock). In addition, if the current is powerful enough, the rock may form a series of compression waves upstream of the obstacle (figure 5.8*c*).

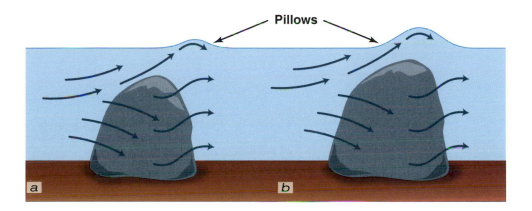

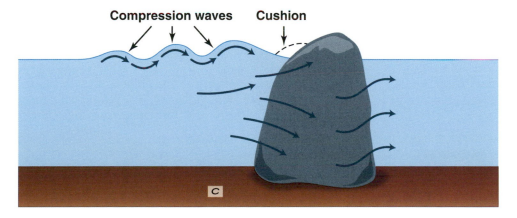

Figure 5.8 Pillows *(a)* downstream of a deep rock, *(b)* over a rock near the surface, and *(c)* upstream of a rock partway out of the water.

Holes

A hole, or hydraulic, occurs in a river where a rock or other obstruction of sufficient width prevents the water from filling the void behind the obstruction from the side, forcing the water to flow over the rock to fill the void or depression. As the water flows over the rock, it plunges down to the bottom of the river and races downstream. As it races downstream, the water shoots back up to the surface, where it moves in one of three directions (figure 5.9). A portion of the water recirculates back upstream to fill the void behind the rock. Farther downstream, some of the water comes up to the surface and continues downstream. This water travels at a slower rate than the general flow of the river and quickly picks up speed as it moves downriver. In between, at the interface of the upstream and downstream flow, the flow is neutral in that it is not really flowing downstream or upstream. This neutral area is called a boil.

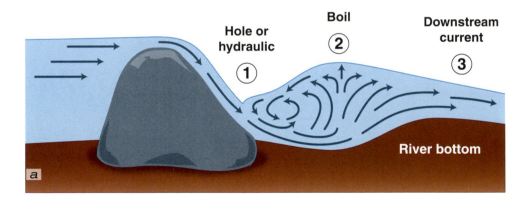

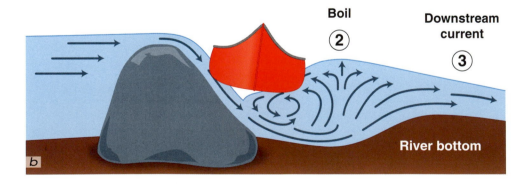

Figure 5.9 *(a)* Hole profile and *(b)* hole profile showing a stuck canoe.

The shape of the hole affects how friendly it is to a paddler. In a smiling hole the center of the hole is farther upstream than the sides (figure 5.10a). This configuration creates the impression that the hole is smiling when viewed from the upstream side. A smiling hole tends to be friendlier to paddlers because they can more easily maneuver the canoe in the hole to the side where they can exit.

In contrast, in a frowning hole, the middle of the hole is downstream of the sides (figure 5.10b). From the upstream side of the hole, the hole looks as if it is frowning. Because the middle of the hole is downstream, the force of the hole tends to move the paddler to the center of the hole where it is strongest and most powerful. These holes are often called keepers because they keep a canoe stuck in the hole. They are difficult to exit because paddlers have to paddle literally uphill to reach the side of the hole where they can extricate themselves.

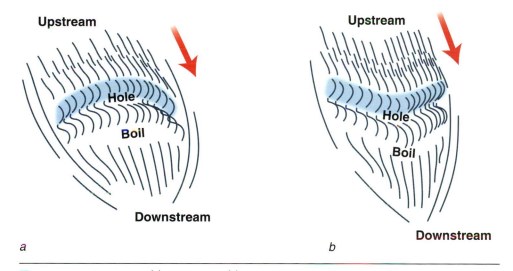

Figure 5.10 Holes: (a) smiling and (b) frowning, when viewed from the upstream side.

PADDLER TIP

Watch a paddler front-surfing a hole or wave. Look at the attitude of the canoe. If the bow is slightly lower than the stern, the canoe is on the wave. If the stern is slightly lower than the bow, the canoe is off the wave. The trim of the canoe is a subtle but good indicator, and watching a canoe in a hole is an enjoyable mental game for the observer.

SAFETY TIP

The differences between holes that are friendly and those that are unfriendly are often subtle. Check with guidebooks and other paddlers before venturing into a questionable hydraulic.

If you are paddling a canoe you can easily feel where you are in the hole. If you are on the upstream side of the boil, you can feel the current pulling the canoe upstream and into the hole. Conversely, if you are on the downstream side of the boil, you can feel the canoe slipping downstream and dropping out of the hole.

If you are sitting on the shore watching a canoe paddle upstream toward the hole in an attempt to surf the wave, you can look closely at the attitude of the canoe and tell where the canoe is in the hole. Look at the trim of the boat. If the bow is lower than the stern, the canoe will move upstream and into the hole. If the stern is lower than the bow, then the canoe is in the downstream portion. Unless the paddler paddles hard, he or she is out of the hole, and might as well ferry to shore and try again. Ferrying is a way of moving the boat back and forth in the current without traveling downstream. You will learn more about ferrying in chapter 7.

Eddies

Eddies form behind rocks or other obstructions in the river. Water flows past the obstruction, creating a void behind the object that the water attempts to fill. An eddy has three distinct parts.

The first part of the eddy is where the water in the main current rushes by the rock so fast that water has to flow back upstream to fill the void (figure 5.11). This action creates a strong current differential between the main current and the current in the eddy. The interface between the downstream current and the upstream current creates an eddy line or, in extremely fast current, an eddy wall. An eddy wall is created when

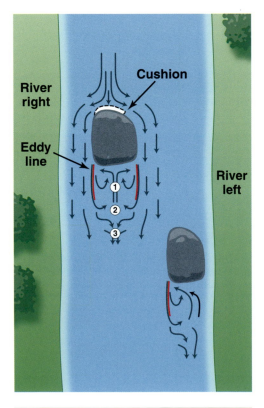

Figure 5.11 Anatomy of an eddy.

there is a vertical height difference between the downstream current and the current in the eddy attempting to fill the void behind the rock. If an eddy wall is present, there is a noticeable downhill current inside the eddy. For a paddler, an eddy of this power can be problematic, and the paddler can find the eddy unfriendly. Most eddies, however, have an eddy line with little or no vertical difference between the main current and the upstream current.

The second part of the eddy is the interface between the current moving upstream and the current moving downstream in the eddy. The current here is neutral. In a strong eddy, this is often the ideal location for paddlers to sit. They aren't plastered against the backside of the rock by the upstream current where it is difficult to exit the eddy, and they aren't falling out of the eddy heading downstream either.

The third part of an eddy is where the water in the main current enters the void behind the rock so far downstream that it continues downstream but at a slower rate than the main current. This area of an eddy can be problematic for paddlers because they may think that they are in the upstream current in the eddy when they are really moving downstream and quickly falling out of the eddy. In addition, because the current is moving downstream in the eddy, no real eddy line is present in this portion of the eddy. Many beginning paddlers prefer to enter an eddy in this area because no current differential is present and the risk of capsizing is lessened.

A river is more than an amenity, it is a treasure.
Oliver Wendell Holmes

PADDLER TIP

When you enter an eddy, look at the shore or some fixed reference point to see whether you are moving upstream or drifting downstream. Better yet, look at the current in the eddy to determine how the water is moving.

Conceptually, the three parts of an eddy have many of the characteristics of a hole. An eddy and a hole are both caused by the river attempting to fill a void. Most eddies are friendly, and paddlers may use them extensively as they travel down a river. In fact, eddy hopping, or traveling deliberately from eddy to eddy, is a good way to move down a challenging section of river.

Remember, however, that some eddies can be violent and unfriendly. Along the edge of the eddy or at the eddy line, water moving in opposite directions creates a current differential. Generally, the water moving upstream in the eddy moves at a slower velocity than the main current outside the eddy. This differential can spin a canoe around. Under normal circumstances paddlers use the current differential to make an eddy turn. But this same differential can easily capsize a canoe. A strong current differential can create an eddy wall, an actual wall of water between the downstream current and the upstream current in the eddy. These eddies are particularly violent and should be avoided.

Paddlers must consider these differentials in moving water, especially when paddling across them. Speed, power, and crossing angles, in addition to size and type of boat, are important when dealing with the effects of a current differential.

Microcurrents

Microcurrents are currents within other currents. Close examination of the current often reveals that smaller currents may be behaving quite differently from the main current around them (figure 5.12).

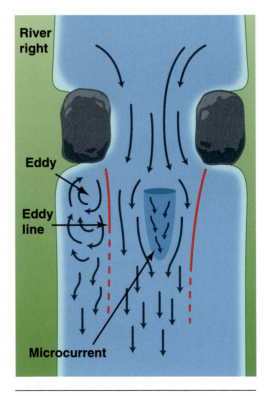

Figure 5.12 Microcurrents.

PADDLER TIP

Recognizing microcurrents is an advanced but important skill. Look at the water and analyze its movement. Look for eddylike currents, slack water, and current differentials behind pillows. These microcurrents can provide refuge for a paddler or, conversely, cause an unwelcome change in the angle of a ferry or other maneuver.

Examination of a chute may reveal a small pillow in it created by a submerged rock. This pillow can be easily overlooked in the water around it. Behind the pillow might be about a boat's length of slack water, which is water that is moving more slowly than the main current surrounding it. A skilled paddler who recognizes this slack water can easily position the boat into the slack water and sit there motionless in the middle of the surrounding fast-moving water.

River Hazards

Rivers present hazards to paddlers for two reasons: Moving water has tremendous power, and rivers can be filled with traps. To appreciate the power of a flowing river, you should understand that water is a heavy element. This weight coupled with movement makes river boating potentially dangerous.

Because water has great weight—1 gallon (3.8 liters) equals 8.3 pounds (3.8 kilograms)—it responds to the physical laws of gravity and inertia. When a river turns, water piles up on the outside of the turn. This bend in the river contributes to velocity differences. The slow-moving water is found on the inside of the bend. On this inside bend the river deposits silt, and shoaling can occur. If the bend is sharp and narrow, water and debris end up churning about violently, creating an extremely dangerous place.

Obstructions and Strainers

As the river flows, the water meets many obstructions. Bridge abutments and rocks are dangerous simply because they don't move and water does. If the water is moving fast enough, a canoe coming against these types of obstructions can be held fast to their upstream sides. When a canoe is pinned this way, escape is difficult and dangerous. Boat damage is certain, and life can be in serious jeopardy.

Another river danger grows from the presence of obstacles called strainers (figure 5.13). Fallen trees, midstream brush, and collected debris between rocks and islands can cause serious problems in river traveling. An accumulation of debris may even block an entire river, especially a narrow one. The problem with

SAFETY TIP

If you capsize upstream of a strainer, make every effort to swim away from it. If you are going to be swept into the strainer, turn over on your belly and swim aggressively up and over the strainer. Your life may depend on getting yourself high enough onto the strainer.

a strainer is that water flows through these objects while boats and people may not. They can become pinned or trapped against the strainer, making escape difficult and sometimes impossible. Maintaining a good lookout and scouting the river is crucial to avoiding these common obstructions.

Strainers are killers! Most commonly formed by trees and rocks, they are extremely dangerous, and paddlers should always avoid them.

Trees are the most commonly encountered form of strainer found on a river. As the current carves out a bend in a river, it undermines the foundation underneath nearby trees, eventually causing them to fall into the river channel. A strainer on a bend of a river is particularly dangerous because the faster current on the outside of the bend can cause a paddler who is flowing with the current to be swept into the strainer.

Rocks can also cause strainers. Usually, the rocks are positioned on the bottom in such a way that water will flow through them to create a strainer. Often, these strainers are referred to

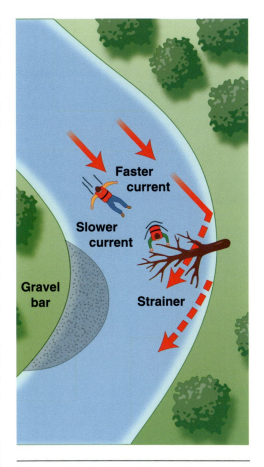

Figure 5.13 Strainer.

as undercut rocks. Seeing a rock in the current of the river without the typical pillow of water piling up on the upstream side is often a good indication of an undercut rock. Always paddle or swim away from strainers.

SAFETY TIP

Low-head dams are called drowning machines because they are efficient at drowning people. This happens because of the way the water recirculates. There are no natural breaks to allow the water to escape. Look for the horizon line and the abutments. Portage well upstream.

High-Water Debris

Spring rain brings flowers, but to the river it brings high water or flood conditions. High water complicates everything already mentioned. Debris that has collected on the bank of the river floats off. Brush, tree limbs, and sometimes entire trees can be floating down the river. Every spring paddlers lose their lives on flooded rivers. Paddlers should avoid rivers in flood stage. Another point to ponder is that spring floodwater is cold water!

Low-Head Dams

Low-head dams are designed to create a perfectly formed hydraulic immediately downstream of the dam, diverting most of the energy of the water toward the surface. In addition, this hydraulic extends from one side of the river to the other, right into the dam abutments. A person caught in the recirculating portion of the hydraulic may recirculate endlessly. An unaided person usually drowns.

A horizon line is the usual indicator of a riverwide obstacle like a waterfall or low-head dam. As you look downriver, you may see a section of calm or smooth-looking water and beyond it a line across the river where the water drops out of sight. Trees on your side of the horizon line will look normal, but trees just downriver from the horizon line often look as if someone cut a section out of their trunks. If a low-head dam forms the horizon line, abutments on each side of the dam usually provide a clear indication of its presence.

Low-head dams have been constructed on rivers both large and small. Most were constructed before people began to use rivers for recreation. The height of the dam is often no more than several feet (a meter or so) above the original channel. Some of the most dangerous low-head dams appear almost level with the water. Low-head dams are potential killers. They are so efficient at this task that they have been called drowning machines.

Waterfalls

Posters and television ads romanticize the adventure of running a waterfall. Running a waterfall, however, is extremely dangerous. Several significant challenges associated with running a waterfall can severely injure you.

- You can land flat in the pool of water below the waterfall and severely compress the disks in your vertebra.
- You can land upside down with the boat on top of you.
- The depth of the pool below the waterfall may not be sufficient.
- If you don't have sufficient speed when you go over the falls, your trajectory could take you straight down, where you'll recirculate behind the waterfall. The rock face of the waterfall will be on one side, and the water from the waterfall will be on the other side.

Look for the horizon line and the portage trail so you can carefully and safely portage around waterfalls (see figure 5.14).

Figure 5.14 Grand Chute waterfalls on the Dumoine River in central Canada.

SAFETY TIP

Be cautious about paddling and playing behind old man-made structures that might contain reinforcing rods, sharp rocks, and other debris.

Foot Entrapment

When standing in swift current, your foot can be pushed into a crevice, snarled root, tree limb, or other object. Stand only where the water is knee deep or shallower and the current is slow enough not to be a factor. Shoreline eddies and areas well away from the current may be the best places to stand. Never stand in the main current of a river or stream. Foot entrapments are life threatening. Do not stand up in current.

Old Man-Made Structures

Most rivers contain man-made structures such as old dams or bridge abutments that have fallen into disuse. Sometimes these structures provide a fun place to play with the canoe. Always use caution around these structures. Riprap (rocks, rubble, or other materials used to reinforce shorelines against erosion) may contain large spikes. Old dams and bridge abutments may contain reinforcing rods or sharp rocks that can create nasty injuries. Check the site for hazards at low water. If you have any doubt, find another place to play.

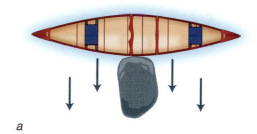

a

Broaches

A pin, or broach, occurs when a swamped canoe is swept sideways into a rock or other obstruction (see figure 5.15). A 5-mile-per-hour (8-kilometer-per-hour) current can exert over a ton of pressure (2,400 pounds, or 1,100 kilograms) on a canoe full of water. When that canoe becomes pinned on a rock,

b

Figure 5.15 *(a)* Center pin and *(b)* double-end pin.

SAFETY TIP

Always swim upstream of the canoe and attempt to keep the canoe parallel to the main current. If there is any question, let the canoe go and rescue yourself.

the force of the water can easily wrap the boat around the rock. In any potential pinning situation, the paddler should avoid getting caught between the canoe and the obstruction. If you are swimming with the canoe, try to keep the canoe parallel to the current. If there is any question, leave the canoe and rescue yourself.

Although a canoe can easily pin and become trapped in a strainer, rocks are more commonly responsible for pinning a canoe on a river. The most common pin is the midship pin, or center pin, in which the rock meets the center of the canoe. If you can influence the pin in any way, try to have the pin occur off the center of the canoe so that extricating it from the rock is easier.

A double-end, or end-to-end, pin is a particularly nasty situation, in which the two ends of the canoe are each caught on a rock and the current pushes the center of the canoe downstream between the rocks.

Drowning-Trap Flows

A river can be hazardous at any water level. Ask knowledgeable people about flow rates to determine the best times and conditions to paddle sections of the river and avoid situations that are particularly dangerous. Most people associate danger with floodlike conditions like muddy water, water flowing over the banks, water in the trees, floating debris, and big waves. Floods and high water are dangerous, and most people recognize the danger and stay off the river.

However, on many rivers, recreational fatalities tend to occur at moderate water levels, when the river is well within its banks and looks perfectly normal. The normal cycle of flows for rivers is that during the summer, when most people visit, the water level drops to the point where moving water is less of a contributing factor in such fatalities. However, as the water level rises, risks increase, and in some cases the river becomes extremely dangerous.

Three components define a drowning-trap flow: depth, velocity, and deceptiveness. At moderate flows the river has the power (depth and velocity) to drown, yet it is deceptive because people tend to associate danger with flood conditions rather than with moderate flows. The cross-sectional profile of a typical eastern river illustrates the relationship between moderate drowning-trap flows, summer low flows, and flood levels that people normally perceive as being dangerous (figure 5.16).

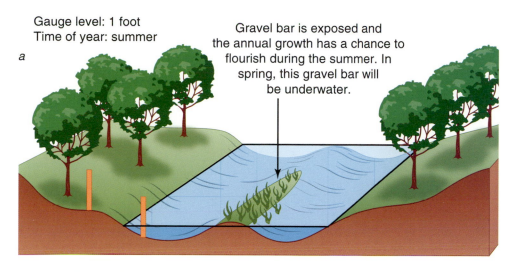

Gauge level: 1 foot
Time of year: summer

a

Gravel bar is exposed and
the annual growth has a chance to
flourish during the summer. In
spring, this gravel bar will
be underwater.

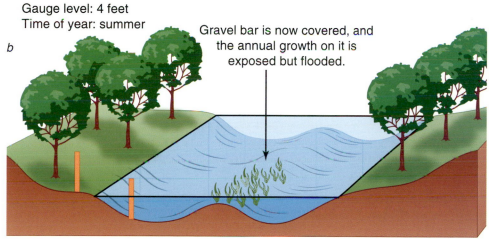

Gauge level: 4 feet
Time of year: summer

b

Gravel bar is now covered, and
the annual growth on it is
exposed but flooded.

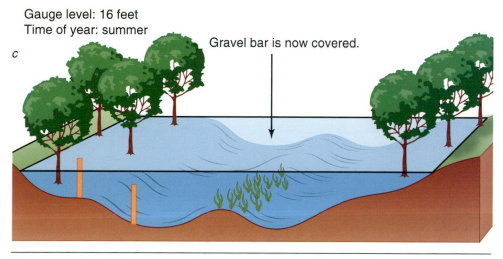

Gauge level: 16 feet
Time of year: summer

c

Gravel bar is now covered.

Figure 5.16 *(a)* Drowning-trap flow with 1-foot (.3-meter) gauge, *(b)* drowning-trap flow with 4-foot (1.2-meter) gauge, and *(c)* flood with 16-foot (5-meter) gauge.

The depth of the water is a key determinant of its velocity and power. Imagine standing in moving water about waist deep. With some deliberate care you can brace yourself against the current and stand in the water. Add another foot of water so that the water is above your waist. Now the river current can easily move you. It may knock you off your feet and sweep you downstream. When the speed of the current reaches that of a person walking fast, it begins to have the power to move you, knock you over, and, depending on circumstances, drown you.

Annual vegetation that invades the gravel bars and other areas of the river during early summer is a good, practical indicator of drowning-trap water levels. Look for areas that were underwater during spring runoff. When vegetation in these places becomes either partially or fully underwater, the river is higher than normal and may be in the drowning-trap flows.

The last component of the drowning-trap flow is deceptiveness. A river well within its banks looks perfectly normal to the casual visitor. However, if that visitor's frame of reference is a once-a-year trip, what is perceived as normal may actually be high water. A river that is not flooding and looks normal may have the depth and velocity to contribute to an accident.

Capsizing

Most paddlers have a story to tell about unexpectedly ending up in the water. Most will laugh and chuckle at the memory of the clumsy mishap. Some may portray it as a narrow escape. A fact of life in paddle sports is that if you spend much time at all on the water, you will eventually take an unexpected plunge. Most of the time, the event is no big deal, especially if you are a swimmer and are wearing a properly fitted life jacket. But if the water is cold and no one is available to assist, a fall overboard can be a risky event and keeping a canoe from capsizing becomes essential.

Understanding boat stability is an important skill in using a canoe. Boat stability is related directly to the below-water hull shape and the height of the center of gravity. The lower and closer the load in the boat is placed to the center line

SAFETY TIP

The number one thing that the paddler can do to stay safe on the water is always to wear a life jacket (personal flotation device, or PFD). Accidents happen fast, even to the most experienced paddlers. Having a life jacket stowed in the canoe is not enough. Drowning remains the leading cause of death in recreational canoeing accidents. Why risk it? Always wear your life jacket. For information regarding proper fit and care of your PFD, turn to chapter 3.

of the boat, the more stable the boat will be, assuming that adequate freeboard remains. If this load is moved off-center, forces created by buoyancy respond to the boat hull to balance the boat. The forces of gravity and buoyancy are equal when the boat is at rest.

The real problem develops when weight is added above the gunwale line (or above the sides of the boat), which raises the center of gravity in the boat. The center of gravity is the point where the total weight of the craft and everything aboard could hypothetically be centered in one spot and produce the same effect on the hull. In a canoe the weight above the gunwale is people—people moving around, people paddling and reaching too far, people doing everything that people do! If this elevated center of gravity is off-center, such as when a person leans over the side of the boat, the force of buoyancy may not be able to counterbalance the change in the location of the center of gravity, resulting in either a swamp or a capsize. In a lightweight canoe, the forces trying to right the boat may kick the craft right out from under the paddler, resulting in a fall overboard and a capsize.

To prevent an unexpected plunge into the water, do the following:

- **Maintain body weight over the center line.** In other words, keep your nose over your navel.

- **Maintain three points of contact while moving around in a canoe**. Like a stable three-legged stool, a person keeping three points of contact retains stability (see figure 5.17). If you move a foot to step forward, you should be holding on to the boat with both hands.

- **Load the boat properly**. Keep the weight centered from both side to side and bow to stern. And you don't want a lot of stuff in your canoe, even on a camping trip. Never overload the craft.

- **Practice proper retrieval**. When retrieving something from the water, use a paddle or move the boat close to the object so that you can grab the item from the water without leaning your shoulders over the side of the boat.

Figure 5.17 Maintain three points of contact for balance.

These techniques take practice, but they will soon become instinctive and protect you from going overboard.

Of course, wind, current, and waves affect the stability of the most carefully loaded and paddled canoe. A wake from a powerboat can surprise even attentive paddlers. If you are not a swimmer, take the time to learn how to swim. Capsizing a canoe is part of the sport. Swimmer or not, always wear your life jacket.

Group Safety

Prepare your boat and equipment for the activity according to the following list:

☐ Make sure that your life jacket fits and that you wear it properly adjusted.

☐ Your boat must have flotation sufficient to float it when swamped.

☐ Inspect your boat and repair any damage before launch.

☐ Install and inspect end lines so that the boat is easy to hold on to when you are in the water.

☐ Inspect your paddles and safety gear such as pumps or bailers, navigational aids, and rescue gear before each trip.

☐ Carry a more-than-adequate supply of food, drinking water, and protective clothing in waterproof containers.

☐ Ideally, every trip should have among its participants several persons certified in CPR (cardiopulmonary resuscitation); first aid or wilderness first response; and boat rescue, capsize, and recovery. Bring a suitable first aid kit and an emergency repair kit and know how to use them.

Prepare as a group and know the responsibilities of group members.

☐ Research the trip. Know the distance, likely conditions, potential hazards, and bail-out points so that you are prepared should conditions worsen.

☐ Know each participant's abilities and goals. Pick an activity level that matches the ability of the group.

☐ The participant with the least experience, skill, and ability must be able to complete the trip safely.

☐ All participants should accept responsibility for their own safety and be ready, willing, and able to assist others in the group as appropriate to their level of training and knowledge.

☐ Identify a trip planner to arrange meeting locations and shuttles, identify equipment needs, and file a float plan for the group.

☐ The group must have the knowledge, skills, and equipment to deal with potential hazards.

☐ Do a group briefing, including an equipment check, at the put-in.

☐ Start as a cohesive group, stay together while under way, and take out as a group. The group's mutual protection promotes individual safety.

☐ See and be seen. Keep a safe distance from other boats. Maintain a route that avoids other boats. Avoid hazards.

Cold-Water Safety and Survival Skills

Paying attention to cold water is a practical thing. You will not have fun if you are cold, so the best thing is to understand the effect of cold water and appropriately deal with it.

Some of the best paddling opportunities occur in spring and fall when cooler weather and cold water increase the risks associated with getting wet. All paddlers should take the precautions necessary to be able to enjoy safe canoeing under these conditions. Carefully read and adhere to the advice on pages 120 through 122 to increase your odds of survival should you capsize or encounter bad weather.

COMMUNICATION

While you are on the water, there may be times when you will not be able to speak or even shout instructions to others in your group. For that reason, it is important that paddlers be able to communicate with others using universal paddle and whistle signals. When given a signal on the water, respond with the same signal to acknowledge your understanding and confirm the signal.

- **Stop**—Hold the paddle horizontally overhead. All paddlers should stop in a safe location and look at the person signaling for more information (photo *a*).

- **Help or emergency**—Wave the paddle from side to side or give three or more long blasts on a whistle. All paddlers should look at the person signaling for more information. Only those trained in rescue for emergency response should directly assist. Other paddlers should remain at a safe distance or in a safe location. In some cases, they may be asked to go for help (photos *b-d*).

- **All clear**—Hold the paddle vertically and stationary. Paddlers may return to normal paddling protocols (photo *e*).

- **Go this way**—Use the paddle to point toward the direction of travel. Point to the clear way, not to the hazard or obstruction. Paddlers responding to the signal should go in the direction indicated (photo *f*).

- **Are you OK?**—Tap the top of your head three times and point to the person whom you are questioning. If the person taps his or her head three times in response, he or she is OK. Otherwise, the person needs assistance (photo *g*).

Avoid Cold-Water Shock and Hypothermia

You should try to avoid two things: cold-water shock and hypothermia. Cold-water shock is a dangerous, sometimes fatal, condition that can result when a person is suddenly immersed in cold water, such as would occur in a capsize. The sudden exposure of the head and chest to cold water typically causes an involuntary gasp for air, a sudden increase in heart rate and blood pressure, disorientation, and possibly, cardiac arrest. The only remedy for cold-water shock is to get the individual out of the water. You should then keep an eye out for symptoms of hypothermia.

Hypothermia is another dangerous and sometimes fatal condition that results when exposure to cold prevents the body from being able to maintain its normal temperature in the core region (heart, lungs, and the rest of the torso). Although this condition can occur through exposure to cold air alone, its onset occurs much more quickly when the body is wet or immersed in water. Paddlers must take special care to protect themselves from this danger when they paddle in cold water, rainy conditions, or cool air temperatures.

The most typical symptoms of hypothermia usually appear in this general order:

1. Shivering
2. Impaired judgment
3. Clumsiness
4. Loss of manual dexterity
5. Slurred speech
6. Inward behavior, withdrawal
7. Cessation of shivering
8. Muscle rigidity
9. Unconsciousness

The method of treatment depends on the severity of the hypothermia. One basic thing to remember is that the individual must be warmed slowly.

• **Mild hypothermia** (victim shivering but coherent): Move the victim to a place of warmth. Replace wet clothes with dry ones from your equipment bag. Give warm, sweet drinks, but no alcohol or caffeine. Keep the victim warm for several hours.

• **Moderate hypothermia** (shivering may decrease or stop): The victim may seem irrational with deteriorating coordination. Use the same treatment as for mild hypothermia but offer no drinks. Keep the victim lying down with the torso, thighs, head, and neck covered with dry clothes, coats, or blankets to stop further heat loss. Seek medical attention immediately.

• **Severe hypothermia** (shivering may have stopped): The victim may resist help or be semiconscious or unconscious. After being removed from water, the victim must be kept prone, on his or her back and immobile. The victim must be handled gently. Cover the torso, thighs, head, and neck with dry covers to stop further heat loss. Do not stimulate the arms and legs in any manner because cold blood in the extremities that suddenly returns to the core may induce cardiac arrest. Seek medical attention immediately.

Reduce Your Exposure

To reduce your exposure to cold water, take the following precautions:

- Dress in layers using synthetic fabrics such as polyester fleece to prevent becoming overheated or chilled from perspiration. Avoid wearing cotton when paddling in cool or cold weather.
- Carry a waterproof jacket designed for splash and rain protection.
- When the water temperature is less than 60 degrees Fahrenheit (15 degrees Celsius), wear specialized insulating clothing capable of protecting you while in the water.
- You should always wear a wet suit or dry suit
    1. If the combined air and water temperatures are below 120 degrees Fahrenheit (49 degrees Celsius),
    2. If the water temperature is below 60 degrees Fahrenheit (15 degrees Celsius),
    3. If you will be far from shore on cold water, or
    4. If in cool or mild weather you expect to be repeatedly exposed to cold water. Keep in mind that the best type of wet suit for paddling is the Farmer John style and that the warmth and comfort range of a dry suit will vary based on the clothing worn underneath it.
- Wear a warm hat that will stay on your head in the water. A fleece-lined skullcap is ideal.
- Have spare dry clothing stored in a sealed dry bag while on the water. If you become wet, change into dry clothing at the first sign of shivering.
- Test your protective clothing in a controlled cold-water environment to understand the level of protection provided.
- Know the water temperature before you set out. Recognize that dam-released water can be significantly colder than expected.
- Always wear your life jacket (PFD).
- Paddle near shore or near others who can help you in the event of a capsize.
- Keep your body well fueled with high-carbohydrate foods and plenty of water.

Know What to Do If You Capsize

In the event of a capsize in cold water:

- Get out of the water and dry off as quickly as possible.

- After you are out of the water, put on dry clothes.

- If you are unable to exit the water quickly, keep calm, remain with your boat, conserve energy and get in the HELP (heat escape lessening posture) position: Fold your arms against your chest, cross your legs, and keep still until help arrives (see figure 5.18).

Figure 5.18 HELP posture.

- If two or more people are in the water, get into the huddle posture: Put your arms around one another, stay close together, and keep still (see figure 5.19).

- Attempt to swim to shore only if

  o the chance of rescue is small or nil,

  o you are in danger of floating into dangerous rapids or other hazards, or

  o you are certain that you can make it.

Figure 5.19 Huddle posture.

Rescue and Emergency Protocols

An experienced paddler never takes safety for granted. Every paddler should practice and be competent at self-rescue and be able to help others with simple assisted rescue techniques. Seek training. Learn quick, uncomplicated methods for helping your paddling buddies and learn how to use a few simple pieces of

SAFETY TIP

Any decision to swim for the shore of a lake should not be made lightly. Physical activity such as swimming or other struggling in the water increases heat loss. Survival time can fall to minutes. Strong swimmers have died before they could swim 100 yards (90 meters) in cold water. In water colder than 40 degrees Fahrenheit (4 degrees Celsius), victims have died before they could swim 100 feet (30 meters). Also keep in mind that judging distance accurately on the water is difficult.

safety gear. All paddlers should wear a properly fitted life jacket, wear appropriate protective clothing including secure footwear, and have a throw rope, knife, sounding device, and bright light for low-visibility conditions.

Self-Rescue

If you capsize close to shore in calm water, first signal others to let them know that you are OK. Hang on to your gear, especially your paddle and boat. If possible, roll your boat upright to make it easier to tow. Place any stray gear inside. If you are close to shore, you may choose to tow your boat. Tow your canoe with your end lines and swim using a strong scissor kick (see figure 5.20).

If you capsize in moving water in a river, assume a defensive position by lying on your back with your legs pointing downstream. Arch your back to stay as close to the surface as possible and avoid bumping the bottom. Keep your feet on the surface to help avoid one of the most common river hazards, foot entrapment (see page 111).

Angle your head toward the closest safe shore and back stroke to safety. If you are being swept rapidly toward a hazard you may need to roll to your side into an aggressive swimming position to reach safety more quickly, but stay flat along the surface until you reach shallow, slow water.

Hold your boat and paddle with one hand and swim with the other if it is safe to do so. Otherwise let go of your gear and take care of yourself first.

Boat-Assisted Rescue

A self-rescue is often the quickest and safest method for a swimmer to reach safety, but a paddler can assist a swimmer in several ways. The simplest method is to paddle over to the swimmer and instruct him or her to hold on to either the bow or stern of the paddler's boat. Both towing and pushing a swimmer work well, but determining which will work best in a given situation requires practice.

SAFETY TIP

Remember these rescue priorities:

- People
- Boats
- Gear

Figure 5.20   Self-rescue.

If towing is called for, have the swimmer hold on to the grab loop, end line, or handle at the stern. Instruct the swimmer to kick and swim to help forward progress, and to stay close to the surface for safety. Paddle to the closest safe shore.

When pushing (bulldozing) a swimmer, have the person hold on to the bow and wrap his or her legs up around the hull. Then paddle to shore. This technique works especially well with panicked or tired swimmers.

Bulldozing an empty boat to shore can work too, although you'll notice the boat will not follow directions well (figure 5.21). Again, practice is crucial. To rescue a paddle, simply pick it up and place it in your boat.

Figure 5.21   Bulldozing an empty boat.

PADDLER TIP

When in position to assist others, use the reach-throw-row-go rescue sequence to minimize risk.

- **Reach.** First reach with your voice. Use a call or whistle blast to get the swimmer's attention to ensure that he or she is OK. Often, reaching a hand to a swimming paddler can bring him or her safely to shore or to your boat. A paddle can extend your reach safely.

- **Throw.** When the swimmer is too far away to reach with a paddle, a throw rope can often aid in the paddler's rescue. Throw ropes are recommended for shore-based rescues.

- **Row.** If the swimmer is beyond range of a throw rope, the rescuer should maneuver his or her boat closer so that a reach is possible. A rescuer in a boat is safer than a swimming one.

- **Go.** As a last option, a trained and properly equipped rescuer can swim to the aid of the swimmer. Bystanders should call or go for help.

Shore-Based Rescue

Ropes can be a useful tool for helping swimmers reach shore. Throw ropes can be stored in a throw bag designed for quick and easy deployment or coiled securely in an area where the paddlers will not be entangled in the event of a capsize. In either case, the rope itself should float and be brightly colored for easy visibility. Because of their simplicity and speed of operation, throw bags are recommended.

Usually between 50 and 70 feet (15 and 20 meters) long, these devices are such important tools that every paddler should carry one. Regular practice with the throw bag is necessary to develop speed and accuracy.

To use a throw bag, first make sure that your footing is secure. Open the bag to allow the rope to run out freely and then grasp the bag in your throwing hand. Hold the free end in your other hand. Shout out to the swimmer. The accepted call is "Rope!" Then throw the bag either overhand or underhand, whichever works best for you in practice. Aim to cross the swimmer with the rope by throwing the rope bag past the swimmer (see figure 5.22). Then steady yourself for a significant force when the rope becomes taut. Sitting down or having another person help you hold steady is a good idea. Pendulum the swimmer (once the rope is pulled taut, the swimmer will swing to your side of the river) into a safe location or pull the person closer if you must help him or her avoid a downstream hazard. Warn the swimmer to stand up only in water that is knee deep or shallower.

Figure 5.22   Shore-based rescue using a throw bag.

All paddlers should be able to swim with a life jacket on and be able to assist a swimmer with either a boat-based rescue or a rope thrown from shore. These skills are essential. Advanced skills, such as wading, either singly or in groups, to rescue entrapped paddlers or pinned boats can be helpful. Being able to set up mechanical systems to rescue people or equipment, swim in difficult conditions, and swim safely over a strainer can be vital for the river paddler. Canoeists on lakes and rivers should learn the necessary rescue and safety skills (and more) in a class setting taught by knowledgeable, experienced, certified instructors. Go to www.americancanoe.org for information about ACA instructor certification.

Other Assisted Rescues

If a swimmer is close, offer the T-grip of a paddle to pull the person to safety. If you are on shore, you can extend branches or boats into the water to offer assistance.

Deep-Water Assists: Canoe-Over-Canoe Rescue

If one boat capsizes in deep water, a second boat can provide rescue assistance without the need to move to shore. The following are general steps for this quick and effective boat-assisted rescue:

1. The rescue boat takes a position alongside the capsized boat. The paddlers who have capsized position themselves. One paddler should position him- or herself at the end of the overturned canoe. A second swimmer should move to the end of the rescue boat and hang on.

2. The rescue boat takes position with its middle at the end of the swamped boat, forming a T.

3. The swimmer at the end of the capsized canoe pushes down on the end. A paddler in the middle of the rescue boat lifts the other end out of the water (see figure 5.23a). They may need to twist the canoe slightly to break the suction.

4. The rescuers pull the capsized boat across the gunwales of the rescue boat, balancing it at the midpoint to allow it to drain. As the boat is pulled in, the swimmer moves to the end of the rescuer boat and holds on (see figure 5.23b).

5. The rescuers roll the boat upright and slide it back into the water, being careful to maintain contact and control (see figures 5.23c and d). The boat is positioned parallel to the rescue boat. The rescuers hold on to its gunwales to stabilize it.

6. One at a time, the swimmers move to the side of their boat and, using a scissor kick and arm strength or with the assistance of a rescue sling, reenter the boat (see figure 5.23e). When both paddlers are safely back in their boat with paddles, the rescuers can let go.

Figure 5.23 Canoe-over-canoe rescue.

Rescue Sling

A method that enables a paddler to climb into a boat without too much difficulty is the rescue-sling technique. Loop over the side of the boat a section of line or webbing long enough to hang into the water. Fasten the loop on a thwart. The paddler then places a foot in the loop, using it like a stirrup. Lifting the hips above the top of the gunwale, the paddler climbs into the center of the boat. The boat should be stabilized by a second boat sitting parallel or by a second swimmer on the opposite side.

SAFETY TIP

All paddlers need to be prepared for these circumstances:
- Low light conditions
- The need to contact help
- Minor medical emergencies
- Outings that extend past the estimated return time
- Weather pattern changes
- Other boat traffic

Summary

Good paddling is about boat control. Mastering control on a lake or river requires thorough knowledge of the various forces involved. Learning to read the weather, rivers, and water enables you to apply the proper strokes and maneuvers to adjust your speed and assess the situation. These essential skills should keep you out of harm's way.

Bear in mind, however, that this text was designed to be used as a supplementary resource to the recreational canoeist. It is not intended to replace on-water instruction by a qualified instructor.

Capsizing

☐ If you realize that you are about to capsize, hold your breath to minimize gasping when entering the water.

☐ Check yourself for injuries and get control of your emotions.

☐ If paddling tandem, check to see whether your partner is OK. If your partner needs assistance, provide what is needed and possible. Focus on staying calm and helping your partner stay calm.

☐ Retrieve paddles, boat, and any other loose equipment.

☐ Stay with the boat while deciding which rescue technique to use.

Self-Tow Rescue

If you are close to shore, swimming and towing the boat is the easiest way to rescue yourself.

- [ ] If a line is attached to the boat, grasp it in one hand. If a line is not attached, try to retrieve one from the boat and attach it.
- [ ] Hold the line with one hand and swim with the other to shore. If no line is available, try pushing the boat and swimming.
- [ ] Slide the boat up on shore and empty it.

Emptying the Boat on Shore

Boats full of water are incredibly heavy. If possible, get assistance in emptying it.

- [ ] Stand near the middle of the canoe, grasp the gunwales, and lift up, tilting the canoe away from you.
- [ ] Lift until you can turn the canoe over and empty it completely.

Reentry in Water

If the boat is floating sufficiently high, reentry in the water is possible.

Unassisted by a second boat

- [ ] If the canoe is upside down, you and your partner swim to the same side of the canoe and lift the gunwales to right it.
- [ ] You and your partner take positions on opposite sides and ends of the canoe.
- [ ] You both grasp near the gunwales and simultaneously pull up, reach across to the far gunwales, and twist your bodies, flopping into the canoe on your buttocks.
- [ ] Bail out as much water as possible.
- [ ] If paddles are not available, use your hands to paddle to retrieve equipment or to go directly to shore.

Assisted reentry

- [ ] The assisting boat pulls up parallel to the capsized boat.
- [ ] If the boat is upside down, the rescuers help the paddlers in the water right the boat by pulling on the gunwale as they turn it over.

☐ The rescuers help the paddlers hold the boat near the gunwale to counterbalance the weight of the paddlers in the water as they pull themselves up from the far side into the boat.

Assisted Towing Rescue

☐ The assisting paddlers secure a line to the capsized boat or grab an existing line on the craft. The line may be attached to the towing boat or the waist of the towing paddler (as long as there can be a quick release from the towing paddler's waist or canoe in the event of another emergency or safety situation).

☐ The paddlers from the capsized craft swim to the far end of the boat and hold on.

☐ The paddlers in the rescue boat paddle to shore towing the capsized boat and paddlers.

PART II

On the Water

CHAPTER 6

Canoeing Techniques, Strokes, and Maneuvers

The canoeist must take the canoe where he or she wants it to go, not where it wants to go."

—Bill Mason

The objective of paddling is to make the canoe go where you want it to go. You use strokes to accomplish that goal. Other issues are efficiency and safety. Some strokes make the canoe go where you want it to go better than other strokes do. This point addresses efficiency. At the same time, you don't want to take a stroke that can potentially dislocate your shoulder. The essence of paddling is to make the canoe go where you want it to go, both efficiently and safely.

In this chapter, you will learn how to properly carry your canoe, fundamentals of boat control and movement, and the basic strokes used in recreational canoeing. You will then learn how to combine these strokes to form new strokes and how to modify them in infinite combinations to make the canoe go where you want it to go.

The structure of this chapter uses three distinct levels of skill development: basic strokes, compound strokes, and customized strokes. These three levels are a useful way to approach skill development. Basic strokes are important because they form the foundation of most of the other strokes that you will perform. Strokes are presented here in their pure form. In reality, most paddling is a hybrid of strokes that allows the paddler to reach the ultimate goal of proper boat placement.

Getting Started

The first step is moving the canoe from the shore to the water. Here are some pointers about accomplishing this without mishap.

Carrying the Canoe

In most instances, a two-person carry is sufficient and convenient. Also, if the paddlers are paddling tandem, the bow paddler can take one end and the stern paddler can take the other end. Paddlers should carry the canoe on opposite sides to help keep the canoe from falling. If youths are carrying the canoe, consider using three or even four people to carry it.

One-Person Carry

A single person executes a solo carry (figure 6.1). The person carries the canoe overhead by placing the center seat, thwart, or a special yoke on the neck and shoulders. Since canoes weigh 60-70 pounds on average, this is a challenging carry for long distances but can be advantageous on winding and tight portage trails.

Suitcase Carry

In the suitcase carry (figure 6.2), two people carry the canoe. They begin by standing on opposite sides of the boat, one at the bow and the other at the stern. Each grabs a deck plate or bow or stern thwart in one hand, and they carry the boat at about thigh level as if carrying a suitcase. Gear can be carried in the boat. Four people, two per side, using the main thwarts as the carry bars, can carry heavier loads.

Figure 6.1 One-person canoe carry.

Figure 6.2 Suitcase canoe carry.

Overhead Portage

Two people, one at the bow and the other at the stern, can carry a tandem canoe overhead (figure 6.3). They rest the boat on their shoulders and support it with their arms bent and their hands on the gunwales. In some instances, the individuals will use the thwarts to rest the boat on their shoulders placing their heads in the overturned hull. The fun part of this carry is that the pair

Figure 6.3 Overhead portage.

can hear each other clearly because sound travels through the overturned hull. The difficulty is that the lead person cannot easily see the path ahead. Another option is to place the deck plate(s) on the shoulder, allowing for better vision, but this can be a bit more difficult for balance. Gear can be carried in backpacks, strapped into the boat, or carried separately on a second trip.

Double-Boat Carry

Two people can carry two boats using a double suitcase carry (figure 6.4). This method is the most efficient way to move two boats at one time.

The two people place the boats parallel to each other, and both then stand between the two canoes. The bow carrier grabs the bow deck of the left canoe in the left hand and the bow deck of the right canoe deck in the right hand. The stern carrier does the same at the stern of the canoes. The double canoe carry works best with boats that are approximately the same length and have narrow profiles. Beamy canoes (canoes that are wide in the middle) will bump into each other, making it difficult to grasp one in each hand unless you have broad shoulders and are strong enough to hold your arms far apart.

Portage Wheels, Canoe Dollies, and Carts

Wheels allow you to move canoes that are just too heavy to carry, and they can facilitate canoe camping by easing the chore of transporting a boat and a week's worth of camping supplies. Portage wheels look like the rear set of wheels on a tricycle. They are designed to strap on to the bottom of the canoe at the center or at the stern. After the wheels are attached, you can roll your canoe (and gear) along a trail in an upright position. Larger diameter wheels

Figure 6.4   Double-boat carry.

seem to work better on an uneven trail through the woods. The smaller sets work well for transporting a canoe over level grass or pavement, say from your vehicle to the water. Make sure that the wheels fold down so that you can store them inside your boat if you will be taking them on the trip.

Keys to Success

- Lift the canoe using your legs, not your back.
- In the two-person carry, one person is on the left side of the canoe and the other is on the right side. This method reduces the likelihood that the canoe will slip and fall to the ground.

Launching and Entering

The easiest and driest way to launch the canoe is for both people to stand amidships with the canoe at a right angle to the shore, grasp the gunwales, and launch the canoe hand over hand into the water. After the canoe is in the water, the bow person stabilizes the canoe for the stern person as he or she enters the canoe. The stern person steps on the centerline of the canoe while placing the left hand on the left gunwale and the right hand on the right gunwale. Once in the stern, the stern paddler should stabilize the canoe for the bow paddler, who enters in a similar manner. See figure 6.5, *a* through *c.*

If the launching area is of sufficient size, the canoe can be boarded and launched by placing the canoe parallel to the shore (see figure 6.5, *d* through *f*). This method allows for greater stability and boat positioning. Once in the water the steps for boarding the canoe are the same as if the canoe were perpendicular.

Keys to Success

- The canoe should be floating freely in the water as you enter it.
- The stern person enters first because, once in the canoe, he or she will face the bow person while stabilizing the canoe for entry.
- The bow person holds and stabilizes the bow as the stern person enters.
- The stern person enters the canoe by placing equal pressure on the left and right hands, which are on the left and right gunwales, respectively. The stern person steps into the canoe on the centerline of the canoe.
- The stern person proceeds to the stern and, once situated, stabilizes the canoe for the bow person, who then enters the canoe.
- If you are entering the canoe on a river, generally face the bow upstream.

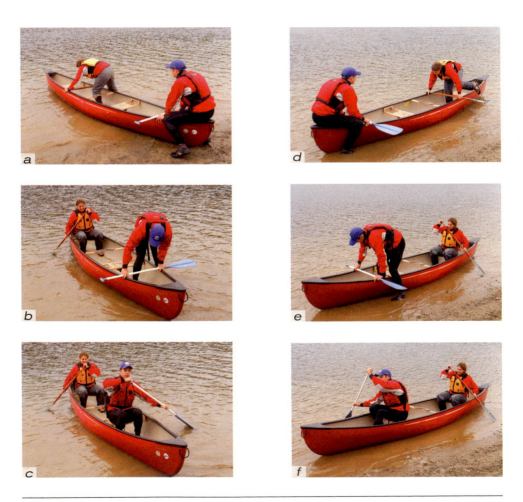

Figure 6.5 Launching the canoe: *(a-c)* perpendicular launch; *(d-f)* parallel launch.

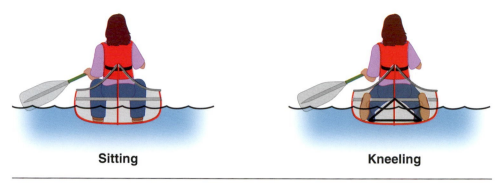

Sitting   **Kneeling**

Figure 6.6   Kneeling versus sitting.

Kneeling Versus Sitting

Normally, kneeling in a canoe offers more stability than sitting on the canoe seat (figure 6.6). For many paddlers, the choice is a tradeoff between comfort and stability. Kneeling in the canoe offers stability more through triangulation than a lower center of gravity. Triangulation is achieved by having both knees on the hull of the boat and by leaning against the seat, resulting in three points of contact. You can easily demonstrate this principle for yourself. In a safe area, try rocking the canoe while sitting on the seat. Then try rocking the canoe while kneeling. You can feel the triangulation created by your legs in the bilge area of the canoe. In addition, check the height of your belly button in the canoe while sitting and then while kneeling. The difference between the two positions is not significant.

Most paddlers compromise between sitting and kneeling. They sit when paddling in calm waters and kneel when the water gets a little rougher.

Trim, Balance, and the J-Lean

Ultimately, trim and balance determine how a canoe will be paddled. Paying attention to trim and balance will position you for successful and efficient paddling.

Trim refers to how the canoe sits in the water from bow to stern (figure 6.7). If either the bow or the stern sits lower in the water than the opposite end, the canoe is said to be out of trim. If the canoe is out of trim, move some of the heavier gear toward the light end of the canoe. If you cannot fix the trim by equalizing the weight in the canoe, having the canoe slightly stern heavy is better.

Balance refers to the lateral stability of the paddler in the canoe. Every time you get into your boat, try doing a J-lean (figure 6.8). Kinesthetically, the J-lean is an important skill to master. Push down with one leg and lift

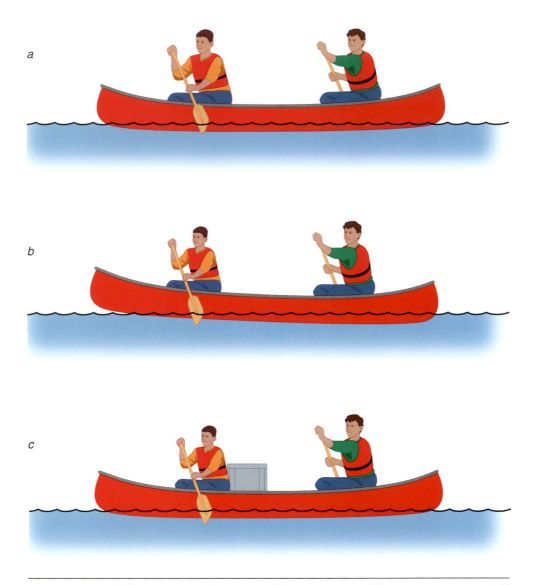

Figure 6.7 *(a)* Canoe in trim with paddlers of the same weight, *(b)* canoe out of trim, and *(c)* canoe in trim with paddlers of different weights.

up with the other leg while keeping your center of gravity inside the canoe. Keep your backbone vertical to the water and angle your hips. You will find that you are exceptionally stable in this position. In addition, you are free to take another stroke rather than having to brace yourself with the paddle. In figure 6.8*c*, the paddler is leaning the canoe instead of her body. This results in the center of gravity being outside the canoe and the paddler is likely to capsize.

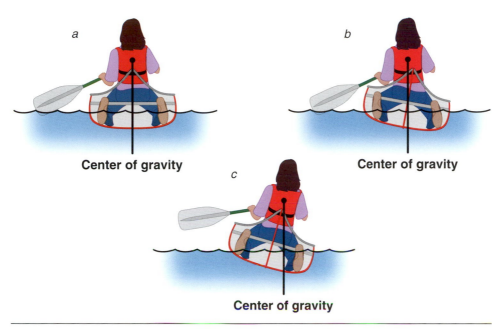

Figure 6.8 *(a)* Balance with no lean, *(b)* balance with a correct J-lean, and *(c)* balance with incorrect body lean.

Concepts of Paddling

The concepts of paddling apply to all paddling disciplines, whitewater and flat-water. These concepts provide the principles of all paddling techniques.

DEFINITIONS

- **Basic strokes**—The power phase of the stroke forms a uniform motion through the water. The blade is perpendicular to the axis of travel.

- **Compound strokes**—Two or more basic strokes are combined to make a compound stroke. Compound strokes can easily be broken down into their basic strokes. For example, a Duffek stroke is a combination of a stationary draw, a draw toward the bow, and a forward stroke.

- **Customized strokes**—Customized strokes are derived from basic or compound strokes, but the blade of the paddle moves through the water at an angle that is not always perpendicular to the stroke. For example, the stationary draw is a customized stroke because the blade requires the forward motion of the canoe.

- **Grip hand**—The grip hand is the hand on the grip of the paddle. The position of the grip hand indicates the angle of the blade in the water. Hence,

(continued)

(continued)

the position of the grip hand and the thumb are good indicators of what the blade is doing. For this reason, the grip hand provides a good reference point for what the paddle is doing in the water.

- **Onside strokes—**A paddler paddling on the left side of the canoe with the right hand holding the grip and the left hand holding the throat of the paddle is paddling on the onside. If a paddler is paddling on the right side of the canoe with the left hand holding the grip and the right hand holding the throat, then the right side of the canoe is the onside.
- **Offside strokes—**The offside is the opposite side of the canoe from the paddler's onside. Examples of strokes used on the offside are the cross-forward stroke and the cross-bow draw.
- **Power face of the blade—**When performing the forward stroke, the power face is the side of the blade that is moving through the water, facing the stern of the canoe.
- **Back face of the blade—**When performing the forward stroke, the back face of the blade is the side of the blade facing the bow of the canoe.

Types of Strokes

Generally, strokes are of three types: dynamic, stationary, or bracing.

- Dynamic strokes are strokes that move in relationship to the position of the paddler. Most strokes are dynamic, including the forward, reverse, and draw.
- Stationary strokes (static strokes) are strokes in which the paddler holds the paddle in a fixed position. To work effectively, stationary strokes require the canoe to be moving through the water or the movement of river current. The stationary draw is an example of a stationary stroke.
- Bracing strokes are primarily used to stabilize the canoe. Examples are the low and high brace strokes.

Turning Circle

Imagine a bicycle wheel turned on its side. If you spin the wheel with your hand, it will rotate on its axle. Imagine this wheel with the axle in the center of the canoe and the rim going through the bow and stern seats of the canoe. Any stroke applied along the outer rim of the wheel will tend to rotate the canoe on its axis (figure 6.9, *a-b*).

As the canoe moves forward, the turning circle moves toward the rear of the canoe (figure 6.9*c*). The faster the canoe is traveling, the farther the turning circle moves toward the stern. In part, this principle explains why the stern paddler can make corrections in steering more easily than the bow paddler can.

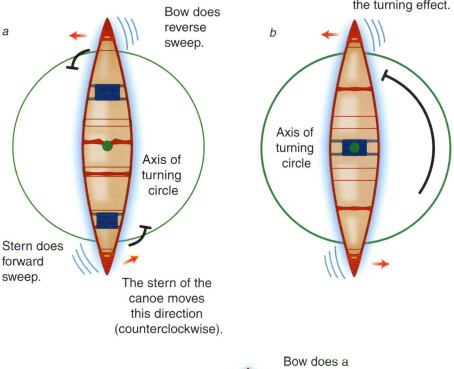

a

Bow does
reverse
sweep.

Axis of
turning
circle

Stern does
forward
sweep.

The stern of the
canoe moves
this direction
(counterclockwise).

Solo paddler does a forward
sweep stroke. It parallels the
turning circle and maximizes
the turning effect.

b

Axis of
turning
circle

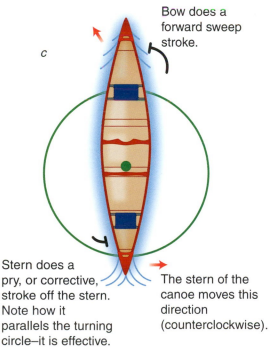

Bow does a
forward sweep
stroke.

c

Stern does a
pry, or corrective,
stroke off the stern.
Note how it
parallels the turning
circle—it is effective.

The stern of the
canoe moves this
direction
(counterclockwise).

Figure 6.9 Turning circle: (a) tandem paddlers, (b) solo paddler, and (c) canoe moving forward.

Moving the Canoe to the Paddle

The objective of paddling is to move the canoe through the water. The paddle is the lever. The water is the fulcrum. You are the effort, and the canoe is the load. Hence, the canoe moves to the paddle. In a real sense, the paddler is levering the canoe through the water. It is easy to lose sight of this fundamental principle when describing strokes and diagramming the stroke moving through the water. The water is an imperfect fulcrum, and as the load becomes heavier, the paddler may seem to be moving the paddle through the water rather than moving the canoe through the water. With the advent of the lightweight equipment, however, paddlers can approach the realization of this principle when they can actually feel the canoe rotating around the paddle.

Basic Canoe Strokes

Basic strokes form the cornerstone of your stroke repertoire. As you develop your paddling skill, you will combine these strokes to form new strokes (compound strokes), and you will learn to modify your strokes in subtle ways to make the canoe go where you want it to go (customized strokes).

In general, basic strokes have two characteristics. First, the power phase of the stroke has a uniform motion through the water. Note that most of the stroke diagrams use a straight line to illustrate the propulsion phase. The sweep strokes are drawn with a uniform curved line.

Second, the blade is perpendicular to the axis of travel throughout the propulsion phase. For this reason, only the position of the blade as it enters the water is shown. In contrast, look at the motion of travel of the J-stroke in figure 6.32 (page 167). Because the blade angle in the water changes throughout the propulsion phase, the different blade angles of the stroke are shown.

Canoe strokes can also be broken down into three parts:

- The catch is the position at which the paddle blade enters the water at the beginning of the stroke.

- The power or propulsion phase is the part of the stroke that moves the canoe through the water.

- The recovery phase comprises the action from the end of the propulsion phase to returning the paddle blade to the catch position for another stroke. The recovery can be done either in-water or out-of-water.

Because the paddler holds stationary strokes motionless in the water, they have a propulsion phase but not a recovery phase. For the individual strokes in this chapter, the description section discusses both the propulsion phase and the recovery phase of the stroke. Where applicable, the catch is also discussed.

Your basic stroke repertoire will consist essentially of three strokes and their complements. These are the forward, draw, and sweep strokes and their complements—the reverse, pry or push-away, and reverse sweep strokes. Add to these strokes the offside strokes like the cross-draw and cross-forward. In a sense, these are not new strokes because you are doing a forward or draw

PADDLER TIP

Your basic stroke repertoire consists of roughly eight strokes that form the basis of most of the other strokes that you will do. These strokes include the forward, reverse, forward sweep, reverse sweep, draw, pry, and push-away. In practice, river canoeing strokes and techniques are modified to best fit the on-water venue.

stroke on your offside. They are included because there are some subtle differences. Also add to these strokes the stationary draw, because it introduces the concept of blade angle and provides an entrée to the customized strokes. In addition, the stationary draw will work only if the boat is traveling through the water.

Forward Stroke

Purpose. The purpose of the forward stroke (figure 6.10) is to move the canoe forward.

Description. The paddle enters the water toward the front of the canoe with the power face of the blade pointing toward the stern of the canoe. To maximize the catch phase of the stroke, the paddler rotates his or her torso, which helps extend the lower arm farther forward. During the propulsion phase, the paddler keeps the shaft of the paddle vertical to the water, which assists in maximizing the forward effect of the stroke. Normally, if the paddler is seated, the propulsion phase of the stroke ends just before the paddle reaches the hip of the paddler. If the paddler is kneeling, the propulsion

Figure 6.10 Forward stroke.

PADDLER TIP

A paddler learning the forward stroke should not expect the canoe to go in a straight line when using just the forward stroke. Additional strokes are required to make the canoe go straight.

phase ends at the knee. Much of the power in the stroke is derived from the torso rotation of the body as it unwinds. A common mistake that paddlers make is taking too long a stroke by extending it past the hips.

The recovery phase of the forward stroke is similar to that used for other strokes. Rotate the paddle so that the shaft moves from a vertical position to a horizontal position. The thumb on the grip hand should point toward the bow of the canoe, and the back face of the blade should point down toward the water. Rotate the paddle back toward the bow, where you take another stroke.

Discussion. The forward stroke is probably the most widely used stroke. Most new paddlers assume that the forward stroke will propel the canoe forward in a straight line. Unfortunately, the forward stroke in its pure form has other effects on the canoe (figure 6.11). Besides making the canoe travel forward, the forward stroke in its pure form will turn the canoe away from the side on which the paddler is paddling. Two points are important here. First, when beginning to learn the strokes, the paddler should not be concerned that the

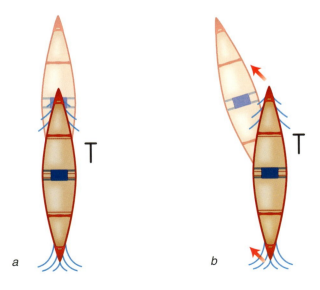

Figure 6.11 Forward stroke effects: (a) Canoe goes forward and (b) canoe turns toward its offside.

canoe is not going straight. Second, a combination of pure strokes, that is, a compound stroke, is required to make the canoe go straight (e.g., forward pry stroke, J-stroke, and so on). After the new paddler recognizes this truth, he or she can put the task of going straight into proper perspective (figure 6.12). Figure 6.13 shows the effects for tandem paddlers.

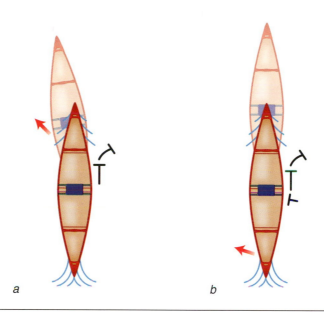

Figure 6.12 Correcting for forward stroke effects: *(a)* the forward stroke component will sideslip the canoe back toward the original track and turn the canoe toward the offside, and *(b)* the correction stroke in the stern pushes the stern to the left, straightening the canoe.

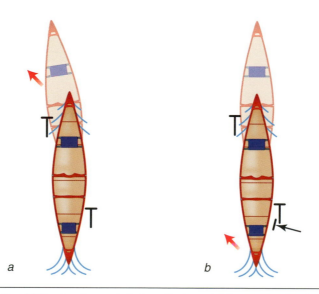

Figure 6.13 *(a)* Tandem forward stroke effects and *(b)* correcting for those effects.

TECHNIQUE TIP

Watch your paddle as you take a reverse stroke. The shaft should be vertical in the water and you should end the stroke at your hips.

Reverse Stroke

Purpose. The complement of the forward stroke, the reverse stroke (figures 6.14 and 6.15) moves the canoe backward.

Description. The paddle enters the water just behind the paddler with the back face of the paddle pointing toward the bow of the boat. The paddler pushes forward while pulling the grip arm back. The thumb on the grip hand is pointing away from the body and the canoe.

The recovery phase of the reverse stroke is similar to that used for other strokes. Rotate the paddle so that the shaft moves from a vertical position to a horizontal position. The thumb on the grip hand should point toward the bow of the canoe, and the back face of the blade should point down toward the water. Rotate the paddle back toward the stern, where you take another stroke.

Discussion. If you are using the reverse stroke to stop the canoe or propel it backward, you will note that the stroke has a strong tendency to turn the bow of the canoe toward your side and that the stern will swing away from your side. An easy solution is to

a

b

c

Figure 6.14 Reverse stroke.

follow the reverse stroke immediately with a draw stroke in the stern that pulls the stern back toward your side. In addition, following the reverse stroke with a draw stroke illustrates the important lesson that you will often have to counter the effect of one stroke with another stroke. The secondary effect of the reverse stroke is that it turns the canoe. You counter this effect by following the reverse stroke with a draw stroke. If for some reason the canoe turns the other way, use a pry in the bow to move the canoe back on line. The lesson for new paddlers is that they need to learn how to combine strokes to make the canoe go where they want it to go. This principle is covered in the discussion of compound and customized strokes.

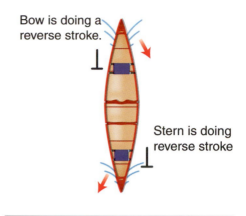

Figure 6.15 Reverse stroke.

Draw Stroke

Purpose.   Used primarily in flatwater, the purpose of the draw stroke (figures 6.16 and 6.17) is to move the canoe sideways toward the paddle. In a tandem canoe, the draw stroke will move the ends of the canoe toward the paddlers and rotate the canoe on its axis.

Description.   The paddler rotates his or her body so that the shoulders are facing toward the side of the canoe, parallel with the gunwale. With the lower arm extended outward and the grip hand extended above the gunwale, the

Figure 6.16 Draw stroke.

paddle enters the water with the power face of the blade facing the paddler and the blade parallel to the keel line. For the propulsion phase of the stroke the grip hand pushes outward and the lower arm pulls inward.

In the pure form of the stroke, there are two types of recoveries. The first is the out-of-water recovery. Before the blade hits the side of the canoe, slice the blade out of the water toward the stern. With the blade parallel to the water and the back face of the blade pointing toward the water, swing the blade out for another stroke.

The underwater recovery is the second form of recovery. Before the blade hits the side of the canoe, rotate the blade so that it is perpendicular to the keel line of the canoe. The thumb on the grip hand points outward, away from your body. Point the edge of the blade where you want it to go, just in front of where you will take the next stroke. Think of the actual motion of the stroke as a tight figure-8 motion.

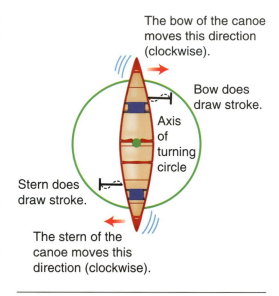

The bow of the canoe moves this direction (clockwise).

Bow does draw stroke.

Axis of turning circle

Stern does draw stroke.

The stern of the canoe moves this direction (clockwise).

Figure 6.17 Draw stroke.

Discussion. The draw stroke is a useful stroke and forms an integral component of several compound strokes (e.g., the Duffek stroke). In addition, just learning to adapt the draw stroke from its pure form will help you make the canoe go where you want it to go. A stern draw is a variation of the draw stroke in which you apply the draw along the turning circle in an effort to pull the stern toward the paddle.

Pry Stroke

Purpose. The purpose of the pry stroke (figures 6.18 and 6.19) is to move the canoe sideways away from the onside of the paddler. This stroke moves the canoe in the opposite direction of the draw stroke. In a tandem canoe, the

TECHNIQUE TIP

When slicing the paddle through the water for an underwater recovery, slice the blade back on itself. You will find that this seeming overreaction will set you up well for your next stroke.

PADDLER TIP

Try the stop-and-go approach when learning the pry stroke. Complete the propulsion phase of the stroke. Stop. Rotate the paddle. Stop. Now slice it back during the recovery phase for the catch. Stop. Rotate the paddle and take another stroke.

Figure 6.18 Pry stroke.

pry stroke will move the ends of the canoe away from the paddlers and rotate the canoe on its center axis.

Description. The paddler rotates his or her body so that the shoulders are facing toward the side of the canoe, parallel with the gunwale. In the pure form of this stroke, the paddle is placed directly against the gunwale with the back face of the blade pointing away from the paddler. The lower hand holds the paddle shaft against the gunwale so that the energy from the pry is transferred directly to the gunwale. The thumb on the grip hand is pointing toward the

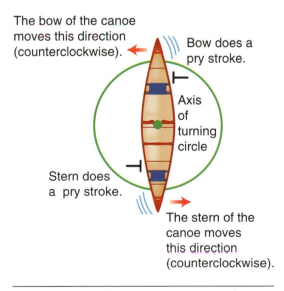

The bow of the canoe moves this direction (counterclockwise).

Bow does a pry stroke.

Axis of turning circle

Stern does a pry stroke.

The stern of the canoe moves this direction (counterclockwise).

Figure 6.19 Pry stroke.

stern. The catch is alongside the canoe with the blade parallel to the keel line and the paddle shaft angled so the blade is slightly under the hull. The paddler then pulls the grip hand back toward the body. When doing the propulsion phase correctly, the paddler feels as if he or she is scooping water through a prying action.

Because the prying action is short, most paddlers use an underwater recovery. For the recovery phase, the paddler turns the blade so that it is at a right angle to the keel line of the canoe. The thumb on the grip hand is pointing away from the paddler; the edge of the paddle slips through the water and sets up the next stroke. As with the draw stroke the paddle motion will make a tight figure-8 motion. This action is evident in the movement of the grip hand.

Discussion.   Most people find that using the pry stroke in its pure form is like being in low gear. A lot of prying is needed to move the canoe as desired. Most paddlers prefer using another stroke in place of the pry, such as the cross-bow draw. In combination with other strokes, however, the pry becomes an extremely useful stroke. When the pry is combined with the forward stroke, it becomes the forward with a pry (similar to the J-stroke), an important stroke used to propel the canoe in a straight line. The reverse J-stroke is another useful stroke, created by combining the reverse stroke with the pry.

Keys to Success

- Pry directly off the gunwale. This technique transfers the energy directly to the canoe.

- If you pry directly off the gunwale, you will find that your grip hand will have a lot of motion to make the stroke work.

Push-Away Stroke

Purpose.   Used primarily in flatwater, the purpose of the push-away stroke (figures 6.20 and 6.21) is to move the canoe sideways away from the paddle. Conceptually, this stroke is the opposite of the draw. In a tandem canoe, the push-away moves the end of the canoe away from the paddle.

Description.   The paddler rotates his or her body so that the shoulders are facing toward the side of the canoe, parallel with the gunwale. With the grip hand extended and the lower arm extended close to the gunwale, the paddle enters the water with the power face of the blade facing the paddler and the blade parallel to the keel line. For the propulsion phase of the stroke, both the grip hand and the lower arm push outward.

There are two types of recoveries. The first is the out-of-water recovery. When the blade becomes extended, slice the blade out of the water toward the stern. With the blade parallel to the water and with the back face of the blade pointed toward the water, swing the blade inward for another stroke.

The underwater recovery is the second form of recovery. When the blade becomes extended, rotate the blade so that it is perpendicular to the keel line of the canoe. The thumb on the grip hand points outward or away from your body. Point the edge of the blade toward the gunwale or where you want it to go.

Figure 6.20 Push-away stroke.

Slice the blade through the water and rotate the blade for another stroke. Think of the motion of the stroke as a tight figure-8 motion.

Discussion. Conceptually, the push-away stroke is the opposite of the draw stroke. But compared with the draw stroke, it is fairly weak because it requires a pushing action away from the body with the lower arm, in contrast to the draw stroke, which requires a pulling action toward the body with the lower arm. Most paddlers find that the pushing action is much weaker than the pulling action and will therefore use another stroke in place of the push-away stroke.

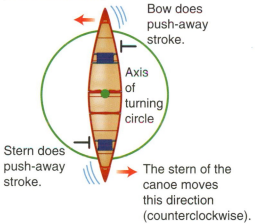

The bow of the canoe moves this direction (counterclockwise).

Bow does push-away stroke.

Axis of turning circle

Stern does push-away stroke.

The stern of the canoe moves this direction (counterclockwise).

Figure 6.21 Push-away stroke.

TECHNIQUE TIP

Both the pry and push-away strokes allow the canoe to move a-beam when the other paddler does a draw stroke. When combined with another stroke, such as the forward stroke, the pry can be used as an additional steering stroke (forward with a pry).

Forward Sweep

Purpose. The purpose of the forward sweep depends on the position of the paddler in the canoe. For a bow paddler, the purpose of the forward sweep is to move the canoe forward and turn the canoe away from the bow paddler's onside (figure 6.22, *a-c*). For the stern paddler, a forward sweep helps to turn the canoe toward the bow paddler's onside while maintaining some forward momentum (figure 6.22, *d-f*). For a solo paddler kneeling in the center of the canoe, the forward sweep turns the canoe along the turning circle, although like the effect of the forward sweep performed by the bow paddler, it will move the canoe forward, only less so.

Description. In its pure form, the forward sweep enters the water well forward of the solo paddler. The blade is perpendicular to the water, and the power face of the blade is facing sternward. The thumb of the grip hand is

Figure 6.22 Forward sweep: *(a-c)* bow and *(d-f)* stern.

pointing toward the sky. In contrast to the draw stroke, in which the shaft of the paddle is vertical, the shaft of the blade during the sweep is more horizontal. The paddler performs the stroke mainly through torso rotation. The blade is at the stern of the canoe at the end of the propulsion phase.

The recovery phase of the forward sweep is similar to that used for the forward stroke. Rotate the paddle so that the shaft moves from a vertical position to a horizontal position. The thumb on the grip hand should point toward the bow of the canoe, and the back face of the blade should point down toward the water. Rotate the paddle back toward the bow, where you take another stroke.

Discussion. As noted in the purpose section of this stroke, the effectiveness of the forward sweep is contingent on the location of the paddler in the canoe. Most paddlers find that using a partial sweep is more effective than using the full stroke as shown in its pure form, in part because the forward sweep has a forward component as well as a turning effect. For the bow paddler, the second half of a forward sweep in its pure form has little effect. The second half of the stroke intersects the turning circle. For the stern paddler, the first half of a forward sweep in its pure form is less effective for a similar reason. For this reason, the bow paddler will use the first half of a sweep stroke and the stern paddler will use the second half of a sweep stroke. Figure 6.23*a* shows the turning circle using full forward sweeps when paddling solo. If paddling tandem, the sweeps are broken into half sweeps, as illustrated in figure 6.23*b*.

Keys to Success
Use a partial sweep if you want to turn the canoe. The bow paddler will find the first half of the sweep useful. The stern paddler will find the second half of the sweep useful.

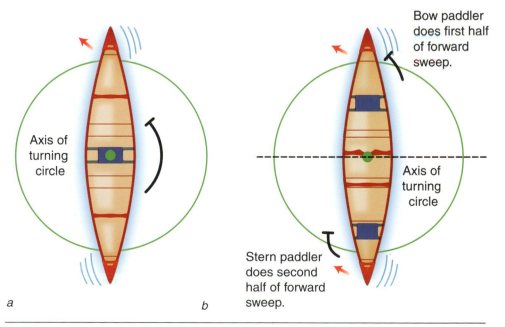

a   b

Figure 6.23 Turning circle (*a*) with full forward sweeps (solo canoe) and (*b*) with half sweeps (tandem canoe).

Reverse Sweep

Purpose.   As with the forward sweep, the purpose of the reverse sweep (figures 6.24 and 6.25) depends on the position of the paddler in the canoe. Most bow paddlers use the first half of a reverse sweep, which will have the effect of moving the canoe toward the bow paddler's onside. For a solo paddler kneeling in the center of the canoe, the reverse sweep will turn the canoe along the turning circle, which will create an effect similar to that of a stern paddler performing a reverse sweep in moving the canoe backward, only less so. For the stern paddler, the reverse sweep spins the canoe toward the bow paddler's offside.

Figure 6.24   Reverse sweep: *(a-c)* bow and *(d-f)* stern.

TECHNIQUE TIP

Sweep strokes can be effective when used in flatwater or in a solo canoe. For tandem canoes and in moving water, the use of a bow or stern draw is more efficient.

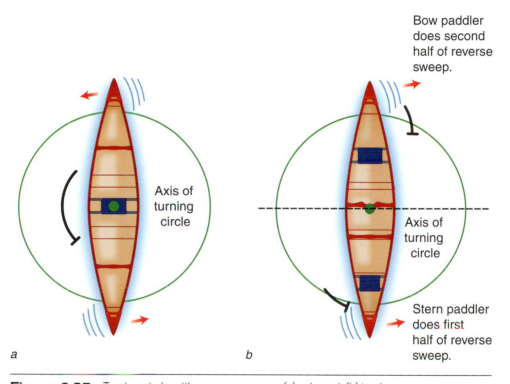

Figure 6.25 Turning circle with reverse sweeps: *(a)* solo and *(b)* tandem.

Description. In its pure form, the reverse sweep enters the water behind the solo paddler. The blade is perpendicular to the water. The thumb of the grip hand is pointing toward the sky. The shaft of the blade during the sweep is nearly horizontal. The paddler performs the stroke mainly through torso rotation. The end of the propulsion phase of the stroke ends with the blade toward the bow of the canoe.

The recovery phase of the reverse sweep is similar to that of the reverse stroke. With the thumb on the grip hand pointing toward the bow of the canoe and the back face of the blade pointing downward toward the water, rotate the paddle back toward the stern, where you take another stroke.

Discussion. As noted in the purpose section of this stroke, the effectiveness of the reverse sweep is contingent on the location of the paddler. Most paddlers find that using a partial sweep is more effective than using the full stroke in its pure form, in part because the reverse sweep has a reverse component as well as a turning effect. For the bow paddler, the first half of a reverse sweep in its pure form has little effect. As shown in figure 6.25, the first half of the stroke intersects the turning circle. For the stern paddler, the second half of a reverse sweep in its pure form is ineffective for a similar reason. For this reason, the bow paddler will use the second half of the reverse sweep stroke and the stern paddler will use the first half of the reverse sweep stroke.

Keys to Success
Use a partial sweep. The bow paddler will find the second half of the reverse sweep useful. The stern paddler will find the first half of the reverse sweep useful.

Stationary Draw

Purpose. Like the draw stroke, the stationary draw (figure 6.26) moves the canoe toward the paddle, but it differs from the draw stroke in two ways. First, as its name suggests, the stroke is stationary in the water. Second, it uses the motion of the canoe traveling through the water to move the canoe.

Description. The paddler rotates the torso slightly toward the onside, places the paddle shaft vertically in the water, and holds it stationary. The power face of the blade engages the water at approximately a 45-degree angle in relation to the canoe, with the leading edge farther away from the gunwale. The thumb on the grip hand should point toward the paddler's nose. The forward momentum of the canoe traveling through the water forces the water against the power face of the blade, which moves the canoe toward the blade.

Discussion. The stationary draw is a useful stroke, and good paddlers often nestle it subtly within other strokes. For example, a paddler might situate it within the beginning of the Duffek stroke or start with a stationary draw and then quickly go directly into a draw stroke for more effect. In addition, in terms of a stroke progression, the stationary draw is useful in showing the concept of blade angle.

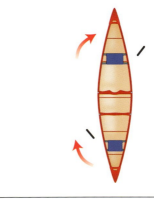

Figure 6.26 Stationary draw.

TECHNIQUE TIPS

- For the stationary draw stroke, the thumb on your grip hand should point toward your nose. Experiment with different blade angles and feel the difference in the force of the water against the blade.

- The stroke before the stationary draw is what counts. Before doing the stationary draw, initiate the turn with a pry off the stern or other stroke. Then the stationary draw will continue the motion that has been initiated.

Stationary Pry

Purpose.   Like the push-away stroke, the purpose of the stationary pry stroke (figure 6.27) is to move the canoe away from the paddle or toward the offside. The stationary pry stroke differs from the push-away stroke in two ways. First, it is stationary in the water. Second, it uses the motion of the canoe traveling through the water to move the canoe.

Description.   The paddler rotates his or her torso slightly outward from the canoe. The paddle shaft is placed vertically in the water and held stationary. The back face of the blade engages the water at approximately a 45-degree angle in relation to the canoe, with the leading edge closer to the gunwale. The forward momentum of the canoe traveling through the water forces the water against the back face of the blade, which moves the canoe toward the offside.

Discussion.   When done it its pure form, the stationary pry will sideslip the canoe to the offside. The paddler can move it forward or aft to increase or decrease its turning effect. You may even place the paddle against the gunwale.

Keys to Success

- In creating a successful stationary draw or pry stroke, the preceding stroke is crucial. Remember, for the stationary draw to work, the

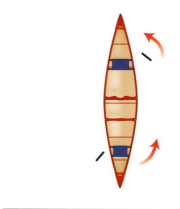

Figure 6.27   Stationary pry.

canoe must have forward momentum. Unfortunately, the forward stroke used to obtain the momentum turns the canoe to the onside, which is in opposition to the stationary draw. Hence, you may need to initiate the stationary draw with a healthy pry off the gunwale, which will turn the bow of the canoe in the direction that the stationary draw will continue to take it.

- For the stationary draw and pry strokes to work, the canoe must be moving through the water.

- Try customizing the stroke by moving the paddle slightly forward or aft or by changing the angle of the blade in the water to see what it does to the canoe.

Cross Strokes

Cross strokes are performed on the solo paddler's offside or the bow paddler's offside in a tandem canoe. The paddler executes a cross stroke without changing the grip hand or the hand on the throat of the paddle. Several subtle differences in the cross strokes result from the paddler having to reach over to the opposite side to take a paddle stroke. A word of caution: Many of the cross strokes require considerable body flexibility, so people who are not accustomed to performing the stroke may have some difficulty.

Cross-Forward Stroke

Purpose.   The purpose of the cross-forward stroke (figures 6.28) is to provide a forward stroke on the offside of the canoe.

Description.   The paddler sets up as he or she does for the forward stroke but then lifts the paddle over the canoe and performs the forward stroke on the offside. Because it is an offside stroke, most paddlers find that the range of the stroke is shorter than it is on the onside, that they use their arms more for the stroke, and that less torso rotation occurs. Generally, the underwater recovery works best. Conceptually, the feathering of the paddle through the water is similar to that used for the draw stroke. Rotate the blade so that the power face is facing the canoe. The thumb of the grip hand points directly toward the bow. Slip the paddle back through the water in a tight figure-8 motion and take another stroke.

SAFETY TIP

The cross strokes require considerable rotation of the body. Many people will not have sufficient body flexibility to perform this group of strokes adequately.

TECHNIQUE TIP

The cross strokes presented here are similar. If you rotate the cross-forward so that it comes in from the side rather than from the front, it becomes a cross-draw. If you lower the shaft from a vertical to a more horizontal position, the cross-draw quickly becomes a cross-bow draw stroke.

Figure 6.28   Cross-forward stroke.

Discussion.   The cross-forward will move the canoe forward and toward the onside. Solo paddlers find this stroke useful for starting their forward movement. Two or three cross-forward strokes start the canoe forward and turn it slightly toward the onside. The paddler then takes two or three forward strokes, which counteract the turning effect and move the canoe forward.

Cross-Draw Stroke

Purpose.   The purpose of the cross-draw stroke (figure 6.29) is to pull the canoe toward the paddle on the paddler's offside.

Description.   The paddler rotates his or her body to the offside so that the shoulders are facing toward the side of the canoe, parallel with the gunwale. The paddler performs a draw stroke as described in the earlier section. In the pure form of the stroke, most paddlers use an underwater recovery because an out-of-water recovery is difficult to perform. The chief characteristic of the cross-draw is that the shaft is vertical to the water.

Discussion.   The cross-draw is a draw stroke performed on the offside. If the cross-draw is performed along the turning circle by dropping the grip hand

TECHNIQUE TIP

The cross-draw is a draw stroke performed on the offside. A key indicator is that the shaft of the paddle is vertical in the water.

a   b   c

Figure 6.29 Cross-draw stroke.

and moving the power face toward the bow of the canoe, it will turn into a cross-bow draw.

Compound Strokes

Most paddlers will use compound strokes to make the canoe go where they want it to go, whether they want it to go straight or to turn.

Compound strokes are formed by adding together two or more basic strokes. For example, the J-stroke and a forward with a pry are each composed of a forward stroke and a prying action off the stern. In the J-stroke, the pry is performed with the power face, whereas in the forward with a pry, the pry is performed with the back face. From an instructional perspective, the ability to describe a compound stroke in terms of the strokes from which it is assembled has considerable value. For example, being able to describe the forward with a pry in terms of a forward stroke and a pry is helpful.

Traveling in a Straight Line

Whether paddling solo or in tandem, paddlers will notice that the canoe has a tendency to veer or turn away from the solo or stern paddler's onside—in other words, not go in a straight line. Why this happens was discussed in the section about the forward stroke (see figure 6.11). The paddler can use several approaches to make the canoe travel in a straight line. These are switching, ruddering, forward with a pry, the J-stroke, and the reverse J-stroke.

Touring Technique

Sometimes referred to as the sit-and-switch approach, switching is a fairly straightforward approach for going straight. Technically, switching is not a compound stroke, but it is included here because it is a way of making the canoe move in a straight line. The bow and stern paddlers take several forward strokes in unison on opposite sides of the canoe. As the canoe begins to turn, they quickly switch sides and take several forward strokes on their opposite side. As the canoe begins to turn, they switch sides again and repeat the process.

Switching is a popular technique among marathon racers, long-distance touring canoeists, and some other paddling groups. It is a relatively efficient method of propelling the canoe forward. Normally, the paddler calling out the commands calls, "Hit" or "Hut," and the paddlers switch sides on the next stroke. The most common mistake that inexperienced paddlers make is waiting too long before switching. The result is that instead of going straight, the canoe tends to swerve toward one side before the paddlers switch and then back the other way after they switch paddling sides. Although switching works, most paddlers will find that they have better control over the path of the canoe if they develop the compound strokes of the forward with a pry or J-stroke.

Ruddering

A common method of steering the canoe is to use a rudder. After taking a forward stroke, the paddler rotates the paddle so that the blade is vertical to the water. The paddler holds the paddle against the stern at an angle to the canoe. Quite simply, the paddler uses the paddle as a rudder to steer the canoe (figure 6.30).

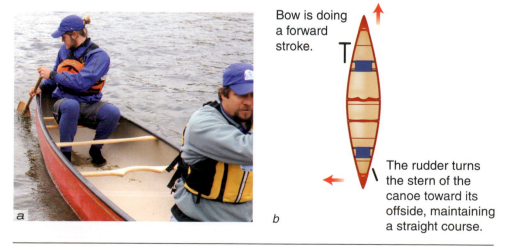

Bow is doing a forward stroke.

The rudder turns the stern of the canoe toward its offside, maintaining a straight course.

Figure 6.30 Ruddering.

Although ruddering will work, several significant drawbacks limit its effectiveness. First, the stern paddler is not taking a forward stroke to propel the canoe forward. This leaves the bow paddler to provide forward momentum, with the full weight of the canoe on the paddle of the bow paddler rather than shared between the two paddlers. Second, the use of the rudder causes considerable drag on the canoe. Third, the rudder works only when the canoe is moving through the water. As the speed of the canoe slows, the effectiveness of the rudder diminishes. Also, as the speed of the canoe decreases, the stern paddler tends to increase the angle of the rudder, which only increases drag.

Forward With a Pry

Purpose. The purpose of the forward with a pry (figure 6.31) is to paddle the canoe in a straight line. The pry off the gunwale in the stern corrects for the turning action created by the forward stroke by literally pushing the stern of the canoe over, which has the net effect of straightening the canoe.

Description. The forward with a pry is literally two strokes that are combined to make a compound stroke. The paddle enters the water toward the front of the canoe with the power face of the blade pointed toward the stern of the canoe. To maximize the catch phase of the stroke, the paddler rotates his or her torso, which helps extend the lower arm farther forward. During the propulsion phase, the paddler keeps the shaft of the paddle vertical to the water to maximize the forward effect of the stroke. In contrast with the forward stroke in its pure form, the propulsion phase of the stroke extends behind the hips to perform the pry component of the stroke.

As the stroke passes the hips, the paddler positions the paddle for the pry. The paddler places the shaft of the paddle against the gunwale. The shaft of the paddle takes a more horizontal position. The thumb on the grip hand points up toward the sky, and the pry is performed with the back face of the paddle. The paddle blade moves no more than 6 inches (15 centimeters) from the hull to prevent the stroke from becoming a reverse sweep and stopping forward momentum. The pry is quick and powerful. When the paddler performs it correctly, he or she should feel the stern of the canoe move sideways in the water.

The recovery phase of the forward with a pry is similar to that of the forward stroke. Rotate the paddle so that the shaft moves from a vertical position to a horizontal position. The thumb on the grip hand should point toward the bow of the canoe, and the back face of the blade should

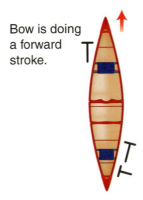

Bow is doing a forward stroke.

The first part of the stroke moves the canoe forward and the pry component straightens the canoe by pushing the stern to the offside.

Figure 6.31 Forward with a pry.

point down toward the water. Rotate the paddle back to the bow, where you take another stroke.

J-Stroke

Purpose.   The purpose of the J-stroke (figure 6.32) is to paddle the canoe in a straight line. Although there are several varieties of the J-stroke, a generic J-stroke is described here. The pry action off the gunwale in the stern corrects for the turning action created by the forward stroke by literally pushing the stern of the canoe over, which straightens the canoe.

Description.   The paddle enters the water toward the front of the canoe with the power face of the blade pointed toward the stern of the canoe. To maximize the catch phase of the stroke, the paddler rotates his or her torso, which helps extend the lower arm farther forward. During the propulsion phase, the paddler keeps the shaft of the paddle vertical to the water to maximize the forward effect of the stroke.

As the stroke passes the hips, the paddler begins to rotate the paddle with the power face of the blade pointing outward. The thumb on the grip hand is pointing downward. This is in contrast to the forward pry, in which the thumb is pointing upward. As the paddler initiates the prying action that is a continuous extension of the forward stroke, he or she may slide the shaft of the paddle 6 to 8 inches (15 to 20 centimeters) along the gunwale.

The recovery phase of the J-stroke is similar to that of the forward stroke. Rotate the paddle so that the back face of the blade is pointing toward the water. The thumb on the grip hand should point toward the bow of the canoe. Rotate the paddle back to the bow, where you take another stroke.

Discussion.   In a review of the canoeing literature, paddlers debate the merits of the forward with a pry versus the J-stroke. Some early authors called the forward with a pry the goon stroke, a rather uncomplimentary name.

a

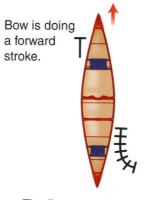

Bow is doing a forward stroke.

The first part of the stroke moves the canoe forward, and the pry component straightens the canoe by pushing the stern to the offside.

b

Figure 6.32   J-stroke.

TECHNIQUE TIP

When performing the pry in the forward with a pry, the thumb on the grip hand points up toward the sky.

The forward with a pry offers several advantages. When done correctly, it provides a swift and powerful corrective stroke. This attribute is useful if the solo paddler is initiating a turn toward the onside of the canoe. The forward with a pry is relatively easy to teach; it is simply a forward stroke followed by a pry stroke.

When done correctly, the J-stroke is generally more efficient than the forward with a pry because its prying action tends to maintain forward momentum. However, the corrective action of the J-stroke is usually less powerful than that of the forward with a pry.

In summary, most paddlers learn both the forward with a pry and the J-stroke and use them interchangeably.

Reverse J-Stroke

Purpose.   The purpose of the reverse J-stroke (figure 6.33) is to move the canoe backward in a straight line.

Description.   For a solo paddler or the bow paddler, the reverse J-stroke combines the reverse stroke and a pry off the gunwale in the bow. The back face of the paddle is used to perform the pry. This is accomplished by rotating the grip thumb out and down toward the elbow of the shaft hand. The shaft hand can also "choke up" slightly on the paddle shaft to assist with the pry portion of the stroke. The amount and direction of the pry depends on how much correction the paddler deems necessary.

Discussion.   When performing the reverse stroke, most learners will experience considerable sideslip in the canoe. If you use buoys, gates, or some other fixed object for a reference point, this sideslip will become obvious. Often a solo paddler will add a far back stroke that begins at the stern and is drawn to the hip, parallel to the keel of

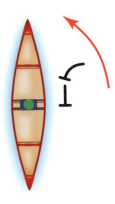

Figure 6.33   Reverse J-stroke.

TECHNIQUE TIP

When performing the pry in the J-stroke, the thumb on the grip hand rotates out and down toward the water.

the canoe, then rotate the paddle 180 degrees and perform the reverse J-stroke. This new stroke is called the compound reverse stroke. The reverse stroke propels the canoe backward, and the pry corrects for the turning action of the reverse stroke.

Spinning and Turning the Canoe

As a paddler's ability to control the forward and reverse directions of the canoe on flat and gently moving water increases, the next step is to work on some of the dynamic strokes and maneuvers that allow the canoe to turn more quickly, or even pivot in place.

Duffek Stroke

Purpose. Originating in the whitewater community, the purpose of the Duffek stroke (figure 6.34) is to turn the bow of the canoe into an eddy or out into the current. On flatwater, the stroke is used to turn or rotate the bow of the canoe.

Description. The Duffek stroke is a combination of three strokes. It starts with a stationary draw, which is followed by a draw toward the bow of the canoe along the turning circle, where it smoothly transitions as it hooks into a forward stroke.

Discussion. The Duffek stroke is the classic stroke used to make an eddy turn or do a peel-out from an eddy. The stroke is very different on flatwater than on a river. On flatwater, the paddler does all the work with the stroke. On a river, it is often just the opposite. The paddler plants the paddle in the eddy, and the current will turn the canoe and paddler around the paddle. The experience

Figure 6.34 Duffek stroke.

of rotating around the paddle creates quite a unusual sensation for the paddler!

Inside Pivot Turn

Purpose. The purpose of the inside (onside) pivot turn (figure 6.35) is to rotate or spin the canoe on a flatwater venue.

Description. For a solo paddler, the inside pivot turn combines three strokes. The paddler starts with half of a reverse sweep that follows the turning circle. The grip hand thumb points up. It stops amidship, where the paddler rotates the paddle to perform a draw toward the bow of the canoe along the turning circle. The grip hand thumb now points down. The third stroke is an underwater onside sweep. The grip hand thumb still points down. This stroke truly is a sweep stroke performed underneath the canoe. When the paddle reemerges at the stern, the paddler rotates the paddle for the next reverse sweep.

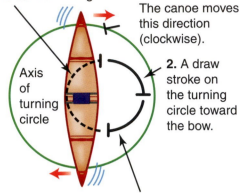

3. An inverted sweep underneath the canoe will actually continue the canoe turning.

The canoe moves this direction (clockwise).

Axis of turning circle

2. A draw stroke on the turning circle toward the bow.

1. Half of a reverse sweep to the center of the canoe, where it converts into the draw.

Figure 6.35 Inside pivot turn.

When paddling tandem, the inside (onside) pivot turn can be completed in two ways:

- Both paddlers complete draw strokes on their respective onsides.
- The bow paddler completes the second half of a reverse sweep and the stern paddler completes the second half of a forward sweep.

Discussion. When you perform the underwater onside sweep stroke correctly, you will feel the canoe continue to rotate. Freestyle paddlers execute this stroke, called a Gimble, as an art form. River paddlers delete the underwater onside sweep stroke and simply feather the paddle from the bow back to the stern, because any stroke under the canoe is likely to catch something and capsize the canoe.

Outside Pivot Turn

Purpose. The purpose of the outside (offside) pivot turn (figure 6.36) is to rotate or spin the canoe.

Description. For a solo paddler, the outside pivot turn is the combination of two strokes: the cross-bow draw and the sweep stroke. The paddler starts with a cross-bow draw along the turning circle toward the bow, lifts the paddle over the bow, and finishes the stroke with a sweep stroke.

For tandem canoes, the outside pivot turn can be completed in two ways:

- Both paddlers complete either pry or push-away strokes on their respective onsides.

- The bow paddler completes the first half of a forward sweep and the stern paddler completes the first half of a reverse sweep.

Discussion. The outside pivot turn is an easy stroke to perform. River paddlers use a variation of this stroke to make eddy turns on their offside.

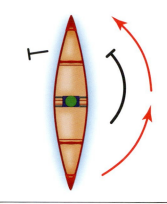

Figure 6.36 Outside pivot turn.

Customized Strokes

The third level of strokes are customized strokes. To a casual observer, customized strokes may look like basic or compound strokes, but they are different. Two significant variations differentiate customized strokes from basic or compound strokes.

First, the motion of the paddle through the water is something other than those pictured as pure strokes in this chapter. For example, the motion of travel of the pure form of a draw stroke (as pictured in this chapter) is at a right angle to the center of the canoe. No rule prohibits a paddler from doing a draw stroke at a 45- or 60-degree angle to the boat or from moving the draw toward the bow or stern of the canoe.

The second characteristic of a customized stroke is that the blade often travels through the water at an angle other than a right angle to the motion of travel. The motion of travel concept is typified by the stationary draw and the stationary pry. In the stationary draw, the motion of the canoe through the water with the blade at an angle has the effect of pulling the canoe toward the blade.

The easiest way to develop your customized paddling skills is to use paddling drills that require you to maneuver in reference to fixed objects such as a dock, buoys, or gates. Paddlers learn quickly that, to make the canoe go where they want it to go in relation to the fixed object, they must adjust and vary their strokes. The use of gates, docks, and other reference points provides immediate feedback. The following drills are typical exercises that learners and instructors can use to develop customized strokes and skills.

Dock Drills and Maneuvers

To practice the strokes described in this chapter and to give paddlers an opportunity to work on linking strokes and creating compound strokes, the following drills and maneuvers can be used in a confined, protected area close to shore. When performing dock drills, be aware of other boaters and people fishing in the area.

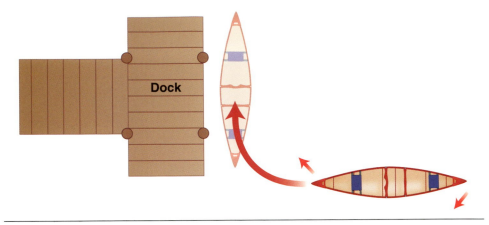

Figure 6.37 Docking drill.

Docking Drill

A dock provides a convenient reference point. Tandem or solo paddlers can approach the dock at a right angle and then turn into the dock so that the canoe stops sideways adjacent to the dock (figure 6.37).

Usually, a bow paddler paddling on the left side will use a cross-bow draw while the stern paddler paddling on the right will use the first half of a reverse sweep to turn the canoe toward the offside and into the dock. If the stern has too much momentum, the stern paddler may use either a stationary draw or a draw stroke to stop the momentum. In addition, the stern paddler may move the paddle slightly aft (rearward) for the draw stroke to stop both the sideways and forward momentum of the canoe.

The point of describing the strokes of the stern paddler is to show how the docking drill in this case assists the paddler in customizing his or her strokes to make the canoe go where he or she wants it to go. The stroke may look like a draw, but it is a customized draw.

The same is true for the bow paddler using the cross-bow draw. The paddler may adjust the blade angle or lift the blade out of the water vertically if he or she wants less stopping action. Or, for increased bite and more stopping action, the paddler may insert the paddle deeper into the water. Again, the stroke looks like a stationary draw, but the paddler customizes it to make the canoe go where he or she wants it to go.

Circle Drill

In the circle drill, learners paddle clockwise and then counterclockwise around an object. They start with a wide circle and then narrow its diameter. This drill is useful in developing the forward-with-correction strokes. If a floating dock is not available, a buoy will work equally well (figure 6.38).

Sideways Docking Drill

With the canoe parallel to the dock, tandem or solo paddlers can move the canoe away from the dock using a series of draw and pry strokes (figure 6.39a). Their objective is to keep the canoe parallel with the dock. Then they can move the canoe back toward the dock.

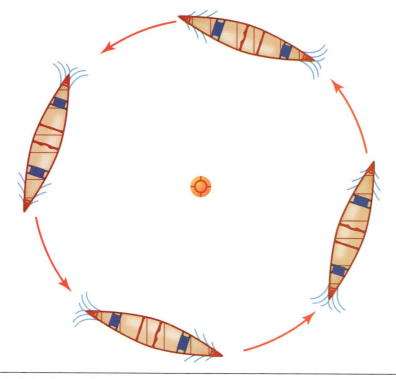

Figure 6.38 Circle drill.

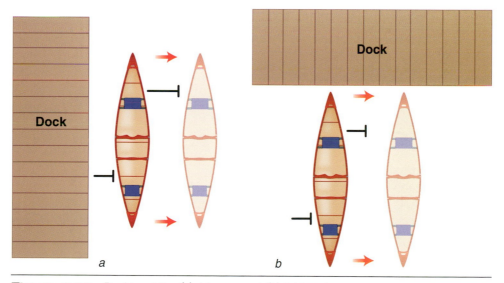

Figure 6.39 Docking drills: *(a)* sideways and *(b)* right angle.

Right-Angle Docking Drill

In contrast to the sideways dock drill, this drill requires tandem or solo paddlers to orient the canoe perpendicular to the dock and move it alongside the dock. The objective is to keep the canoe perpendicular to and the same distance from the dock as it moves (figure 6.39*b*).

Sideslip Drill

Using the dock as a reference point, the paddlers paddle parallel to the dock and then sideslip the canoe toward the dock, keeping the canoe parallel to it (figure 6.40). To sideslip to the offside, the bow paddler uses a stationary pry and the stern paddler uses a stationary draw. Flip the drill around and approach from the other direction. The bow paddler then uses a stationary draw, and the stern paddler uses a stationary pry.

The sideslip drill with the dock is an excellent drill for learning the stationary draw and stationary pry. The dock provides a useful reference point for both the paddlers and the instructor. The paddlers learn the effect of changing the blade angle of the stationary strokes. Second, they learn the importance of where the stroke is placed in relation to the canoe and themselves. The use of the dock aids the instructor because the first part of instruction is for the learners to determine how well they are doing the skill. Next, after offering suggestions, the instructor can evaluate the effectiveness of those suggestions by noting the learners' performance of the skill.

Wiggle Courses

A wiggle course uses a series of single buoys to create a sequence of maneuvers for the learner. For example, two buoys can be placed the length of the canoe plus a couple of feet (half a meter) apart. Tandem or solo paddlers can paddle the canoe sideways through the buoys without touching them (figure 6.41). Using the same setup, the paddlers could paddle a figure 8 through the buoys.

Two or more buoys can establish a course similar to that shown in figure 6.42. Paddlers can perform a series of

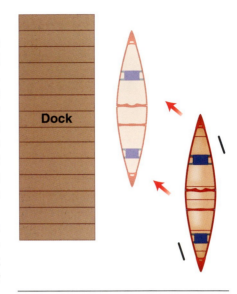

Figure 6.40 Sideslip drill.

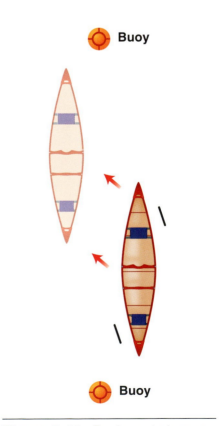

Figure 6.41 Two-buoy wiggle course.

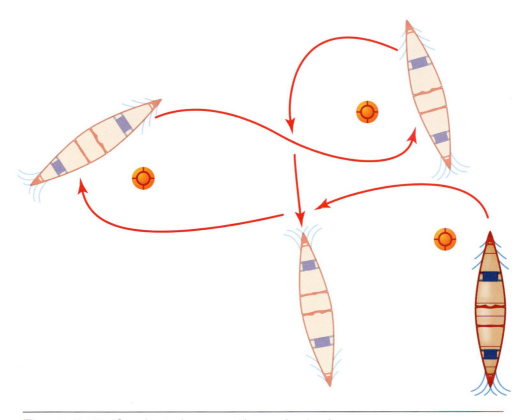

Figure 6.42 Sample wiggle course with more than two buoys.

turns, sideslips, and other maneuvers through the course. A wiggle course offers the beginning learner an advantage over gates because negotiating the course requires less precision. For this reason, buoys make a good intermediate step before the learner uses gates. Also, a wiggle course is easier to set up because each point requires only one buoy.

Gates

Derived from racing, gates provide a higher degree of feedback to the student because the learner needs to maneuver both the bow and stern through the gate without touching it. A simple four-gate setup (figure 6.43) can provide almost an infinite variety of courses. Gates require greater precision on the part of the learner.

An important note on the use of gates: As presented here, the purpose of using gates is to develop general paddling skills. At some point, running gates encourages a level of technique that is specific to running gates, not to paddling in general. This is OK, but both learners and instructors should be aware of it when they are reaching this point.

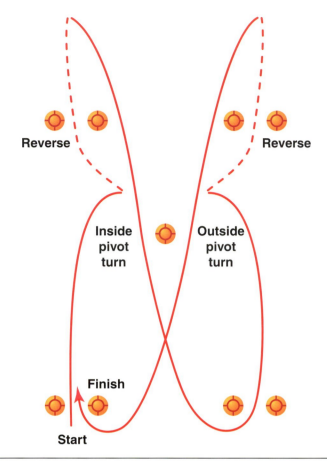

Figure 6.43 Sample gate sequence.

When constructing a gate course, the distance between buoys should be no less than 4 feet (1.2 meters) (figure 6.44). To start, the width can be greater, and as abilities improve, the width can be narrowed.

Summary

To borrow again from Bill Mason's quote, "The canoeist must take the canoe where he or she wants it to go, not where it wants to go." Developmentally, the three-tier approach to strokes presented in this chapter can help learners make the canoe go where they want it to go. The basic strokes are the foundation of your stroke repertoire. Unfortunately, the basic strokes will not normally make your canoe go straight. By using compound strokes you learn to combine

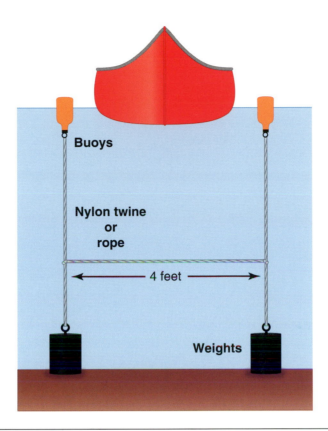

Figure 6.44 Gate construction using buoys.

basic strokes to make the canoe go where you want it to go. Commonly used compound strokes often receive their own names. The J-stroke, Duffek, and forward with a pry are examples of compound strokes. Compound strokes can be easily broken down into their component parts, or basic strokes. You can use a compound stroke such as a J-stroke or forward with a pry to make your canoe go straight. You create customized strokes, the third level of strokes, by learning to modify the basic and compound strokes in infinite combinations to make the canoe go where you want it to go. Maneuvering around docks and other reference points, wiggle courses, and gates can develop your skills because to do so you will have to go beyond the compound strokes and into using the customized strokes.

It is important to remember, though, that this text was designed to be used as a supplementary resource to the recreational canoeist. It is not intended to replace on-water instruction by a qualified instructor.

CHAPTER 7

River Trips

Take everything as
it comes; the wave
passes, deal with
the next one.

*Tom Thomson
(1877–1917)*

The hand-painted river gauge on the side of the bridge indicated that the water level was perfect for paddling. We launched four canoes for the daylong run and set off for sights we had only read about in the guidebooks. We were well equipped but somewhat anxious because only one of the group of eight had run this section before. Mark would be in the lead boat and show us where to scout the big drops. Our most experienced paddler would be in the last, or sweep, boat to make sure that the other boats would have support if needed.

The focus before the launch had been to make sure that we were prepared. The real adventure lay downstream in a 6.5-mile (10.5-kilometer) wilderness run accessible only by boat. We were to see spectacular sights available only to the lucky few who had the skills and sense of adventure to float by boat.

With the right preparation, you can launch and travel downriver far from the put-in. The farther you travel from quick access to emergency services, the higher the level of adventure and risk. Adventure is largely about managing risk.

Although casual paddlers do not require the same level of skill and knowledge as the most adventurous, they should emulate the adventurers' approach to managing risk. Developing paddling skills, understanding the environment in which the trip will take place, and taking safety precautions (such as wearing a life jacket) are the practices of the most capable athletes. Failing to do so are the practices of the foolhardy.

Paddling on moving water builds on the skills obtained on flatwater. You should practice strokes on flatwater to develop boat control and balance.

In this chapter we build on the strokes covered in chapter 6 and add the dynamic of moving water. Canoeists must understand the force of moving water. A gallon of water weighs about eight pounds (a liter weighs one kilogram). River volume is measured in cubic feet per second (CPS). One cubic foot

SAFETY TIP

Although adventure and exploration are important in the history of many nations, in recent years participation in adventurous outdoor activities has grown like never before. The variety of adventurous activities available to the public is remarkable. Common tickets to adventure include mountain biking, rock climbing, backcountry skiing, scuba diving, backpacking, mountaineering, surfing, ice climbing, skydiving, wilderness canoeing, ocean kayak touring, and whitewater kayaking.

These activities, while diverse, share the allure of adventure and its many benefits. Outdoor adventure teaches self-reliance and personal responsibility. It causes participants to challenge themselves physically and mentally, and rewards the effort with unique personal satisfaction. For those who are not enticed by these adventurous activities, the pursuit of them may seem too risky, or even crazy. That view is typically an uninformed one, resulting from a lack of knowledge or understanding of the training and skill level of those engaging in such activities.

of water equals 7.5 gallons (28.4 liters), weighing a total of 63 pounds (28.4 kilograms). The faster water flows, the greater the kinetic energy, or force, it creates. Hundreds, even thousands, of pounds (kilograms) of force can be created against a boat hull. Understanding the characteristics of the moving-water environment helps you develop respect for the power of the current. Because of the higher element of risk involved in paddling in moving water, you should take a river-paddling course from a certified ACA instructor before venturing out.

Canoeing on Moving Water

Chapter 5 covered how to read a river; in this chapter we will apply that information. Many maps and guidebooks give a river difficulty rating for flow under a variety of conditions, ranging from flatwater to classes I through VI. The rating is a measure of the force, speed, and difficulty of moving water. Many rivers do not fit neatly into a system because water levels fluctuate, and hazards come and go. To use the river classification system, you must know both your own abilities and the prevailing conditions. If the water is extremely cold, for instance, you should add another level of difficulty to the rating. Start with the lowest levels of the system to gain experience and travel with experienced paddlers who know the local area.

The river difficulty system provides a solid reference for paddlers new to a river or to paddling moving water. Just as skiers know to use caution on black diamond ski slopes, paddlers should use extra caution on rivers rated class III or higher. If you are getting started in river paddling, start with easier class I or II water. Master your paddling skills at these levels before venturing on to class III or above. Rivers rated class II and above require specialized outfitting and rescue gear, such as flotation bags, thigh straps, and helmets. Paddlers need solid skills to avoid capsize on rivers rated class III or higher. On class II water you can develop solid river-reading and scouting skills. Scouting, or looking at a rapid from land to determine the best route before running it, is required before running drops at higher classifications.

RIVER DIFFICULTY CLASSIFICATIONS

- **Class I: Easy**. Fast-moving water with riffles and small waves. Few obstructions, all obvious and easily missed with little training. Risk to swimmers is slight; self-rescue is easy.

- **Class II: Novice**. Straightforward rapids with wide, clear channels that are evident without scouting. Occasional maneuvering may be required, but rocks and medium-sized waves are easily missed by trained paddlers. Swimmers are seldom injured, and group assistance, while helpful, is seldom needed.

(continued)

(continued)

- **Class III: Intermediate**. Rapids with moderate, irregular waves that may be difficult to avoid and can swamp an open canoe. Complex maneuvers in fast current and good boat control in tight passages or around ledges are often required; large waves or strainers may be present but are easily avoided. Strong eddies and powerful current effects can be found, particularly on large-volume rivers. Scouting is advisable for inexperienced parties. Injuries while swimming are rare; self-rescue is usually easy, but group assistance may be required to avoid long swims.

- **Class IV: Advanced**. Intense, powerful, but predictable rapids requiring precise boat handling in turbulent water. Depending on the character of the river, it may feature large, unavoidable waves and holes or constricted passages demanding fast maneuvers under pressure. A fast, reliable eddy turn may be needed to initiate maneuvers, scout rapids, or rest. Rapids may require "must" moves (maneuvers required of the paddler to run the drop without mishap) above dangerous hazards. Scouting may be necessary the first time down. Risk of injury to swimmers is moderate to high, and water conditions may make self-rescue difficult. Group assistance for rescue is often essential but requires practiced skills. A strong roll (ability to right the boat after capsize without leaving the seated position) is highly recommended. (Note: A roll requires specific outfitting in the boat and skills learned from a skilled instructor teaching on flatwater.)

- **Class V: Expert**. Extremely long, obstructed, or very violent rapids that expose a paddler to above-average endangerment. Drops may contain large, unavoidable waves and holes or steep, congested chutes with complex, demanding routes. Rapids may continue for long distances between pools, demanding a high level of fitness. What eddies exist may be small, turbulent, or difficult to reach. At the high end of the scale, several of these factors may be combined. Scouting is mandatory but often difficult. Swims are dangerous, and rescue is difficult even for experts. A very reliable roll (meaning it is successful almost 100 percent of the time), proper equipment, extensive experience, and practiced rescue skills are essential for survival.

- **Class VI: Extreme**. One grade more difficult than class V. These runs often exemplify the extremes of difficulty, unpredictability, and danger. The consequences of errors are very severe and rescue may be impossible. For teams of experts only, at favorable water levels, after close personal inspection and taking all precautions. This class does not represent drops thought to be unrunnable, but may include rapids that are only occasionally run.

Courtesy of American Whitewater www.americanwhitewater.org.

River Maneuvers

Paddlers use specific maneuvers on moving water to work with (not battle against) the energy of the river current. Paddler strength is no match for the tremendous force exerted on a boat hull by moving water. Use of these techniques allows the paddler to use the power of the water to his or her advantage. The added benefit is that these maneuvers are great fun! Practice of these techniques will result in a high level of grace and finesse in your paddling.

Downcurrent J-Lean

A capsize in moving water often happens when a boat crosses an eddy line and rolls into the oncoming current. Avoid this by using a J-lean to expose the boat bottom to the oncoming current. This action neutralizes the drag caused by current rushing under the hull. Without neutralizing this river force, water can pile up against the boat and roll the paddler and boat upstream. Whenever you cut across current, keep a slight downcurrent lean on the boat using the J-lean technique. Press against your downcurrent knee (if kneeling) or against your downcurrent buttock (if sitting) while maintaining good upright posture by keeping your nose vertical over your belly button. Proper execution of the J-lean exposes the hull of your boat to the oncoming rush of current, allowing water to pass safely under the boat. Lack of a downcurrent J-lean may result in a flip when cutting across forceful eddy lines.

Ferries

Ferrying is possibly the best method of crossing current without losing headway downstream. Ferrying is useful for maneuvering around obstructions, for boat scouting, for lining up properly for a drop or chute, and for avoiding unsafe obstacles. The ferry uses the energy of the water deflected off the side of a properly angled canoe. Proper paddle strokes prevent the canoe from moving downstream, while the force of the current provides the push to move the boat to the other side of the river (see figure 7.1).

The key to ferrying lies in keeping the boat angle to the oncoming current balanced with paddle speed. If you begin with the boat facing directly into the current, the angle of the boat is 0 degrees. To ferry, you widen the angle of the boat to the current up to 45 degrees, but no more. The upstream end of the boat

TECHNIQUE TIP
Getting Started in the Forward Ferry

Start against the shore with your boat facing upstream into the current. Angle the upstream end of the boat slightly toward the opposite shore. If the current is slow, angle the boat no more than 45 degrees in relation to the downstream flow. If the current is fast, use a smaller angle. Holding the angle, paddle upstream into the current. The stern paddler uses steering strokes to keep the angle consistent as the current speed varies across the river. The bow paddler continues paddling forward, and the stern paddler assists with forward paddling and angle correction. Continue paddling until you reach the other side.

points in the direction that you wish to travel in the ferry. The slower the current, the greater the angle can be, up to 45 degrees. In fast current, the boat angle may be as little as 15 or 20 degrees.

In a forward ferry, the boat faces upstream to the oncoming current, meaning that the boat and paddler are turned around facing upriver. The forward ferry is easier to master than the reverse ferry because the paddler can see the angle of the current to the boat and make needed adjustments. For a forward ferry, the solo paddler uses a forward stroke and steering strokes to keep the boat at the proper angle (less than 45 degrees) to the oncoming current. For tandem paddlers, the bow paddler provides power while the stern paddler is primarily responsible for the boat angle in the current.

A reverse ferry is typically more difficult to execute. In a reverse ferry, the boat and paddlers face downstream. The stern paddler provides power using reverse strokes. The bow paddler sets the angle by steering the stern 15 to 45 degrees toward the direction to be traveled and holds the angle in the current

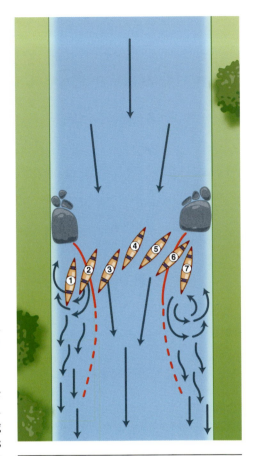

Figure 7.1 Ferrying.

using reverse strokes and reverse steering strokes toward the bow of the boat. Reverse ferries are generally used while traveling downstream in midcurrent to view obstacles and determine the best course of travel.

Eddy Turns

Eddy turns are ways to park your boat in the middle of fast-rushing current. Being able to complete an eddy turn is a critical skill to safe river paddling, because successful execution of the technique allows you to maintain control of your craft. Eddies offer a resting place for lunch, bailing, or water breaks, or a place to scout or set up a rescue rope.

Boat speed, angle, and lean are key components to entering an eddy. Position the boat so that you will enter the eddy at an angle appropriate for the difference in current speeds (see figure 7.2). Remember that you are aiming at a moving target! Lean the canoe as if you are leaning a bicycle through a turn. Enter with enough speed to cross the eddy line near the top of the eddy and allow the river current to assist in turning the boat. If you do not have enough speed, you may not make it into the eddy.

Figure 7.2 Eddy turn. As the tandem canoe crosses the eddy line, the bow paddler completes a Duffek while the stern paddler completes a forward sweep or stern draw, pivoting the craft into the eddy, facing upstream. Proper lean, or heeling of the canoe, is crucial in this maneuver.

Peel-Outs

A peel-out is a way to leave an eddy. Just like the eddy turn coming in to an eddy, the technique provides a safe way to cross the eddy line and use the force and momentum of the river current to carry your boat. Peel-outs are sometimes the only safe way to leave an eddy into a powerful jet of water. The technique provides you with good speed to enter the oncoming current without capsizing.

Boat speed, angle, and lean are key components. You need enough speed to cut across over the eddy line into the oncoming current. Cross the eddy line with an angle appropriate to the current speed (see figure 7.3). The faster the

Figure 7.3   Peel-out. As the canoe crosses the eddy line, the bow paddler completes a Duffek or bow draw while the stern paddler completes a forward sweep and stern draw. Once in the downstream current, the forward stroke can be used.

current, the quicker the peel-out will be. As the current catches the front half of the boat, the boat will peel out, turning downstream in the current. Paddle through the turn to make sure that the boat is out of the eddy and then continue paddling downstream. A properly executed J-lean keeps the boat upright as it enters the faster current.

Surfing

Just like surfing on a board at a coastal beach, surfing in a canoe is a blast. Surfing has practical applications for cutting across river currents, but primarily it is a maneuver to be enjoyed for the fun of it.

Forward surfing on a standing wave is really a modification of the forward ferry combined with the force of gravity pulling your boat to the low point of the wave trough. Simply forward ferry into the trough of the wave and then point your boat directly into the current (see figure 7.4). If the wave is big enough and you have positioned your center of gravity on the upstream side of the wave, you will balance the canoe at a point where gravity will pull you upstream while the current tries to move you downstream. Remember to lean downstream if your boat is kicked to one side or the other. Side surfing a big wave is a great way to practice your J-lean.

Figure 7.4 Forward surfing.

River Sense

Paddlers need to develop a sense of the river. Moving water is an ever-changing force that you must treat with respect. Before starting the trip, consult maps, guidebooks, and people knowledgeable about the river. Maps reveal much about the river, including the average gradient, dams or other obstructions, and access points for emergencies and rescue.

Guidebooks usually give a detailed account of the river along with shuttle information. Always check the date that the guidebook was published. A major flood can significantly change the river, making some rapids more difficult and others easier. Check with knowledgeable people like conservation officers, members of local paddling clubs, or outfitters who are familiar with the river on a daily basis.

Be sure to check the stream flow or the river gauge before embarking on the trip. The U.S. Geological Survey (USGS) provides real-time online stream gauge readings for thousands of streams in the United States. Stream volumes can change quickly after a summer thunderstorm or an unseen event upstream, so always be prepared for rising levels and the characteristics of water as it changes depth and force.

When you are on the water, assign a lead boat and a sweep boat. The lead generally is the person most familiar with the lake or river. The sweep boat carries first aid and safety gear and should carry one of the most highly skilled and experienced paddlers on the outing. All remaining boats stay between the lead and sweep boats. On a river, paddlers should never lose sight of the boat following. If that boat goes out of sight, the paddler should pull over and wait. Likewise, the boat ahead should pull over and wait, and so on throughout the group.

The sweep boat assists any paddlers who need assistance. On a regular basis, the lead boat should pull over to initiate a rest break and allow the following paddlers, including the sweep, to catch up. These rest periods keep spirits high and give the trip leader an opportunity to make sure that participants are drinking fluids, eating high-energy foods, and are not suffering from environmental conditions.

Vision, Scouting, and Decision Making

A paddler must learn to look downstream. This sounds like common sense, but novice paddlers often focus on what is happening immediately under them. With practice a paddler raises his or her vision and starts looking downstream or forward. Tunnel vision causes mishaps that can be avoided. Be aware of the need to look downstream constantly.

Remember two rules of thumb for running rivers:

1. Never paddle anything that you would not want to swim.
2. When in doubt, get out and scout.

Scouting involves beaching the boat above a rapid, getting safely ashore, walking down to look at the rapid, and planning a route (see figure 7.5). Each paddler in the group has the opportunity to make a decision. After viewing the rapid, they can choose to run it or walk it. Paddlers who decide to walk a rapid (portage) should be congratulated for their decision, not scoffed at or laughed at. Each person should determine if he or she feels up to running a rapid and risking a swim or other mishap.

If paddlers choose to run a rapid, the group will often set up safety lines below the drop by positioning paddlers on shore with rescue throw ropes. Rescue ropes should be positioned so that boaters have room to surface after a capsize, collect their wits, grab on to paddle and boat, and then look for a rope thrown to them. The rescuer with the rope should be positioned to pull the paddler and boat into a slow-moving eddy.

Carry a throw rope when scouting. All paddlers should keep their life jackets on and zipped while scouting a rapid. Riverbanks can be slippery, and many people have taken a swim while scouting.

When you have found a good position to see the entire rapid, determine where you want to end up at the bottom of the rapid (hopefully upright). After determining your desired end point, look carefully at the river current to determine how you will get there. You will often need a combination of eddies, peelouts, ferries, and other maneuvers to get where you want to go, all while avoiding holes and other hazards. Using combinations of river maneuvers is river running at its best! By practicing paddling maneuvers in less risky conditions, you gain the confidence and skills needed to perform them when they count the most.

Figure 7.5 Get out, scout the river, and plan your route before a big rapid.

Leader's Preparedness and Responsibility

☐ Know the river or lake to be paddled. Guidebooks and topographic maps are valuable references in trip planning. Know about the difficult parts of the trip, including rapids, open-water crossings, and low-head dams. Be aware of wind and river levels. Plan alternatives in case conditions are too windy, too high, or too low.

☐ Choose locations for put-in and take-out along with a possible lunch break stop. Consider time and distance. Planning a trip that is too short is better than planning one that is too long. Arrange the vehicle shuttle.

☐ Limit the size of the group to a number that you can comfortably control. Designated group leaders should be experienced paddlers. Decisions on the participation of inexperienced boaters should be based on total group strength. Remember that the welfare of the group is your major responsibility, and a balance of experienced paddlers with less experienced ones will result in a more enjoyable trip for all.

☐ Plan so that all necessary group equipment is present on the trip.

☐ If the trip is into a wilderness area or for an extended period, file plans with appropriate authorities or with someone who will contact them after a prescribed time. The establishment of a late return phone number can save time and worry for everyone involved.

Participant's Preparedness and Responsibility

All members of the group have specific responsibilities to ensure personal and group safety. As a member of the group you should:

☐ Be a competent swimmer with the ability to handle yourself underwater. If you are not a strong swimmer, you must be confident in the water so that you do not panic if you are involved in a capsize.

☐ Wear a properly fitted life jacket when on or around the water.

☐ Be suitably equipped.

☐ Keep your craft under control. You must always be able to stop or get to shore before reaching any danger. Know your boating ability. Do not enter a rapid unless you are reasonably sure that you can safely navigate it or swim the entire rapid in the event of a capsize.

☐ Be sure to keep an appropriate distance between canoes. This distance may vary based on conditions. Keep the canoe following you in sight. Never get ahead of the assigned lead boat or behind the assigned sweep boat. Experienced paddlers with knowledge of the water being traveled should occupy both the lead and sweep positions.

☐ Keep a lookout for hazards and avoid them.

☐ Respect the rights of anglers, private property owners, and others. Be courteous.

River Trip Planning

Planning a river trip involves more than just river skills. A bit of research will ensure that you are prepared to comply with all local, state, and federal laws. These laws may include launch permits or fees, state boat registration requirements, and zoning regulations of certain waterways. Check with local authorities before launching your boat.

Plan a trip no longer than a half day for your first river outing. A short trip covering 2 to 3 miles (3 to 5 kilometers) gives you a chance to hone skills and river maneuvers without the worry of being on the water too long. A trip of modest length also provides a good opportunity to check equipment and train muscles new to the sport.

The All-Important Shuttle

The paddlers' shuttle is an activity that precedes most downriver trips. This is when the group plans and places a vehicle (or vehicles) at a designated take-out downstream. Paddling trips do not always end up at the spot where you started. On rivers and lakes, traveling from point A to point B is part of the fun of exploration. Watching participants new to the sport sort out how to execute a shuttle can be comical. Many a paddler has ended up at the take-out having left the car keys in a vehicle at the put-in!

Here are foolproof steps for setting up a shuttle:

1. Travel to the put-in and drop off canoes and all gear needed on the river. Remember the essentials: boat, paddle, life jacket, protective gear, and food and water.

2. Participants drive all vehicles to the take-out. Some group members should stay with the gear for safety and security.

3. Leave all vehicles except those needed for the return. Be sure to leave dry clothes in vehicles at the take-out. Remember to take your vehicle keys.

4. Drive back to the put-in in as few vehicles as possible (don't overload, and use your seat belts).

5. Pack your vehicle keys in a secure place at the put-in (of course, carry with you the keys for the vehicles at the take-out).

6. Paddle and enjoy the trip.

7. Take out and load all canoes.

8. Travel back to the put-in.

9. Pick up vehicles left at the put-in. Transfer canoes if needed or return to the take-out to pick up the remaining boats.

10. Travel home.

Wherever there is a channel for water, there is a road for the canoe.

Henry David Thoreau

PADDLER TIPS

Take on only those challenges for which you are physically and mentally prepared.

- Honestly assess your skill level and the risks associated with each paddling endeavor.
- Be willing to walk away at any time from a challenge for which you feel unprepared.
- Never allow peer pressure to override sound judgment.
- Be sure to consider any health issues, fatigue, or mental distractions that could increase your risk.

Possess rescue skills necessary to assist others in your group.

- Know how to assist a capsized paddler with righting and reentering the craft.
- Know basic or wilderness first aid and CPR (cardiopulmonary resuscitation).
- Whitewater paddlers should be practiced in using a throw bag in swift water.
- Take a course that teaches proper rescue techniques from an ACA-certified instructor.

Plan for emergencies.

- Have an evacuation plan that you can use should someone become injured.
- Have a first aid kit appropriate to the type of paddling activity that you are doing.
- Think through worst-case scenarios and prepare proper responses in advance.

Paddling With Children

Paddling with children is rewarding, but it can be a lot of work if not properly planned. Even when you do everything right, your role as teacher, leader, or parent requires more than just paddling knowledge and skill. You should approach an outing with children as an activity for them, not you. If you plan and approach it with that attitude, you will have an enjoyable experience and the children will have great fun that will keep them involved and excited about paddling for a lifetime. Structure everything around their safety, well-being, and concerns. Make sure that they have dry, comfortable places to sit and soft, warm pads to sleep on.

Figure 7.6 Children must wear properly fitted life jackets at all times when canoeing.

First, make sure that the child has a properly fitted life jacket (see figure 7.6). Details on the different types of PFDs are provided in chapter 3. Although the orange horse-collar type II devices are inexpensive, they are uncomfortable to wear. Invest in a child-size type III or V device. Take the child with you and let him or her pick out a life jacket with a favorite cartoon character. The child will be proud to wear it. Set a good example by wearing yours, too.

A boat cushion makes an ideal seat that provides insulation and keeps the child off the bottom of the canoe and out of any water that accumulates there. A closed-cell foam pad, along with a fleece blanket, provides a warm place to lie down and nap. A raincoat or poncho can protect the child if conditions turn wet. A cheap rain poncho can be cut to size with scissors and worn right over the life jacket as a weather protection layer. Be sure to dress the child in layers (remember wicking, warmth, and weather layers) and bring extra dry clothing along in a dry bag.

Carry a short, lightweight paddle for the child's use so that he or she can share in the fun! To a child, having fun is more important than paddling correctly, so be patient and enjoy the moment.

Child-strength bug spray and sunscreen are important for personal comfort. Remember to bring plenty of snacks and drinks in nonbreakable containers.

Keep your outings short (2 to 3 hours) with stops on shore to explore and play. Diapers are best changed on shore. Gentle riffles shallow enough to walk are OK, but avoid deep, fast water until the child is old enough and strong enough to handle an unexpected swim without assistance.

Summary

The river can be a very dynamic and exciting environment. Without a complete understanding of how the water and current moves within the river banks, paddlers can find themselves going quickly from a fun float down the river to a potentially life-threatening situation. The information shared in this chapter creates a framework that paddlers can use to eliminate many of the potential hazards found on rivers and to cope with those that cannot be eliminated.

Simply put, when you decide to pursue river canoeing, it is essential that you build your knowledge and skills accordingly. Take a course from a certified instructor.

CHAPTER 8

Overnight Camping Skills

> You won't get where you want to go if you travel only on sunny days.
>
> *Anonymous*

Seeing a moose drinking water as it stands majestically in the middle of the Allagash River in Maine. Falling asleep to the soothing sounds of the rapids on the Dumoine River in Quebec. Noting the contrast between the sun-parched landscape of brown hues and the cool wet river on a float down the Rio Grande. Watching the sun both set in the west and rise in the east from your campsite on Cape Sable, the southern point in the Everglades. These are some of the unique experiences and benefits that the canoe camper enjoys.

We are backcountry astronauts traveling through outdoor space. We have our comfort zones, and we bring with us the amenities of home to make our trips more enjoyable. But no convenience stores are available if we become hungry, and when the sun goes down, darkness comes. To survive and be comfortable in this new environment, the canoe camper needs to plan every aspect of the trip, including shelter, food, navigation, the cargo-carrying capability of the canoe, and even recreation. What you take on your voyage is what you will have, no more and no less.

This chapter focuses on some of the skills and techniques that will help you to plan a safe and enjoyable canoe camping trip. In addition, canoe campers need to ask the question, Why do I go outdoors? In response to this question, canoe campers should program activities that they and their companions can do during the trip.

Trip Planning for Canoe Camping

In the United States, most canoe campers use land and water resources managed by a federal, state, or nonprofit agency. These include national parks, national forests, Bureau of Land Management lands, Army Corps projects, state parks, and wildlife refuges. The point is that resource managers administer most of the waterways visited by canoe campers. Each area has its own rules, regulations, and procedures. Therefore, the first stop in most trip planning is at the Web site or printed literature of the agency that manages the resource. If you are working through an outfitter, they will usually have most of the information that you will need for your trip. Their information includes typical trips and routes, campsite locations, procedures for obtaining permits, hazards, sights to see, and things to avoid.

Even the experienced canoe camper should rely on the information provided by the resource manager or outfitter. The manager or outfitter has information unique to the area that will enhance your enjoyment of the trip, as well as the information regarding rules, regulations, and campsite reservations that you will need for a successful trip. Here are some steps in planning your canoe camping trip:

- Start your planning efforts with the information provided by the outfitter or agency that manages the resource. They have the specifics in terms of rules, regulations, general practices, and what to bring or not to bring on your trip.
- Obtain a good set of maps or charts with which to plan your trip. Consult guidebooks, topographic maps, water trail information, and other materials to provide reference information for the water you plan to travel.

The rivers flow not past, but through us, thrilling, tingling, vibrating every fiber and cell of the substance of our bodies, making them glide and sing.

John Muir

- For planning purposes, figure an overall rate of travel by canoe of roughly 1.5 miles (2.5 kilometers) per hour. This estimate includes water and snack breaks. Tides, currents, wind, portages, and the size of the group affect the average speed.

- As a rule of thumb, allow one to 1 to 1.5 hours per portage. Remember that two carries on a .25-mile (.4-kilometer) portage require .75 mile (1.2 kilometers) of walking.

- Backcountry travel is a physical activity that requires the canoe camper to fuel the furnace. Allow at least 2,000 calories a day per person.

- Remember the shuttle in terms of time and cost. Unless you do a loop trip, you will need to run a shuttle. A typical shuttle will cost from $25 to several hundred dollars per vehicle if you use the outfitter or another service to deliver your vehicles to the take-out. In addition, when running the shuttle on your own, allow sufficient time in your trip planning for the shuttle, which often requires one-half to a full day.

- File a trip plan with the resource manager or with your own family or friends. Allow an extra day or half day as a buffer. If you are not out of the backcountry at the designated time, they will come looking for you. Remember to notify them when you exit the backcountry so that they don't search for you in vain after you are back in civilization. A false search is an embarrassing event, it is time consuming, and it can be costly.

Equipment

As a backcountry canoe camper, what you take with you is what you will have on your backcountry trip. For this reason, you must have the necessary equipment with you to make it an enjoyable trip, and even to survive. You depend on your equipment. A damaged canoe can impede travel. A wet sleeping bag can result in a sleepless night, and that, in turn, can result in sloppy judgment leading to an accident. Not having adequate mosquito netting can result in a bug attack that makes life miserable. A group of raccoons that gets into your food supply because it wasn't adequately protected or cached can wreak havoc on your cuisine for the remainder of your trip. Whether for enjoyment or survival, carefully consider the equipment that you take with you.

The equipment list forms the backbone of the camping experience because if you don't bring it with you, you won't have it. A fairly comprehensive backcountry equipment list is provided at the end of this chapter. You will not need to take everything listed on your trip, but you can review the list and use it to develop your own abbreviated or personalized equipment list. You can eliminate items from the list that you don't need and add items that you think you do need. The purpose of the list is to stimulate your thinking about what you might take rather than to suggest absolutes. For example, you may not think of taking money with you into the backcountry. If you have an emergency evacuation, however, a credit card and some paper currency are useful items (most people will want to leave their wallets in a safe place in the front country). If you are using a stove for cooking, you may find that you have little need for a saw or axe (figure 8.1).

Figure 8.1 Take with you the necessary equipment to enjoy your trip.

Pack gear and supplies based on usage. Tents and sleeping gear can be packed together for access at the campsite. You might pack your sleeping gear and clothing together. Next, pack items based on accessibility. Pack items that you might need during the day where you can easily get to them in your pack. This list may include a flashlight, sunscreen, bug repellent, rain gear, and a first aid kit. In addition, if you are planning any portages that will require you to carry your pack, make sure to place soft objects next to your back.

Under the kitchen items, plan on using 1 gallon (3.8 liters) of water per person per day for drinking, cooking, and washing dishes. If you are traveling in an area where potable water is unavailable, you will need to carry this water with you. A 6-day trip will require 6 gallons (22.7 liters) of water for each person, or 48 pounds (22.7 kilograms) of weight in the canoe. A tandem canoe will carry nearly 100 extra pounds (45 kilograms) of weight. If you plan to use river or lake water on the trip, you should seriously consider treating it to make it potable. Methods of treating the water include pumping it through a filter (2-micron minimum), using iodine, or boiling it. Remember, pumping 10 gallons (38 liters) of water per day for a group of 10 people can take some time, and boiling the same amount of water can consume considerable fuel.

Try using a food container to eat out of in place of a flat plate. Several options are available. For example, try using a 3.2-cup (.75-liter) rectangular food storage container. The rectangular container is preferred over a round one because it is easier to hold. The container is excellent for providing temporary storage. You can save the leftovers from breakfast and have them for lunch, or you can save the leftovers from dinner and have them for breakfast. Also, containers and mugs with screw-on lids are designed for this purpose.

When examining the bedroom and bathroom sections of the list, consider a pee bottle. Using a Nalgene bottle of a different color than your drinking bottle can work well. To take it a step further, some backcountry campers use a bottle of a different size or shape, or they add something to change the "feel" of the bottle, to make sure they can distinguish the difference between their

PADDLER TIP

Consider the following when determining how to pack your gear.

- Does the pack keep its contents dry in case of capsize or a downpour?
- Is the pack easy and comfortable to portage?
- Does the pack easily fit into the canoe? Note that rigid items like barrels or pack frames don't pack easily into a canoe. In contrast, a Duluth pack or Bill's Bag conforms to the interior of the canoe.
- Does the pack provide protection from scavengers like raccoons or bears?

water and pee bottles in minimal light conditions. Opening the tent and going outside to relieve yourself not only exposes you to insects but also causes you to lose considerable body heat that you will need to regenerate when you are back in your sleeping bag. The pee bottle, though not commonly thought of, is a convenient item to have with you.

In the clothes closet section, most canoe campers will find that they need considerably less clothing than in the front country. Generally, you will need your paddling clothes, the clothes that you wear around the camp, and your sleeping wear. Your sleeping wear should not be the clothes that you wore during the day. The perspiration in them would evaporate as you slept, so that clothing would cool you rather than keep you warm.

Most items listed in the accessories section are self-explanatory. You can easily subdivide packs into the different types of packs that you might use. Refer to chapter 3 for more information on how to select gear.

Insects and Pests

Usually, insects (mosquitoes, black flies, no-see-ums, horse flies, bees, yellow jackets, and so on) will cause you the most problems. Generally, there are two approaches to protection. You can wear protective clothing, including mosquito netting, or you can use chemical repellents. Each approach has its advantages, and most people use a combination of both. The advantage of the chemical repellents is that they seem to keep the insects and pests away from the body. However, one key disadvantage is that some repellents can actually remove the waterproof coating or nylon from garments. When using protective clothing, and depending on the conditions, you can be a bit hotter wearing long sleeves and long pants, but you will avoid chemicals. And when the bugs are no longer around, you can easily remove some layers. As a group, it is extremely important to learn whether any trip participants have an allergy to bites and stings and to bring the appropriate treatment.

Camp Activities

Devote some attention to items used for recreation. A trip is more than just the number of miles covered in a day. Plan activities that help the group interact with the natural surroundings or that bond members together through a common experience. A tree or bird identification book is recreational as well as educational. Try reading an outdoor story around the campfire. Storytelling, an art form that has almost been lost, also works well. A few simple objects can significantly enhance the quality of the backcountry experience.

Alcohol and Tobacco

Normally, a trip in the backcountry is not a good time to go cold turkey or attempt major behavior modification. The outdoor environment places enough stresses on the body. However, alcohol and boating should not be combined.

Never boat under the influence. Also, remember that cigarette filters are not biodegradable and should be carried out of the backcountry.

Keys to Success

- Remember that you are a backcountry canoe camper. For the most part, what you bring with you is what you will have on the trip, no more and no less. If you didn't bring a needle and thread, you will not be able to sew the button back on your pants.

- Don't overpack. The equipment list provided provides a starting point for you to develop your own list of items.

- Plan on a gallon (3.8 liters) of water per person per day. If the waterway on which you are traveling is not potable, you will need to carry water with you into the backcountry or use portable filtration systems to ensure your health and safety.

- A trip into the backcountry stresses the body, so trying to eliminate vices or make major behavior modifications is unwise.

- Consider an evening program. Stories read or told around a campfire can provide a highlight to the backcountry trip. Think beyond traveling, eating, and sleeping and address the question of why you are taking people outdoors. Incorporate the answer to this question in your program. (Note: Consider using a small lantern as a surrogate for a campfire. Lanterns may be the best choice where firewood is scarce.)

Selecting a Campsite

Start thinking about your next campsite in the morning. Resource managers often locate campsites roughly a day's travel apart so that the region can accommodate several groups. If you meet other people in your course of travel, ask them where they are planning to camp for the evening. If you are not in an area where you have assigned sites, you may need to coordinate or even negotiate site occupancy with those whom you meet along the way.

Start looking for a campsite early in the afternoon. High ground (dry ground), fresh water, and pleasing surroundings are all considerations when selecting a site. Selection of a campsite late in the day may cause the group to settle for an undesirable location. With proper planning, you may find an appropriate location by studying a topographic map or nautical chart.

Proper campsite selection can provide shelter (figure 8.2). A southern exposure can help warm the campsite on a brisk fall day and a northern exposure can help shield the site from a hot summer sun. An eastward-looking site may provide protection from a threatening storm moving out of the west. Enclosing the site in the trees of a forest can help break the wind of a storm. In contrast, an exposed campsite on a small point may allow a gentle breeze to circulate through the campsite and reduce insect problems. Even on a still day the temperature differential between the cool water and the sun-warmed earth can create convectional air flow through the campsite.

TECHNIQUE TIP

Shelter is anything that protects the body. Clothes, tents, and campsite attributes are all forms of shelter. A campsite can reduce heat loss and conserve body heat, or it can cool the body with a gentle breeze.

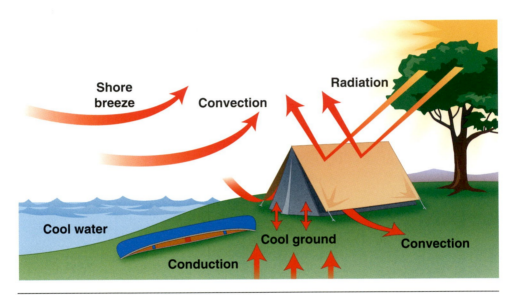

Figure 8.2 Proper campsite selection can provide or enhance shelter. You can lose or gain heat through convection currents, radiation, or conduction.

In many areas, campsites are predetermined, and the canoe camper selects all campsites before the trip. Hence, campsite selection depends more on availability than desirability. Some areas use a reservation system through which you reserve your campsite location over the Internet or phone before arrival. Other areas have no reservation system, and campsites are allocated on a first-come, first-served basis. Still other areas will permit you to make campsite reservations for your trip only on the day that you enter the backcountry. For example, the Everglades National Park uses this last method, and many a good plan for a trip has been significantly modified because someone else who is already in the backcountry has reserved a particular site. Regardless, the canoe camper must find out which system the resource manager is using and then adapt trip planning accordingly.

Keys to Success

- Think of your campsite as a form of shelter. Site characteristics can help protect you from heat, cold, and even insects.

- Be prepared for additional visitors for the night. You may need to share your site with another group of canoe campers who didn't make their planned destination for the day. The site can become crowded. Always be gracious.

Setting Up Camp

Think about the organization of your campsite much as you would the rooms in your house. Set up a kitchen area, a dining area, a bedroom area, a bathroom area, and a garage or storage area.

First is the kitchen, or cooking area. Because of top-heavy stoves, pots of boiling water, and food being cooked, locate the kitchen away from the main routes of travel. Even so, for a group of hungry campers, this area is likely to be the center of attention, and it will attract many people.

Second, your campsite should have a dining room, or eating area, where people can eat their food after it is prepared. Usually, the eating area should be separate from the cooking area. This separation prevents people from inadvertently knocking over the stove or dropping something into the food as it cooks. Generally, however, you should keep the eating area in proximity to the cooking area because the functions are closely related.

The next area is the bedroom, or where the tents are located. As a rule, provide some separation between the tent area and the cooking and eating areas, particularly if you are cooking over an open fire. This recommendation is more important if you are camping with a group rather than by yourself. You don't want sparks from the fire burning a hole in a nylon tent, nor do you want people tripping over the lines securing the tents.

Use trees to your advantage. Locating your tent in an open area encourages air circulation that creates a cooling effect and may discourage insects. Pitching the tent among the trees may reduce heat loss and increase comfort on a cool evening (see figure 8.3). The canopy overhead can help block the rays of the hot sun during the day. When pitching the tent among trees, avoid dead limbs that could break off in a storm and cause tent damage or physical injury.

When selecting your tent location, be sure it will be above the high-water mark (river or tidal). To find that mark, look for the remains of floating debris. Often, the tide or river pushes debris toward the shore when it is rising and deposits it there when the water begins to recede. This process may also leave a line along the shore. Allow a margin for error because the next tide or flood could reach a higher level on the shore. Some management practices recommend camping 200 feet (60 meters) from a body of water, but doing so is not always possible. In any case, you should know how to identify the high-water mark.

Figure 8.3 Trees can keep you cooler during the day or warmer at night.

The fourth area is the bathroom, or latrine. In some areas outhouses or a variation of them are provided. If they are provided, use them. Some areas require users to bring portable toilets and carry out their wastes. If so, locate the toilet close enough to the camp that people will use it rather than the natural environment, yet far enough away from the camp to provide privacy and enough distance from odors. If your area allows onsite disposal, dig a cat hole and make sure to cover your waste with soil. The rule of thumb for onsite disposal is to allow a minimum of 200 feet (62 meters), or about 70 adult steps, from water, the trail, and the camp (www.LNT.org).

The last area is the garage, or canoe storage area. Your canoe is your transportation in the backcountry and the vehicle that will take you back to the front country. Just as you wouldn't park your vehicle with the doors unlocked in a place where someone might steal it, you need to park your canoes where a rising tide, a dam release, or a storm upstream won't float them away. In addition, you should turn your canoes over on their sides and tie them to a secure object and consider storing them where they are visible from camp.

SAFETY TIP

If you have any doubt about where the high-water mark is located when securing your canoes, pull them even farther up on shore, turn them over on their sides, and tie them to a secure object. A rising tide or rising river that floats your untied canoes away will leave you without transportation. Nothing is more embarrassing or potentially dangerous than waking up in the morning to find that your canoes have drifted away in the night.

Keys to Success

- Be sure that your campsite and equipment is located well above the high-water mark (river or tidal), typically indicated by a deposit of floating debris left as the water level recedes.

- Secure your canoes by turning them over on their sides. Tie the painters or endlines to a secure object such as a tree.

- Reduce your environmental and site impacts. Don't trench around tents. If you dig cat holes, make sure that the soil is returned over the cat hole in its natural state.

- Be prepared for nonhuman visitors during the evening, including raccoons, bears, and other animals. Store your food in plastic barrels that are varmint proof or cache the items by suspending the food pack 15 feet (5 meters) off the ground. Check with the local resource manager regarding the types of animals that you may encounter and the practices used to keep them out of your food.

Breaking Camp

The guiding rule for breaking camp is to leave the campsite better than how you found it. If you are camping in a wilderness area with no designated campsites and you are practicing a Leave No Trace ethic, you would attempt to leave the campsite as if you had never been there. For example, when camping on a sand beach, you might rake the sand with a paddle to eliminate footprints and the grooves made in the sand by dragging the canoes past the high-water mark. The objective is to remove all traces of your presence so that the next visitor has the opportunity to camp at a pristine site. Consult the Leave No Trace Web site (www.LNT.org) for more information.

In many areas, however, developed campsites are the norm. You will have little doubt that you have arrived at the campsite. A metal sign may mark the site. The center of the site may contain a stone fire ring. Logs may be placed near it to serve as benches. A close examination of the site usually reveals the effects of long-term use. For example, tree roots may be exposed by heavy foot traffic. In contrast to the Leave No Trace approach, proper etiquette at developed sites is to leave some wood next to the fire ring for the next group and, of course, to remove any trash and litter.

Although the two approaches seem in direct opposition to each other, they have in common the idea that canoe campers should leave the campsite in better condition than when they found it (see figure 8.4).

Keys to Success

- The following is the golden rule of canoe camping. *Canoe campers should leave the campsite in better condition than it was in when they found it.* You should observe this rule whether you are leaving the site as if you were never there or leaving a stack of wood next to the fire ring for the next camper.

- Clean out the burned cans in the fire ring and other trash left in the campsite.

Figure 8.4 Canoe campers should follow the golden rule of camping: Leave the campsite in better condition than it was when you found it.

- Sweep the campsite before you leave for trash, litter, and, most important, items that someone may have inadvertently left behind.
- If you used a campfire, douse the fire with water. Stir the coals and make sure that the fire is completely out.

Camping Safety

Think of safety as an integral part of everything that you do. In a real sense, everything discussed in this chapter relates to safety. Many people think of safety as simply wearing a personal flotation device (PFD) or carrying a throw rope. Safety is something that they add to what they do. But safety should permeate everything that you do. Good trip planning enhances safety. Selection and use of the proper equipment enhances safety. Good campsite selection enhances safety. Many of the "Keys for Success" listed in this chapter are really safety issues. Hence, your first line of defense in terms of safety is good trip planning and the preparations that you make for your canoe camping trip. The implementation of your equipment list relates directly to your safety. This attitude and approach toward safety forms a backdrop for everything that you do in the backcountry.

Although many people perceive backcountry canoe camping as a low-risk activity, it generally involves high risk because it usually occurs more than several hours from a hospital or medical facility. A mishap that is simple or relatively easy to remedy in the front country could be life threatening or lead to a permanent disability in the backcountry. For example, a dislocated arm in the front country where the patient is less than an hour from the hospital is a simple stabilize-and-transport situation. Splint the shoulder, transport the victim to the hospital, and let the doctors set the dislocated shoulder. However, in the backcountry where the victim is more than an hour from a hospital, a shoulder dislocation could lead to permanent neurological damage if left unset. In the backcountry, resetting the dislocated shoulder becomes a viable option, as long as someone in the group has the proper medical training.

SAFETY TIP

Safety permeates everything that you do during your canoe camping experience. Safety begins with trip planning and procuring the appropriate equipment. It includes route selection, campsite selection, and everything that you do on your trip. And, of course, it includes wearing your PFD. It ends once you have unloaded the canoes, unlocked the front door, and entered the safety of your own home . . . until it is time to do the laundry!

For this reason, the canoe camper should think conservatively. Although you may have the skills to run class III rapids in the front country, consider portaging in the backcountry. If you can paddle 12 miles (20 kilometers) in the front country, plan to travel 10 miles (16 kilometers) in the backcountry. If you travel 10 miles rather than 12 miles, you reduce fatigue. Fatigue often leads to poor thinking and bad decisions that can easily cause an accident or mishap. So think and act more conservatively than you might otherwise. Your survival might depend on it.

Against this backdrop, consider some of the specific suggestions regarding camp safety that follow.

Keys to Success

- In most canoe camping situations, you are more than an hour from a hospital. Therefore think safety and be more conservative than you might be otherwise. Consider portaging a rapid that you might normally run (figure 8.5).
- Portage your gear and run the rapid without the gear (figure 8.6). If you capsize, your gear is safe. In addition, paddling the lighter canoe is more fun.

Figure 8.5 In the backcountry, it makes sense to portage a rapid you might normally run, to reduce the risk of injury.

Figure 8.6 Running Big Steel rapid dry after portaging gear.

- Practice a capsize and rescue in a safe location before the trip to simulate what you might experience in your backcountry travel.

- Stoves and campfires are inherently dangerous. Always think about where the pot of boiling water is going to fall if someone or something knocks it over, and then position yourself somewhere else.

- Check with your resource manager or outfitter regarding the typical hazards that you will encounter and then prepare for them accordingly.

- When you select a campsite, take a moment to survey the site for potential hazards, including deadfalls (dead tree limbs or dead leaning trees that could fall on your tent), ant colonies, and beehives.

- Bring a first aid kit. Most problems encountered on backcountry trips involve sunburn, insect bites, and blisters from paddles or incorrect or new footwear. Store the first aid kit in a waterproof container.

- Filter your water with a pump, use iodine or other chemical treatments, or use other approved treatments to purify your water. Boiling water works but is inefficient and consumes considerable energy.

- Wear your life jacket, or personal flotation device (PFD), while on the water.

Camping With Children

Canoe camping can open up the backcountry for a family with children because the children are along for the ride in the canoe. You can take children of almost any age on a canoe camping trip as long as you observe the proper precautions. Although backpacking with small children is often impractical, a canoe can easily carry the extra weight of a small child.

Consider the following important items when taking children on a canoe camping experience:

- Buy comfortable life jackets for your children and require them to wear the life jackets at all times in the canoe. You have almost no control over when a child will suddenly fall out of the canoe.

- Scale back your trip expectations. Plan to stop approximately every hour for breaks and exploring opportunities. Children will appreciate the breaks.

- If you camp near the water, insist that children wear their life jackets around the campsite. A wrong step can put a child in the water. With a life jacket on, a child will float to the surface.

- Consider children's need for recreation. Don't expect them to be as awed by the beautiful scenery as you are. They are more interested in playing with something tactile (figure 8.7).

Figure 8.7 Chldren would rather play with something tactile than passively admire the scenery.

- You will need to think for young children. You need to protect them. For example, you will need to protect them from sun, dehydration, and insects because they won't recognize these dangers on their own.

Camping With Dogs

People often want to camp with their dogs. Canoe campers may believe that their dogs can run free, but the reality is usually something else. Taking your dog into the backcountry is like taking another person along on the trip. You will have to do the following:

- Feed the dog.
- Clean up its feces. The same policies and practices regarding waste disposal for humans apply to your dog. If you use a cat hole, dig a cat hole for your dog's feces. If you are required to carry out your feces, you will probably need to carry out your dog's feces as well.
- Provide it with a place to sleep.
- Control its behavior. You don't want your dog chasing down wildlife or attracting wildlife that could be harmful to you.

Think long and hard before taking your dog into the backcountry. Check with the resource manager regarding rules and procedures for pets. Generally, these regulations will determine whether you can take your dog, and if so, what you must do.

Keys to Success
- Check with the resource manager to determine the policies and procedures regarding bringing pets into the backcountry.
- Keep your dog under control at all times. You may need to keep your dog on a leash or closely supervise it so that it doesn't chase other animals.
- Think of your dog as another passenger on the trip. You will need to bring food for it to eat. Also, plan on carrying your dog's wastes out from the backcountry.

Summary

A canoe camping trip offers you a chance to experience beautiful landscapes and vistas and an opportunity to bond with people in your group. Each resource area to which you travel will have different rules, regulations, and policies that will affect your trip. In addition, resource managers may have suggestions about equipment that you should bring to the backcountry. As a self-contained backcountry canoeist, your equipment list is critical to a successful trip. What you bring with you is what you have, no more and no less. If you plan your travel conservatively; bring the right food, clothes, and equipment; and think safety, you will have an enjoyable and safe trip. That's what it's all about.

Equipment List

Kitchen

- ☐ Food
- ☐ Condiments (salt, pepper, and so on)
- ☐ Water purification tablets
- ☐ Water pump or purifier
- ☐ Canteen, water bottles
- ☐ 2-liter or larger water containers for multiday storage (1 gallon, or 3.8 liters, per person per day)
- ☐ Mesh laundry bag
- ☐ Cooking pots and pans
- ☐ Spatula and cooking spoon
- ☐ Cup
- ☐ Plates (Rubbermaid or Tupperware containers)
- ☐ Knife, fork, spoons
- ☐ Large knife
- ☐ Matches
- ☐ Waterproof matches
- ☐ Fire starters
- ☐ Can opener (or pocket knife)
- ☐ Stove
- ☐ Gas bottles
- ☐ Funnel for gas
- ☐ Stove windscreen
- ☐ Backpacker oven
- ☐ Dining fly

Bedroom and Bathroom

- ☐ Tent and fly
- ☐ Ground cloth
- ☐ Air mattress
- ☐ Sleeping pad
- ☐ Sleeping bag
- ☐ Pillow
- ☐ Pee bottle
- ☐ Toilet gear (shovel, toilet paper, hand sanitizer, zipper bags, and so on)
- ☐ Toiletry bag (toothbrush, toothpaste, biodegradable soap, dental floss, shaver, and so on)

Clothes Closet

- ☐ Shore boots or sneakers
- ☐ Socks
- ☐ Sandals
- ☐ Paddling footwear
- ☐ Socks
- ☐ Underwear
- ☐ Undershirts
- ☐ Poly underwear, pants
- ☐ Poly underwear, top
- ☐ Sweater (not cotton)
- ☐ Shorts
- ☐ Long pants
- ☐ Belt

- [ ] Jacket
- [ ] Rain gear (rain pants, jacket, parka, poncho, paddling top and bottom)
- [ ] Hat
- [ ] Gloves
- [ ] Bandanna
- [ ] Swimsuit
- [ ] Towel

Tools

- [ ] Multitool or pocket knife
- [ ] Folding saw or axe
- [ ] Duct tape
- [ ] Watch
- [ ] Thermometer
- [ ] Maps
- [ ] Map case
- [ ] Compass
- [ ] GPS device
- [ ] Shovel
- [ ] Signaling mirror
- [ ] Whistle
- [ ] Scissors

Accessories

- [ ] Pack
- [ ] Dry bags
- [ ] Flashlight
- [ ] Spare batteries
- [ ] Spare bulb

- ☐ Candle lantern
- ☐ Candles
- ☐ Sunglasses
- ☐ Spare prescription glasses
- ☐ Binoculars
- ☐ Camera
- ☐ Suntan lotion
- ☐ Insect repellent
- ☐ Lip salve
- ☐ First aid kit
- ☐ Fishing tackle (rod, reel, lures)
- ☐ Ropes
- ☐ Nylon twine
- ☐ Nylon cord
- ☐ Recreational items
- ☐ Reading material
- ☐ Cards
- ☐ Notebook or journal
- ☐ Pencils and pens
- ☐ Needle and thread
- ☐ Rubber bands
- ☐ Spare plastic bags
- ☐ Wallet
- ☐ Money
- ☐ Calling card number
- ☐ Car keys
- ☐ Cell phone
- ☐ Prescribed medicines

Transportation

- [ ] Canoe or kayak
- [ ] Paddle
- [ ] Spare paddle
- [ ] Life jacket (PFD)
- [ ] Throw bag and rope
- [ ] Portage yoke
- [ ] Portage cart
- [ ] Bilge pump
- [ ] Wet suit or dry suit
- [ ] Helmet
- [ ] Roof rack for vehicle
- [ ] Air bags or flotation
- [ ] Air pump (for bags)

CHAPTER 9

Pursuing Paddle Sports: Pass It On

Land was created to provide a place for boats to visit.

Brooks Atkinson

The opportunities to explore the world by canoe are as varied as the landscape itself. From outrigger canoe competitions in Hawaii to wilderness canoe trips in the Boundary Waters Canoe Area to short outings with a local livery or outfitter, nearly every part of the globe has paddling options for your enjoyment.

But the paddling lifestyle is not one that we should take for granted. Each day, access to water resources is being purchased, developed by private developers, and locked away from the common adventurer who does not own part of the access. Paddling clubs and conservation and stewardship organizations work hard to ensure that the paddling public retains rights to access our precious waterways. We as paddlers must do our part to care for and protect our waterways for our children and future generations.

Use and Stewardship of Resources

Paddle sports are accessible to people of all abilities, races, and income levels. You need only the desire and a mentor, instructor, or guide to gain exposure to the possibilities. If you have experience, be a mentor to those who have not shared in the world of rivers, lakes, estuaries, ponds, and tidal areas. Paddling clubs exist around the world, and they are a perfect way to meet new friends, connect with experienced people willing to share knowledge, and become part of a social network of paddling partners.

The consensus is that resource stewardship (caring for and protecting the waterways) is a by-product of awareness. Awareness develops largely through experience with the resource, and one would be hard pressed to name an activity that provides more experience with a water resource than paddling. In other words, to ensure that recreational paddling has a future in our society, enthusiasts should care enough to pass the legacy of these lifetime pursuits on to the next generation. We each have a role to play in investing in the future of paddle sports. It is up to each of us to pass it on.

Many paddlers are so committed to the paddling lifestyle that it would be hard to imagine what they would do if they could not think, plan, and dream about paddling. A number of groups work in direct support of the shared water resource and are worthy of support. See "Web Resources" at the end of this book for more details.

Paddlers who have developed the necessary skills to explore wild, remote, or challenging waterways safely and responsibly on their own have invested time, effort, and money to be able to enjoy self-reliant outdoor experiences. Commercial outfitters have likewise invested time, effort, and money to provide paddlers with services that enable them to enjoy an experience on wild, remote, or otherwise challenging waterways. Liveries and outfitters can be viewed as the community's gatekeepers because they introduce the majority of entry-level paddlers to paddle sports on local and less challenging waters.

Safe, responsible, and ethical use of the nation's rivers is a shared concern of resource management agencies and the greater paddle sport community.

Limitations of Use

On some rivers, paddlers must obtain a user permit. Permit systems regulate the number of paddlers who can access the waterway on any given date or time. Recreational demand and use patterns are constantly changing, so allocation systems must accurately adjust to such changes. Historic use patterns on use-limited rivers may not accurately reflect the true level of demand generated by all user groups.

Semipublic and educational groups such as clubs, camps, and institutional programs have not always enjoyed equitable access to use-limited waterways. Agencies that manage use-limited rivers have often allocated use without the benefit of a reliable demand study or other scientific information.

Decisions to limit access to and use of the nation's waterways should never be taken lightly. The American Canoe Association (ACA) recognizes that on some waterways the public demand for use is greater than the resource can accommodate without degrading the resource and compromising recreational experiences. The number of people participating in canoeing, kayaking, and rafting has increased substantially in recent years. All people who seek to explore waterways by canoe, kayak, or raft should have an equitable access opportunity.

To ensure paddling opportunities in the future, the paddling community must be involved on a local level with issues regarding waterway access.

Paddler Environmental Ethics

Paddlers should provide role models of ethical behavior (see figure 9.1). Here are some tips. You can also consult the Leave No Trace Web site (www.LNT.org) and local resource managers for additional guidance.

1. Never litter and always pack out trash.
   - Carry a bag or container specifically for trash removal.
   - Secure trash in your boat so that it will withstand wind or capsize.
2. Conduct all toilet activity at least 200 feet (60 meters) from any water body.
   - Bury all solid human waste 4 to 8 inches (10 to 16 centimeters) deep or pack it out.
   - Pack out used toilet paper or sanitary napkins. In wet conditions, where no wildfire hazard exists, you may burn toilet paper in the hole with waste (cat hole) before filling in the hole with soil.
   - Urinating directly in the water may be advisable on certain deserted waterways or at sea (consult Leave No Trace, www.LNT.org, for specific guidelines).
   - Never dispose of any foodstuff in the same location as human waste because food will prompt animals to dig up the waste.
   - Exact procedures vary depending on the specific environmental characteristics (climate, soil, and so forth) of your paddling or camping

Figure 9.1 Practicing environmental ethics is every paddler's responsibility.

location. Consult Leave No Trace (www.LNT.org) for specific guidelines and check with the local resource manager for location-specific guidance.

3. Pack out human waste in sensitive or heavily used environments.
   - Raft-supported trips should carry portable toilet systems designed for river use.
   - Portable toilet systems should be compatible with locally available dump stations.
   - Paddlers on canoe- or kayak-only trips can carry specially designed disposable bags to facilitate packing out solid waste (such as the WAG bag from Phillips Environmental Products).

4. Do not disturb wildlife.
   - Observe wildlife quietly from a distance.
   - Use binoculars or telephoto camera lenses to obtain closer views.
   - Maintain a distance of 50 to 100 yards (meters) between you and marine mammals.
   - Never attempt to feed wildlife.
   - Never leave food or trash accessible to wildlife.
   - On multiday paddling trips in bear country, store food and trash in specially designed bear-resistant bags or canisters.
   - Watch for and avoid any wildlife dens, nesting areas, or spawning areas.
   - Never allow your craft to drift into wading or swimming wildlife.

5. Minimize impacts to shore when launching, portaging, scouting, or taking out.
   - Do not drag boats on the ground when launching or taking out.
   - Launch and take out on sandy beaches or rocky areas.
   - Avoid disturbing (marring) soft ground, especially on sloping terrain such as riverbanks.
   - Try to avoid stepping on vegetation.

6. Avoid building campfires, except in officially established fire rings or in emergencies.
   - For overnight trips use a camping stove for cooking.
   - If you must build a fire, use established fire rings if available.
   - Obey all resource management agency guidelines and regulations regarding campfires.
   - Thoroughly douse campfires with water and verify that they are completely extinguished before leaving them unattended.
   - Scatter ashes and return any disturbed terrain features to their original condition.

Reprinted courtesy of the American Canoe Association (ACA).

Paddler Standard of Conduct

Members of the paddling community conform to a common standard of conduct. Observing these commonsense principles will show others that you are serious about your sport.

1. Obey all rules and regulations.
   - Be informed about all applicable rules and regulations before launching your vessel (see figure 9.2).
   - When paddling on multiple-use waterways, know the generally accepted rules of navigation (the rules of the road for boating), available from the U.S. Coast Guard.
   - Avoid paddling near areas of heightened security, such as military bases, dams, and nuclear power plants.

2. Respect private property. Use only public lands and access points.
   - Do not cross or occupy private property without permission from the owner.
   - When using private property with permission, never litter or engage in any behavior likely to upset the landowner.
   - Help landowners police and maintain access areas that they make available for public use.
   - Be informed about the navigability status of the waterway and what constitutes the high-water mark.

Figure 9.2 Paddlers should learn the applicable rules and regulations of their venue before launching their canoes.

3. Be considerate of others on the water.
   - Paddle in control and avoid drifting into others.
   - Avoid interfering with the recreational activities of others.
   - Be courteous and polite when communicating with others.
   - Never engage in lewd or inappropriate behavior.
   - When playing in hydraulic river features such as waves or holes, whitewater paddlers should yield the right-of-way to boats traveling downstream.
4. Give anglers a wide berth.
   - Pay attention to the location of anglers and their fishing lines.
   - Avoid passing within the casting range of anglers when possible.
   - If one must pass within casting range, time passage to when the angler has reeled in the line.
   - Pass by anglers as quickly and quietly as practicable.
5. Never change clothes in public view.
   - Use available changing facilities or restrooms.
   - When no changing facility is available, use vehicles, tents, changing apparel, or landscape features to change clothes beyond the view of others.
6. Respect local culture and standards of conduct.
   - Respect local community standards of decency.
   - Always assume that public nudity may offend others.

- Avoid using offensive language.
- Enrich your experience by learning about the heritage and culture of the places where you paddle.
- Support local businesses with your patronage whenever practicable.

7. Give back to the waterway.

- Volunteer for organized waterway cleanups and improvement projects.
- Report pollution or other waterway degradation to appropriate officials and ACA.
- Support causes and organizations that are working to safeguard the nation's recreational waters.

Reprinted courtesy of the American Canoe Association (ACA).

Paddling Opportunities

The Paddlesports Industry Association (PIA) is the premier trade association promoting paddle sports. PIA serves the paddle sports industry, including boat rentals, retailers, liveries, outfitters, manufacturers, and distributors. PIA members help outdoor enthusiasts experience the fun and joy of rafting, kayaking, and canoeing the lakes, rivers, whitewater, streams, creeks, bays, and coastal waters of the United States and internationally. To locate an outfitter in your area, visit www.paddlesportsindustry.org.

Paddlers have organized clubs in many communities across the United States and Canada. Many are ACA Paddle America Clubs or ACA Club Affiliates (see figure 9.3). These clubs organize instruction, stewardship, and recreational events. For a list of paddling clubs in your area, visit www.americancanoe.org.

AMERICAN CANOE ASSOCIATION

The American Canoe Association (ACA) is a nationwide, not-for-profit organization that serves the broader paddling public by providing education on matters related to paddling, supporting stewardship of the paddling environment, and enabling programs and events to support paddle sport recreation. The ACA has actively promoted paddle sports across the United States since 1880. The ACA is uniquely qualified to help individuals and organizations understand how paddle sport can contribute to the quality of life through enabling safe and positive paddling experiences. The objective of the ACA is to be the recognized primary resource to individuals, organizations, agencies, and regulators for information and guidance on all aspects of paddling.

(continued)

(continued)

The ACA's strategic tenets are education, stewardship, and recreation.

1. **Education.** The ACA has long been a leader in the area of paddle sport education, promoting gateway paddling education to reach the broader public as well as mastery-level programs for the paddle sport enthusiast. The ACA's cadre of certified instructors and trainers are the gold standard in the paddlesport industry.

2. **Stewardship.** The ACA is a recognized leader of conservation and stewardship efforts on behalf of paddlers. The ACA maintains and enhances both the natural and regulatory environments for paddlers at the national level.

3. **Recreation.** Since its inception in 1880, the ACA has been actively involved in paddling recreation, events, and competition. Serving all segments of the paddling public, the ACA promotes the value and healthy benefits of paddling, as well as the activity itself.

For complete information, visit the ACA Web site at www.americancanoe.org.

Figure 9.3 Paddling clubs have been organized in communities across the United States and in Canada.

Summary

People paddle for many reasons. We canoe for relaxation, to be close to nature, to be with friends and family. We canoe for the camaraderie, the fellowship, the adrenaline, the togetherness brought about through being on the water. We can experience another level of satisfaction by passing on the enjoyment of paddle sports to others.

Somewhere around you, a child is waiting to be introduced to paddle sports and a neighbor is looking for a way to spend more time with his or her family. Make a resolution to share your interest in paddling with someone new. Become a mentor and pass on the passion of paddling.

Web Resources

International Paddling Organizations

American Canoe Association (ACA)
www.americancanoe.org
Primary resource for individuals, organizations, agencies, and regulators for information and guidance on all aspects of paddling.

Asian Canoe Confederation (ACC)
www.canoeacc.com
Extensive list of brief news items about Asian canoeing competitive events and participants, as well as a link to subscribe to the ACC newsletter.

Australian Canoeing
www.canoe.org.au
Paddling education, competition, clubs, paddling in Australia, and international paddling trips.

British Canoe Union (BCU)
www.bcu.org.uk
Links to paddling clubs in England, Northern Ireland, Scotland, and Wales.

Confédération Africaine de Canoe (CAC)
www.kayakafrica.org
Contact information for African canoeing and kayaking organizations, championship results, information on recent CAC congress decisions, and links to additional international federations, events, retailers, and tour companies.

European Canoe Association (ECA)
www.canoe-europe.org
ECA news and competition calendar; statutes; competition rules, results, and records; and links to member federations and regional organizations, divided by country.

International Canoe Federation (ICF)
www.canoeicf.com
Headquartered in Lausanne, Switzerland, an umbrella organization of all national canoe organizations that administers aspects of the sport worldwide.

New Zealand Recreational Canoeing Association (NZRCA)
www.rivers.org.nz
Searchable Web site with extensive links to information on New Zealand river and lake conservation, safety, and access; canoeing and kayaking education and clubs; NZRCA newsletter; news releases and archives; and membership forum.

Paddle Canada
www.paddlingcanada.com
Membership and instructor information; news and events listing; outlines of programs of instruction offered by Paddle Canada in canoeing, kayaking, and sea kayaking; water film festival schedule; and job postings.

General Interest

America Outdoors
www.americaoutdoors.org
International trade association for adventure travel outfitters, tour companies, and outdoor educators and their suppliers.

American Canoe Association Member Clubs
www.americancanoe.org/Recreation/clubs.lasso
This Web site has a list of paddling clubs in your area.

American Rivers
www.americanrivers.org/site/PageServer
Organization that serves as an advocate for healthy rivers, conducting campaigns to clean up, restore, and protect the nation's rivers.

American Whitewater
www.americanwhitewater.org
National organization with a mission to conserve and restore America's whitewater resources and to enhance opportunities to enjoy them safely. Links to news articles, success stories, river information, and action items. Dedicated to river stewardship, river safety, and protecting public access to rivers in the United States.

Canadian Canoe Museum
www.canoemuseum.net/heritage/default.asp
Located in Peterborough, Ontario, exhibits include more than 600 canoes and kayaks and 1,000 related artifacts. Site includes information on exhibits, canoeing cultures, and building a canoe, as well as paddler profiles, and links to photos.

Canoe/Kayak Olympics

www.olympic.org/uk/sports/programme/index_uk.asp?SportCode=CA

Provides information on the Olympic disciplines of flatwater and slalom canoeing and kayaking, including competition format, equipment, glossary, and history.

Cliff Jacobson

www.cliff-jacobson.com/bwcaw.shtml

Most-published canoe camping expert of this century. Contains links to articles, books, and videos.

FreeStyle Canoeing

www.freestylecanoeing.com

Includes links to events, brochure, and competition standings for freestyle canoeing, a style that emphasizes smooth, efficient flatwater paddling and precision boat control.

Go Paddle 4 Fun, LLC

www.gopaddle.com

Aims to attract new paddlers to recreational canoeing, kayaking, rafting, and tubing through its online international directory of paddlesports outfitters.

National Association of State Boating Law Administrators (NASBLA)

www.nasbla.org

Professional association whose mission it is to strengthen the ability of United States boating authorities to reduce death, injury, and property damage associated with recreational boating.

National Safe Boating Council

www.safeboatingcouncil.org

Provides information to advance and promote the safety of the recreational boating experience, including a boating safety instructor certification course and a close-quarters boat handling course, as well as links to many other safe-boat-handling courses.

Paddlesports Industry Association

www.paddlesportsindustry.org

Nonprofit trade association serving the paddlesport industry. Members include outfitters, liveries, retailers, manufacturers, and other professionals involved in paddle sports.

United States Canoe Association

www.uscanoe.com

Nonprofit educational association encouraging the growth of paddling as a competitive sport and recreational activity.

USA Canoe/Kayak
www.usack.org
News and updates on athletes, coaches, and competitions from the national governing body for the Olympic sports of flatwater sprint and whitewater slalom and the official U.S. federation of the International Canoe Federation.

Wooden Canoe Heritage Association (WCHA)
www.wcha.org
Nonprofit membership organization devoted to preserving, studying, building, restoring, and using wooden and bark canoes and to disseminating information about canoeing heritage throughout the world.

Water Trails

ACA Water Trails Database
www.americancanoe.org/recreation/watertrails.lasso
Database that includes an abundant list of water trails in the U.S. and Canada, including the ACA-Recommended Water Trails, providing each trail's location, waterways, contact information, and Web sites, sorted by state and province.

Boundary Waters Canoe Area Wilderness (BWCAW)
www.bwcaw.org
Online application for permits and reservations, data on availability by entry point and date, trip-planning guide, and information about the lottery process as well as rules and regulations for visitors.

North Forest Canoe Trail (NFCT)
www.northernforestcanoetrail.org
News, volunteer opportunities and recognition, trip planner, and online store with maps, books, and other products related to this 740-mile water trail following Native American travel routes from Old Forge, New York, across Vermont, Québec, and New Hampshire, to Fort Kent, Maine.

U.S. and Canadian Water Trails
www.seakayakermag.com/community/water_trails/_watertrails.htm
Links to water trails in the U.S. and Canada.

Fitness

GreatOutdoors.com
www.greatoutdoors.com/published/healthfitness
Lots of articles for outdoor-related fitness, including a section for paddling-specific health and fitness articles.

Men's Health

www.menshealth.com

Catering to men, this Web site offers free videos, tips about getting started, and lots of ways to change, enhance, or improve your workout.

Whole Fitness

www.wholefitness.com

Offers a good summary of exercises, stretches, and diet tips for those who want to learn more about physical fitness.

Women's Health

www.womenshealthmag.com

This is the women's version of the *Men's Health* site, focusing on issues relating to women's fitness and health.

Governmental Agencies

Bureau of Land Management

www.blm.gov/wo/st/en.html

Bureau within the U.S. Department of the Interior that is responsible for carrying out a variety of programs for the management and conservation of 40 percent of all land managed by the Federal government.

Federal Recreation Areas

www.recreation.gov

Provides campground and tour reservation services and trip planning information for Federal recreation sites.

National Park Service

www.nps.gov

Bureau within the U.S. Department of the Interior charged with preserving the natural and cultural resources and values of the national park system.

National Weather Service

www.nws.noaa.gov

National point-and-click map with weather watches, warnings, and advisories from the National Oceanic and Atmospheric Association's national weather service.

U.S. Coast Guard Auxiliary

www.cgaux.org

Volunteer organization that provides safety patrols on area waterways, meeting regularly with the boating public at marinas and in classrooms. Assists the U.S. Coast Guard in non-law-enforcement programs such as search and rescue and marine environmental protection.

U.S. Coast Guard Boating Safety Division
www.uscgboating.org
Division the U.S. Coast Guard whose mission it is to minimize loss of life, personal injury, property damage, and environmental impact associated with the use of recreational boats in order to maximize safe use and enjoyment of U.S. waterways by the public.

U.S. Department of the Interior
www.doi.gov
The federal government's principal conservation agency.

U.S. Forest Service
www.fs.fed.us
An agency of the U.S. Department of Agriculture that manages public lands in national forests and grasslands.

U.S. Geological Survey
water.usgs.gov
Provides extensive, detailed current and historical water information, including publications, data, maps, and applications software.

Success Checks

Chapter 1

1. Canoeing evolved from a means of transportation to a sporting activity.
    a. true
    b. false

2. *Paddle sports* is a general term that includes which of the following?
    a. canoeing
    b. kayaking
    c. paddleboats and rowboats
    d. canoeing and kayaking

3. What does *tandem* mean?
    a. paddling a kayak with a two-bladed paddle
    b. two people paddling a canoe

4. People often choose a certain type of canoeing based on the water available to them. Match the water to the type of canoeing that could take place on it.

    _____ winding stream   a. canoe camping
    _____ large lake   b. whitewater
    _____ small pond   c. freestyle
    _____ marsh and lagoon   d. river touring
    _____ frothy river   e. fishing

5. Your best source for verifying up-to-date information about hazards, put-ins, take-outs, water levels, and trip difficulty is
    a. the Internet
    b. paddling club publications
    c. retailers
    d. guides or local paddling experts
    e. published guidebooks

Chapter 2

1. Being physically fit enables you to take care of yourself on the water.
    a. true
    b. false

2. Physical exhaustion has no effect on one's ability to think clearly.
   a. true
   b. false

3. Stronger, more muscular canoeists are better canoeists because they have more power.
   a. true
   b. false

4. A paddler who is flexible is less likely to be injured than a paddler who is stiff and cannot easily adapt to a variety of circumstances.
   a. true
   b. false

5. Cardiorespiratory fitness helps in all components of physical fitness.
   a. true
   b. false

6. Stretching should be done only on land because standing in a canoe is not recommended.
   a. true
   b. false

7. You should drink just enough water so that your urine runs clear.
   a. true
   b. false

8. A good rule for determining caloric intake is that calories in should exceed calories out.
   a. true
   b. false

9. Competitive paddlers take training and nutrition seriously.
   a. true
   b. false

10. Entering nonpaddling competitions such as triathlons or bike races is an excellent way to stay in shape and add variety to your workouts.
    a. true
    b. false

11. Which of the following is *not* a component of physical fitness?
    a. strength
    b. flexibility
    c. energy
    d. endurance
    e. cardiorespiratory fitness

12. Listening to your body means
    a. even though it hurts, you should keep doing it
    b. putting your wrist to your ear and listening for a tiny, quiet voice
    c. being aware of how physical activity affects you body and knowing when to stop
    d. none of the above

13. Which of the following would be a good choice of food while canoeing?
    a. potato chips
    b. dried fruit
    c. ice cream
    d. granola bar
    e. *b* and *d*

14. Which of the following should you *not* do while stretching?
    a. Take consistent, deep breaths.
    b. Bounce so that you can touch your toes.
    c. Warm up to get the blood flowing.
    d. Hold your stretch for 10 to 15 seconds.

15. Which of the following can be used to assist in stretching?
    a. tree
    b. paddle
    c. buddy
    d. all of the above

16. Which of the following is *not* a good example of a cardiorespiratory workout?
    a. swimming
    b. bicycling
    c. heavy lifting
    d. running

17. Which of the following muscle groups are engaged by push-ups?
    a. chest
    b. triceps
    c. shoulders
    d. all of the above

18. Which of the following muscle groups relates to your body's core?
    a. biceps
    b. calves
    c. abdominal muscles
    d. shoulders

19. Which of the following is *not* a component of a good training program?

   a. action

   b. quality

   c. variety

   d. fun

   e. none of the above

20. Which of the following is *not* a good resource for learning more about physical fitness?

   a. physician

   b. personal trainer

   c. the Internet

   d. library

   e. none of the above—all are useful resources!

Chapter 3

1. The main constructional components of the canoe are the hull, seats, thwarts, and _____.

   a. end lines

   b. gunwales

   c. freeboard

   d. rocker

2. Which of the following is *not* one of the four areas of canoe design that affect performance?

   a. speed

   b. maneuverability

   c. capacity

   d. comfort

3. What type of canoeing is considered technical, quiet-water paddling?

   a. recreational

   b. freestyle

   c. whitewater

   d. touring

4. Regardless of material used for construction, which of the following is *not* a recommended method of storage?

   a. Store the canoe upside down.

   b. Store the canoe out of the sun.

   c. Store the canoe outdoors.

5. Identify the part of the canoe paddle where the blade and shaft meet.
   a. throat
   b. yoke
   c. grip
   d. tip

6. What blade shape is most commonly used for whitewater paddling?
   a. beaver tail
   b. bent shaft
   c. wide and short
   d. long and thin

7. Federal law requires that each paddle have one of these. The ACA recommends that paddlers wear them anytime they are on the water.
   a. seat belts
   b. helmets
   c. proper footwear
   d. life jackets

8. What type of life jacket is approved for flatwater use but not for moving-water or whitewater paddling?
   a. inflatable (type III or V)
   b. offshore (type I)
   c. rescue vest (type V)
   d. horse-collar (type II)

9. Identify the layer of clothing to avoid.
   a. wicking
   b. weather
   c. warmth
   d. wet

10. When you are packing your canoe, what should you use to keep gear dry and secure?
    a. mesh bags
    b. dry bags
    c. duffel bags
    d. garbage bags

Chapter 4

1. When planning a paddling trip, you should gear the experience toward the skill level of
   a. the trip leader
   b. the strongest paddler

c. the overall group

d. the weakest paddler

2. The _____ paddler can perform an assisted canoe-over-canoe rescue and deep-water reentry and, if paddling whitewater, can negotiate class II rapids.

 a. first-time

 b. beginning

 c. intermediate

 d. advanced

3. The river and open-water classification systems rate rivers based on

 a. difficulty

 b. environment

 c. aesthetics

 d. location

4. Which of the following is *not* an individual paddling role?

 a. lead paddler

 b. rescue

 c. trip leader

 d. shuttle driver

5. When paddling at night, which of the following is not an acceptable form of light?

 a. headlamp

 b. shoulder-mounted light

 c. flashlight

 d. flare

6. Canoeists should always travel within the marked channels of shipping lanes.

 a. true

 b. false

7. When should trip leaders assess the safety conditions?

 a. pretrip

 b. during the trip

 c. posttrip

 d. at all times

8. Who should be notified of your float plan?

 a. friends

 b. family

 c. park ranger (or other authority)

 d. all of the above

9. List three questions you can ask to assess the abilities of your group.

10. Based on the various levels of paddlers, where would you self-assess your abilities?

Chapter 5

1. If you are not experienced in paddling in moving water, the two important things that you should do before venturing out are obtain training (take a class) and travel with someone who is experienced (go with a group who has paddled the river before).

    a. true

    b. false

2. What simple, practical method can you use to help predict the weather?

    a. Know what jet vapor can tell you about the weather.

    b. Know what the various clouds or lack of them can tell you about the weather.

    c. Trust the weather report without question.

    d. both *a* and *b*

3. The National Weather Service, a branch of the National Oceanic and Atmospheric Administration, supplies the 24-hour weather broadcast service.

    a. true

    b. false

4. You cannot get into trouble with bad weather when fair weather is forecast.

    a. true

    b. false

5. Rivers can be dangerous to paddlers because they have tremendous power and might contain hazards.

    a. true

    b. false

6. When a river turns, does water pile up on the outside or the inside of the bend in the river?

7. What is the name of the feature that is created behind an obstruction that is protruding from a fast-moving river?

8. Speed, power, and the crossing angle are all important considerations when crossing the current differentials on a river.

    a. true

    b. false

9. Common types of strainers that can cause serious problem in rivers include

    a. fallen trees

    b. low-head dams

    c. bridge piers

    d. all of the above

10. If you capsize upstream of a strainer, you should make every effort to swim away from it. If you are going to be swept into the strainer, turn over on your belly and swim aggressively up and over the strainer. Your life may depend on getting yourself high enough onto the strainer.

    a. true

    b. false

11. A horizon line is the usual indicator of a riverwide obstacle commonly referred to as a

    a. pillow

    b. waterfall or low-head dam

    c. foot entrapment

    d. strainer

12. What river hazard is called the drowning machine because it is efficient at drowning people if they become caught in one?

    a. strainer

    b. pothole

    c. low-head dam

    d. bridge pier

13. You should never try to stand in fast-moving water that is above the level of your knees because you could possibly experience a threatening situation known as

    a. drowning

    b. hypothermia

    c. pinning

    d. foot entrapment

14. Unless you are familiar with the area, you should avoid paddling and playing behind old manmade structures because they might contain reinforcing rods, sharp rocks, and other debris that could cause injury.

    a. true

    b. false

15. The circumstance that results when a canoe is swept sideways into a rock or other obstruction is called a

    a. pin or broach

    b. capsize

    c. strainer

    d. drowning machine

16. The main thing that any paddler can do to stay safe on the water is to wear a life jacket (personal flotation device, or PFD) at all times.

    a. true

    b. false

17. To prevent an unexpected plunge or capsize into the water, you should
    a. maintain three points of contact while moving around in a canoe and load the boat properly
    b. practice proper retrieval techniques so that you can recover anything that you drop over the side into the water
    c. both *a* and *b*
    d. none of the above

18. Explain the difference between cold-water shock and hypothermia.

19. List the most typical symptoms of hypothermia in the general order of occurrence.

20. All paddlers need to be prepared for
    - low light conditions,
    - ways to contact help,
    - minor medical emergencies,
    - outings that extend past the estimated return time,
    - weather pattern changes, and
    - other traffic.
        a. true
        b. false

Chapter 6

Mark each statement as true or false.

1. The purpose of canoe strokes is to make the canoe go where you want it to go.

2. There are three levels of strokes—basic, compound, and customized.

3. A compound stroke is defined as a stroke made up of two or more basic strokes.

4. The forward, reverse, and draw strokes are examples of compound strokes.

5. The J-stroke, forward pry, and Duffek strokes are examples of customized strokes.

6. One indication that a paddler is performing a customized stroke is that the paddler is continuously adjusting the blade angle and the motion of travel of the blade to make the canoe go where the paddler wants it to go.

7. In a stationary or static stroke, the paddle remains stationary and the force of the water against the paddle moves or turns the canoe.

8. A dynamic stroke has two phases: the propulsion phase and the recovery phase.

9. If the paddle is a lever, you are the effort, the water is the load, and the gunwale is the fulcrum.
10. A stroke applied along the turning circle will turn the canoe.
11. Having both knees on the hull and leaning against the seat provide more stability in a canoe than simply sitting on the seat.
12. When the canoe is sitting level in the water front to back, it is said to be in trim.
13. One indicator that you are doing the forward stroke correctly is that the shaft is vertical in the water.
14. A stationary draw or stationary push-away relies on movement of the canoe through the water to turn the canoe.
15. A cross stroke involves crossing over to perform a stroke on the other side of the canoe without changing the grip hand on the paddle.
16. If you take a forward stroke in a canoe, three things normally occur. First, the canoe goes forward. Second, the canoe turns toward the paddler's offside. Third, the canoe sideslips through the water by moving sideways but parallel to its original course of travel.
17. When doing the J-stroke, a technique tip to remember is that the thumb on the grip hand is pointing down when doing the pry at the end of the stroke.
18. When doing the forward pry stroke, a technique tip to remember is that the thumb on the grip hand is pointing up when doing the pry at the end of the stroke.

Chapter 7

1. The farther you travel from quick access to emergency services, the higher the level of adventure and risk.
    a. true
    b. false
2. Paddling on moving water requires a set of skills different from those obtained on flatwater, so practicing strokes on flatwater first provides no benefit.
    a. true
    b. false
3. You should take a river-paddling course from a certified instructor before venturing out on moving water.
    a. true
    b. false
4. Scouting, or looking at a rapid from land to determine the best route before running it, is a must for running drops at higher classifications.
    a. true
    b. false

5. A capsize in moving water often happens when a boat crosses an eddy line and rolls into the downstream current.

   a. true

   b. false

6. Using a J-lean to expose the boat bottom to the oncoming current helps to neutralize the drag caused by current rushing under the hull.

   a. true

   b. false

7. What technique is a critical skill for safe river paddling because it allows you to maintain control of your craft and park your boat in the middle of flowing current?

   a. forward ferrying

   b. eddy turn

   c. peel-out

   d. reverse ferrying

8. Which skills are among the paddler's responsibilities when paddling a river?

   a. keeping the sweep boat in front

   b. keeping the lead boat in back

   c. keeping track of the boat behind you

   d. all of the above

9. Decisions about the participation of inexperienced boaters should be based on total group strength.

   a. true

   b. false

10. Streams can change volume quickly after a summer thunderstorm or an unseen event upstream, so you should always be prepared for rising levels and the characteristics of water as it changes depth and force.

    a. true

    b. false

11. Which statement is part of the trip-planning process?

    a. Take on only those challenges for which you are physically and mentally prepared.

    b. Have rescue skills necessary for assisting others in your group.

    c. Plan for emergencies.

    d. all of the above

12. For a forward ferry, the paddler uses a forward stroke and steering strokes to keep the boat at the proper angle (more than 45 degrees).

    a. true

    b. false

13. Whenever cutting against current differentials, the paddler should
    a. lean downstream
    b. lean upstream
    c. stay upright
    d. none of the above

14. Rescue ropes should be positioned so that boaters have room to surface after a capsize, collect their wits, grab on to paddle and boat, and then look for a line thrown to them to assist.
    a. true
    b. false

15. Which of the following are among the rules to follow in running rivers?
    a. Never paddle anything that you would not want to swim.
    b. Never swim anything that you would not want to paddle.
    c. When in doubt, get out and scout.
    d. both *a* and *c*
    e. none of the above

Chapter 8

Mark each statement as true or false.

1. The term *backcountry astronaut* refers to the notion that what you take on your voyage in the backcountry is what you will have—no more and no less.

2. For planning purposes, a canoe travels roughly 1.5 miles (2.5 kilometers) per hour.

3. For planning purposes, a person can easily consume 2,000 calories per day.

4. For planning purposes, use a gallon (3.8 liters) of water per person per day.

5. Think of organizing your campsite as you would organize rooms in your house by separating the kitchen, dining room, bedroom, and bathroom from one another.

6. In general, you can use two methods of protecting yourself from insects such as mosquitoes. The first is to place a barrier of clothes between the insects and you, and the second is to use chemical repellents.

7. Normally, a backcountry trip is a good time to go cold turkey on your vices.

8. Shelter is anything that protects the body.

9. Clothes, tents, and campsite attributes are not considered forms of shelter.

10. A debris line left on the shore by floating debris is often an indicator of the high-water mark.

11. Secure your canoes overnight by turning them over on their sides and tying the painters or endlines to a tree or other fixed object to prevent them from floating away.

12. Digging trenches around your tent is a recommended practice.

13. Leave the campsite in better shape than you found it.

14. One view of a backcountry experience suggests that it is a higher-risk activity than most people believe because it occurs more than 1 hour from the nearest hospital.

15. Always wear your PFD when in your canoe on the water.

16. Safety should permeate everything on your trip, including trip planning and procuring the appropriate equipment.

Chapter 9

Mark each statement as true or false.

1. Each paddler has an opportunity and a responsibility to care for the water resource.

2. Only healthy people should paddle.

3. Canoeing is an activity available only to the wealthy.

4. Canoeists have unrestricted access to the nation's waterways.

5. Paddlers should be concerned about all activities that affect the resource, including personal toilet activity.

6. Urinating directly in the water may be advisable on certain desert waterways or at sea.

7. You should plan to dispose of any foodstuff in the same location as human waste to consolidate the spread of waste.

8. To view wildlife, allow your craft to drift into any that you find swimming or wading.

9. To minimize impacts to the shore when launching, portaging, scouting, or taking out, do not drag boats on the ground and avoid stepping on vegetation.

10. Paddlers need to know the rules of navigation when they paddle on multiple-use waterways.

11. The three strategic tenets of the American Canoe Association are education, stewardship, and recreation.

12. Paddling clubs are a great way to continue paddling and gain extensive experience.

Answers

Chapter 1: 1. true; 2. d; 3. b; 4. winding stream = d, large lake = a, small pond = c, marsh and lagoon = e, frothy river = b; 5. d

Chapter 2: 1. true; 2. false; 3. false; 4. true; 5. true; 6. false; 7. true; 8. false; 9. true; 10. true; 11. c; 12. c; 13. e; 14. b; 15. d; 16. c; 17. d; 18. c; 19. e; 20. e

Chapter 3: 1. b; 2. d; 3. b; 4. c; 5. a; 6. c; 7. d; 8. a; 9. d; 10. b

Chapter 4: 1. d; 2. c; 3. a; 4. d; 5. d; 6. false; 7. d; 8. d; 9. See page 78. 10. Self-assessment based on information on pages 78 to 79.

Chapter 5: 1. true; 2. d; 3. true; 4. false; 5. true; 6. outside; 7. eddy; 8. true; 9. a; 10. true; 11. b; 12. c; 13. d; 14. true; 15. a; 16. a; 17. c; 18. Cold-water shock can result from the sudden exposure of the head and chest to cold water, which typically causes an involuntary gasp for air, a sudden increase in heart rate and blood pressure, disorientation, and possibly cardiac arrest. Hypothermia results when exposure to cold (cold air or cold water) prevents the body from being able to maintain its normal temperature in the core region (heart, lungs, and so on). 19. 1. shivering, 2. impaired judgment, 3. clumsiness, 4. loss of manual dexterity, 5. slurred speech, 6. inward behavior, withdrawal, 7. cessation of shivering, 8. muscle rigidity, 9. unconsciousness; 20. true

Chapter 6: All statements are true except 4 (basic strokes), 5 (compound strokes), and 9 (water is the fulcrum).

Chapter 7: 1. true; 2. false; 3. true; 4. true; 5. false; 6. true; 7. b; 8. c; 9. true; 10. true; 11. d; 12. false; 13. a; 14. true; 15. d

Chapter 8: All statements are true except 7, 9, and 12.

Chapter 9: 1. true; 2. false; 3. false; 4. false; 5. true; 6. true; 7. false; 8. false; 9. true; 10. true; 11. true; 12. true

Photo Credits

About the Editors

Pamela S. Dillon, American Canoe Association executive director from 2002 to 2007, has been an avid paddler since the early 1970s. She has served as an ACA instructor trainer (IT) in canoe and kayak.

Appointed as chief of the Ohio Department of Natural Resources Division of Watercraft in 2007, Pamela returned to her roots, where she began as a state watercraft officer in 1977. With ODNR she assisted in the development of the Ohio River Rescue Training program, the first state-sponsored training program of its kind in the United States. Pamela served as chair of the National Safe Boating Council (NSBC) from 1991 to 1993. In 2005, she was appointed to the National Boating Safety Advisory Council (NBSAC) and was reappointed for a second term through 2009. She was named to the National Boating Safety Hall of Fame in 2006.

For her work, Pamela has received recognition from the U.S. Coast Guard, National Association of State Boating Law Administrators, National Safe Boating Council, National Water Safety Congress, Professional Paddlesports Association, and United States Power Squadrons. She has also received numerous federal, state, and local awards.

Jeremy Oyen is the national director of safety education and instruction for the American Canoe Association. He has worked in the paddlesports and outdoor education field for over 20 years. He has served as a wilderness canoe guide, whitewater canoe and kayak instructor, manager of a specialty outdoor retail shop, paddlesports buyer, owner of Lake Erie's first sea kayak guide company, and manager of Cleveland Metroparks' nationally recognized Institute of the Great Outdoors, where he received the International Boating and Water Safety Summit's National Boating Education and Advancement Award in 2005. He holds a secondary education teaching license in the State of Ohio and ACA certifications as an instructor of moving water canoe (solo and tandem), an instructor of essentials of river kayak, an instructor trainer educator of coastal kayak, and instructor trainer in adaptive paddling.

About the Contributors

Wyatt Boughter, a former professional in the paddle-sport industry, resides with his wife and black Lab in Minneapolis, where he makes his living as a graphic designer and professional blogger. Wyatt is proud to be an ACA lifetime member and instructor of both canoe and kayak. When the waters aren't frozen and the mosquitoes don't block the sun, he can be seen paddling his way across one of Minnesota's countless waterways.

Virgil Chambers has been the executive director of the National Safe Boating Council since 1996. He is retired from the State of Pennsylvania, where he was the chief of the Boating Safety and Education Division for the Pennsylvania Fish and Boat Commission from 1978 to 1996. He developed and started the Pennsylvania Public School Boating and Water Safety program. He is the founder of the National Association for Search and Rescue (NASAR) water rescue training program and was the director of this national program from 1987 to 1997. He received the National Association of State Boating Law Administrators boating safety education award in 1994 and has been recognized with many other awards by national and international organizations for his work in boating and water safety education. He is in the Pennsylvania Swimming Hall of Fame at Pennsylvania State University. He was chair of the Ohio-Penn Division of the American Canoe Association from 1996 to 2002. Virgil is certified as a lifeguard instructor, water safety instructor, canoeing and kayaking instructor, and boating safety instructor with the American Red Cross, American Canoe Association, and National Safe Boating Council, respectively.

Dr. Robert Kauffman is a professor and chair of recreation and park management at Frostburg State University. As part of his academic responsibilities, he coordinates the FSU component of a collaborative program with Garrett Community College in adventure sports. Recently, he served on the board of directors of the American Canoe Association, where he served as secretary for the association. In addition, he served on the ACA's council between 1980 and 1989 and obtained the Coast Guard grants for the hypothermia film *Cold*,

Wet and Alive and the river rescue film *Heads Up*. Under a Coast Guard grant, he authored a boating safety text for use in state boating safety programs, titled *Boating Fundamentals: A Manual for Safe Boating*. His paddlesport-oriented articles have appeared in *Park and Recreation* magazine, *Camping* magazine (the official publication of the American Camping Association), *Trends* magazine, and *American Canoeist*. He has done extensive research on river users and conducted an in depth study for the State of Maryland on boating fatalities on the main stem of the Potomac River. As an instructor trainer educator, he has taught numerous courses in canoeing, rafting, and river rescue. He has been a canoe-ist for over 25 years, and his involvement in canoeing includes competition, river canoeing, canoe camping, river rescue, education, safety conservation, and recreational boating.

 **Laura Liebel** is an avid multiseason instructor and life-long outdoor enthusiast. Based in the Niagara Region of New York, she spends spring through fall conducting both instructor certification workshops and skills training for camp counselors, retailers, and paddling enthusiasts throughout upstate New York, in the Adirondacks, and in adjacent states. Laura is an American Canoe Associa-tion–certified instructor trainer in canoe and kayak and operates the WeKaNu paddling school (www.wekanu. com). When not teaching paddling or leading outings for local clubs, she winds down by camping and hiking with her family in and around the Adirondacks, their favorite adventure destination. As a person who is committed to sharing the outdoors, she also volunteers as a nature walk leader for the local Audubon Center and conducts Nordic walking sessions.

When the lakes and rivers freeze, Laura moves into her other passion, teach-ing skiing as a level II PSIA-certified instructor for a ski resort in Glenwood, New York. Before teaching others to enjoy outdoor activities, she had a successful career in training and development and management in both the financial services industry and as president of her own consulting firm, Counterpoint Consulting, which still provides specialized management consulting services to organization leaders and leadership teams.

Laura has a degree in education from Geneseo State University in New York. She was recognized by the Niagara Frontier chapter of the American Society for Training and Development and was awarded Trainer of the Year. Frequently tapped as a workshop and clinic leader, she has a great drive to help people more fully enjoy and benefit from the outdoor experience.

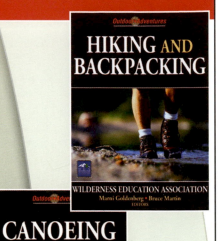
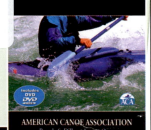